Ayu
Watanabe

L♥DK
エルディーケー

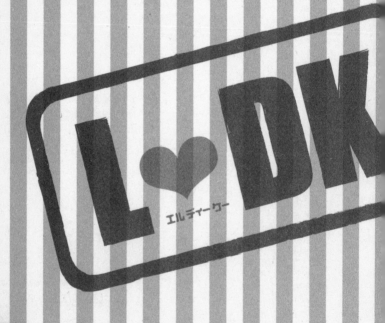

5

L♥DK
Ayu Watanabe
5

c o n t e n t s

#17 Mean...?

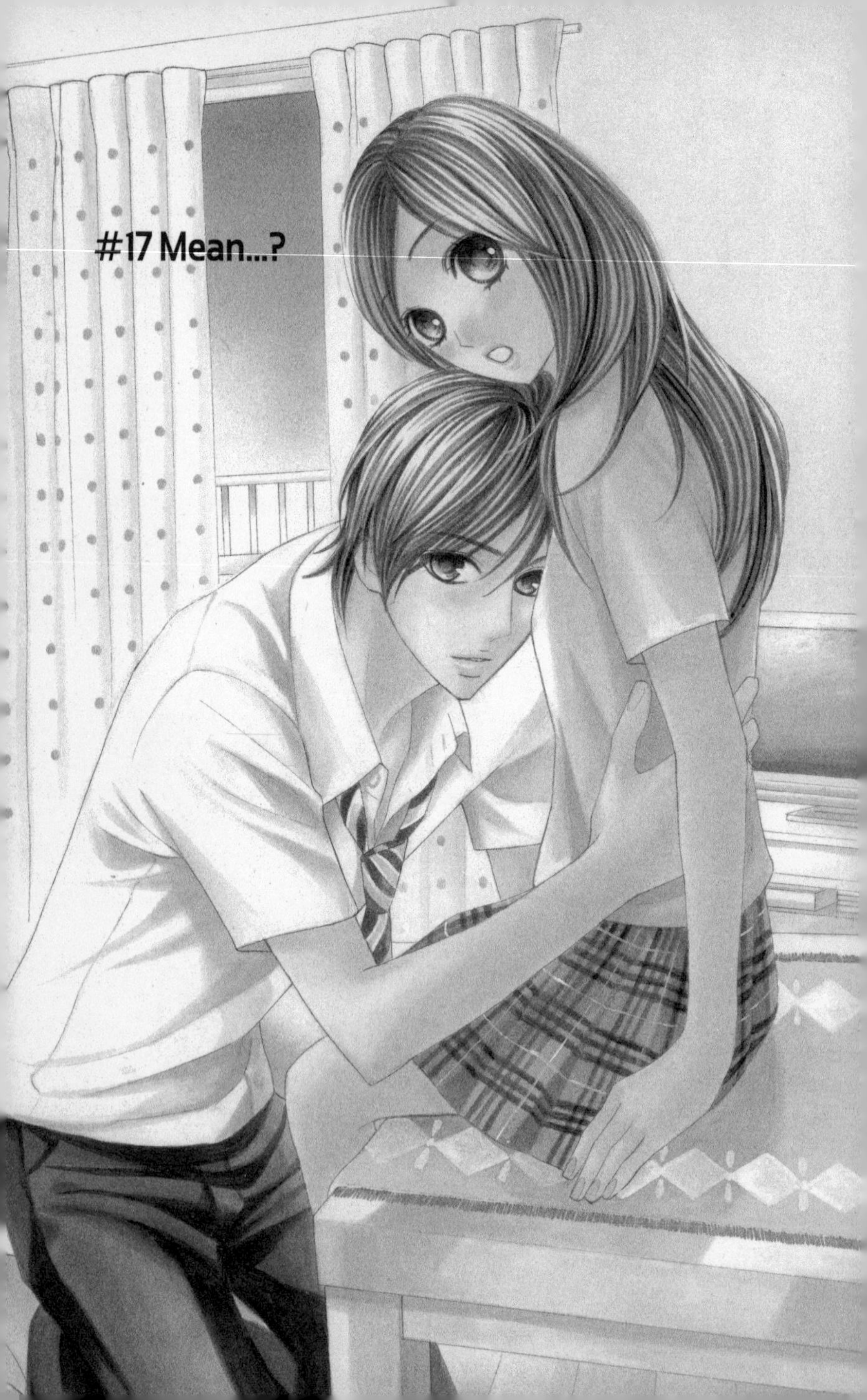

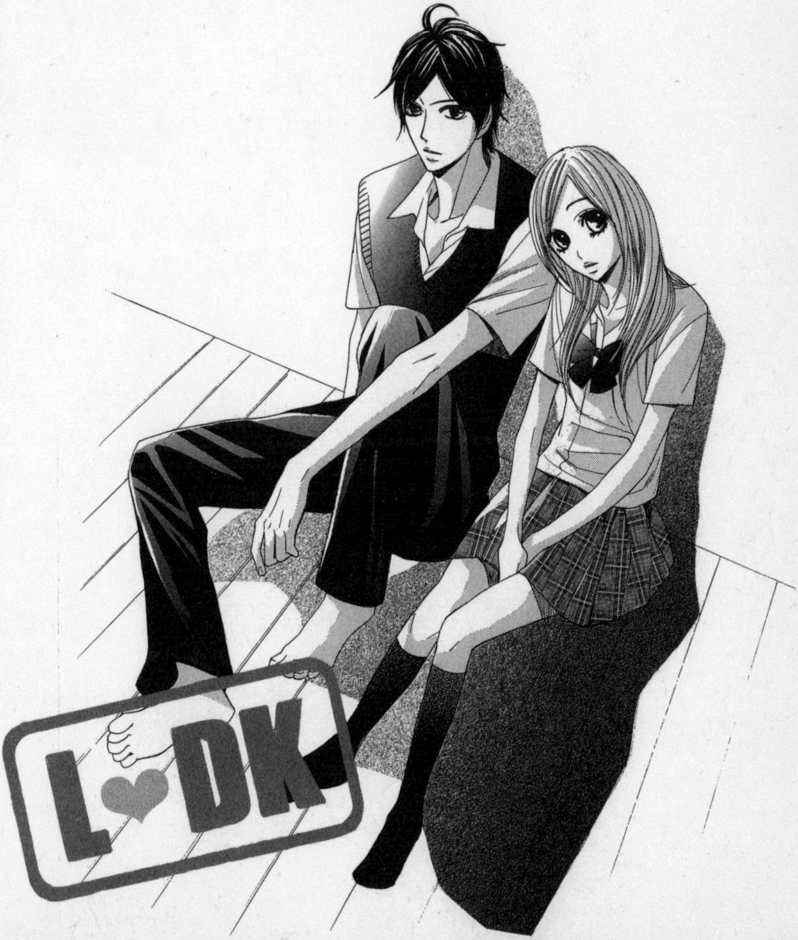
L♥DK

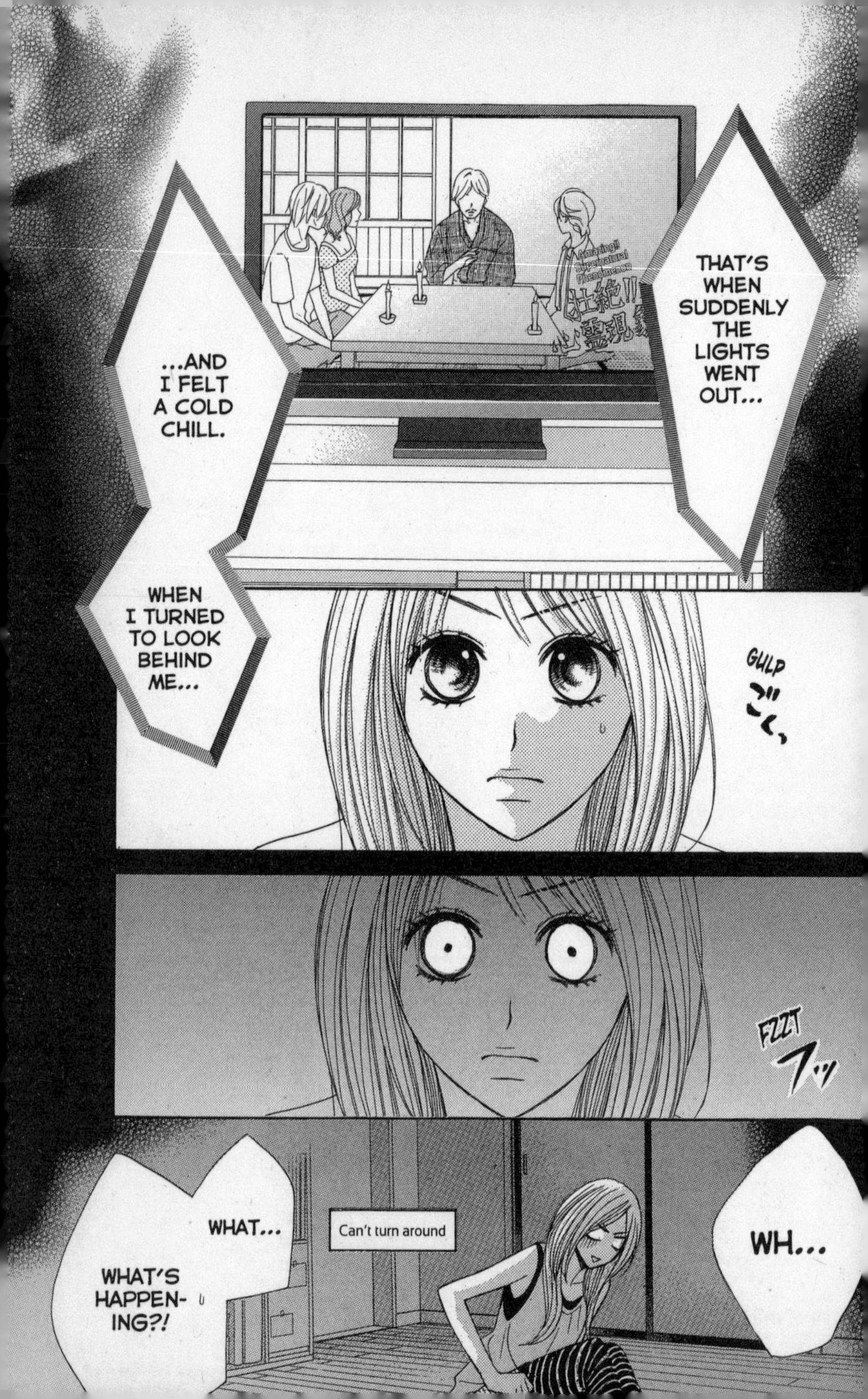
Amazing!! Supernatural Phenomenon
THAT'S WHEN SUDDENLY THE LIGHTS WENT OUT...
...AND I FELT A COLD CHILL.
WHEN I TURNED TO LOOK BEHIND ME...
GULP
ごくっ
FZZT
フッ
WH...
Can't turn around
WHAT...
WHAT'S HAPPENING?!

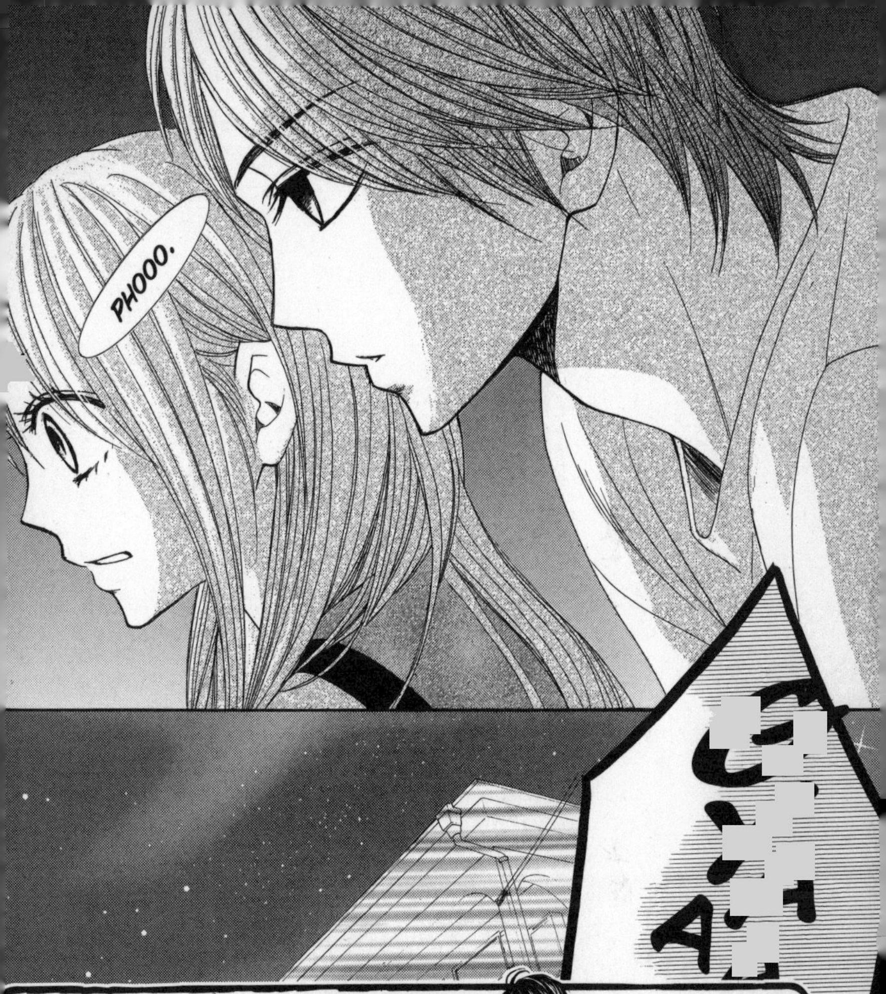
PHOOO.

The Story So Far

L♥DK

Story

Aoi begins the secret arrangement of sharing an apartment with the class hottie, Shusei. It's one heart-racing escapade after another, and soon Aoi realizes she has feelings for Shusei. But she's afraid that if she ever confesses her love to him, their rooming situation will end. That's when Aoi's little brother, Kento, finds out about their secret cohabitation! Kento, shocked and dismayed, throws a punch at Shusei, but Shusei declares he has no intention of leaving Aoi...?!

Cast

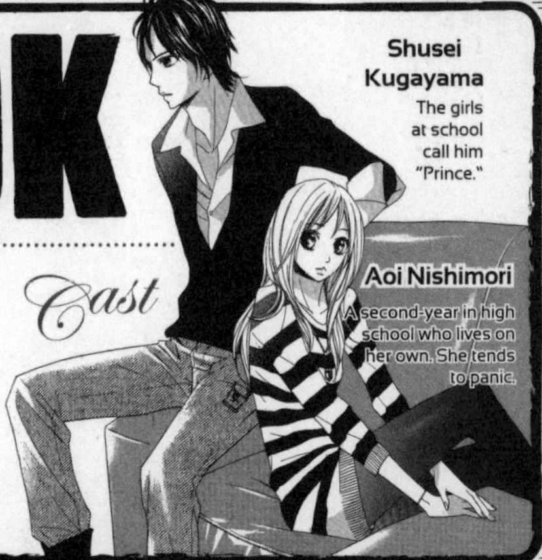

Shusei Kugayama

The girls at school call him "Prince."

Aoi Nishimori

A second-year in high school who lives on her own. She tends to panic.

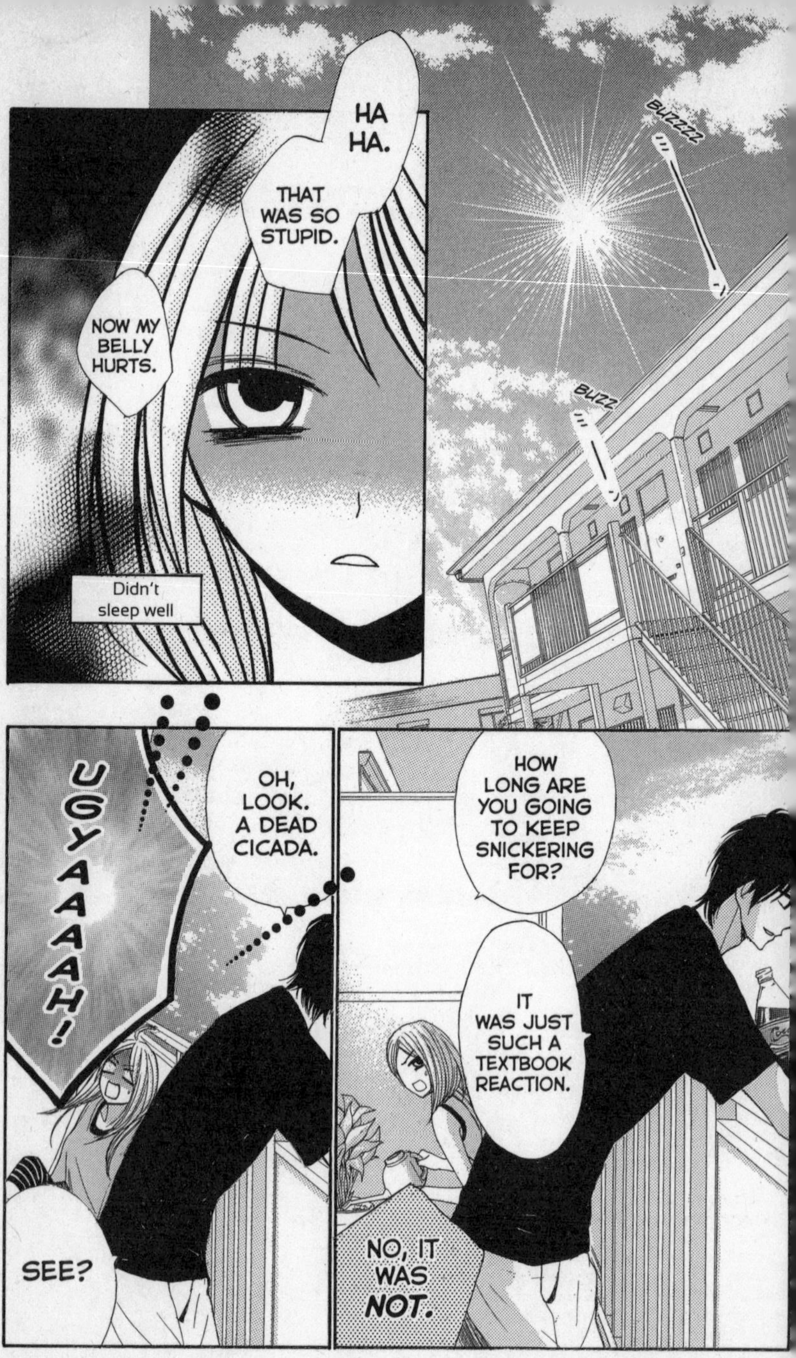
BUZZZZZ
BUZZ
HA HA.
THAT WAS SO STUPID.
NOW MY BELLY HURTS.
Didn't sleep well
HOW LONG ARE YOU GOING TO KEEP SNICKERING FOR?
IT WAS JUST SUCH A TEXTBOOK REACTION.
NO, IT WAS NOT.
OH, LOOK. A DEAD CICADA.
UGYAAAAAH!
SEE?

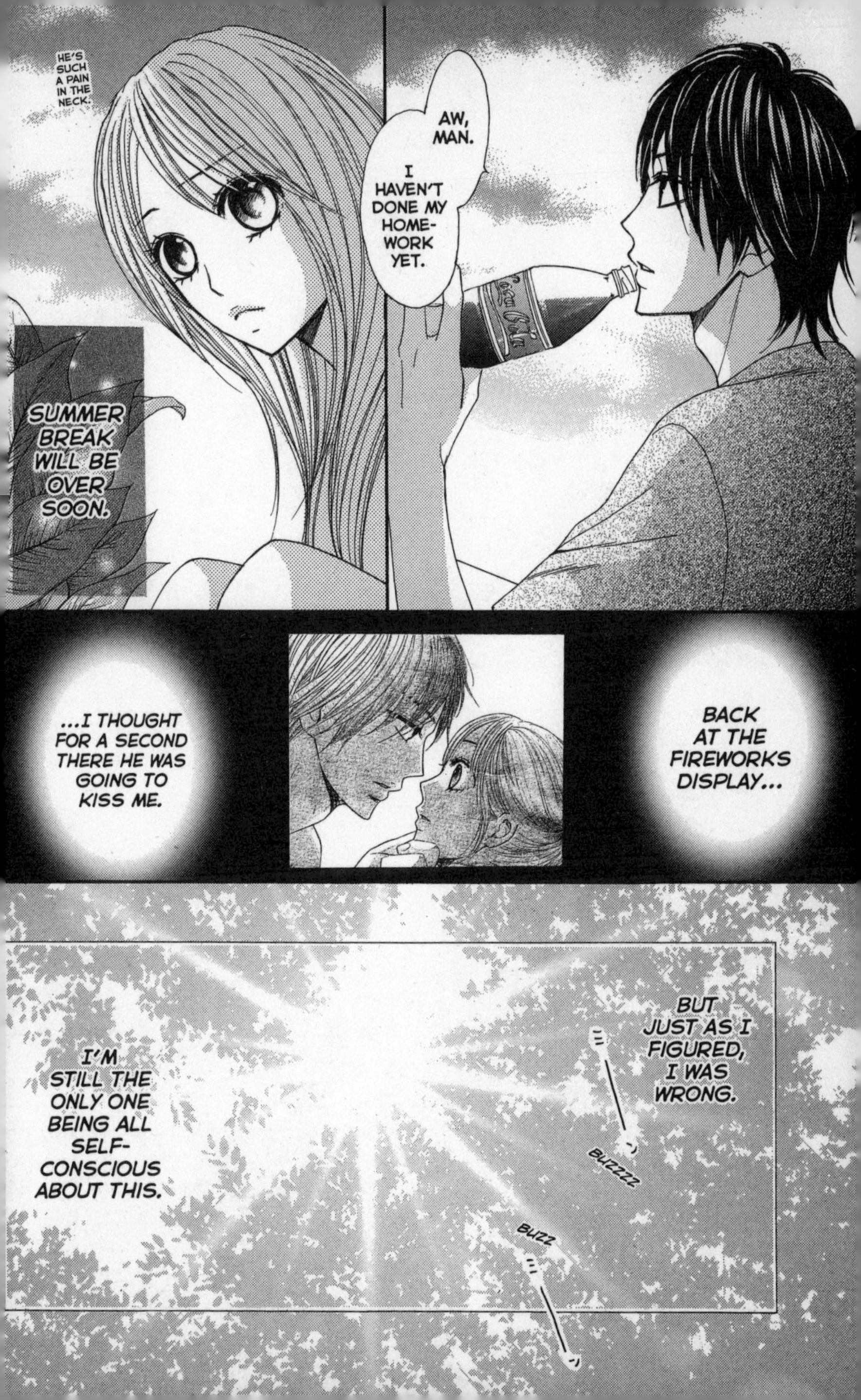
AW, MAN.
I HAVEN'T DONE MY HOMEWORK YET.
HE'S SUCH A PAIN IN THE NECK.
SUMMER BREAK WILL BE OVER SOON.
BACK AT THE FIREWORKS DISPLAY...
...I THOUGHT FOR A SECOND THERE HE WAS GOING TO KISS ME.
BUT JUST AS I FIGURED, I WAS WRONG.
BUZZZZ
BUZZ
I'M STILL THE ONLY ONE BEING ALL SELF-CONSCIOUS ABOUT THIS.

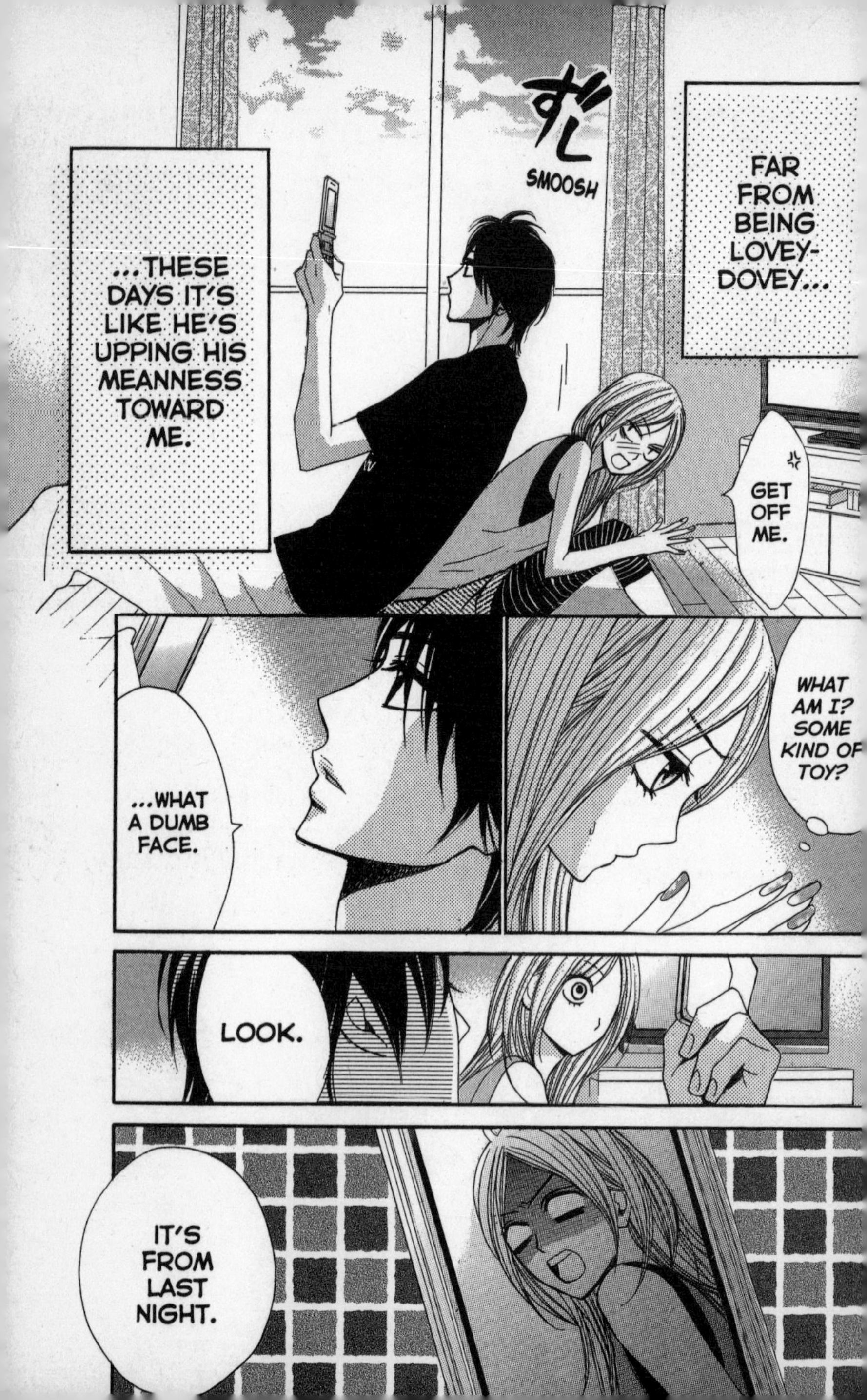
FAR FROM BEING LOVEY-DOVEY...
ずし
SMOOSH
...THESE DAYS IT'S LIKE HE'S UPPING HIS MEANNESS TOWARD ME.
GET OFF ME.
WHAT AM I? SOME KIND OF TOY?
...WHAT A DUMB FACE.
LOOK.
IT'S FROM LAST NIGHT.

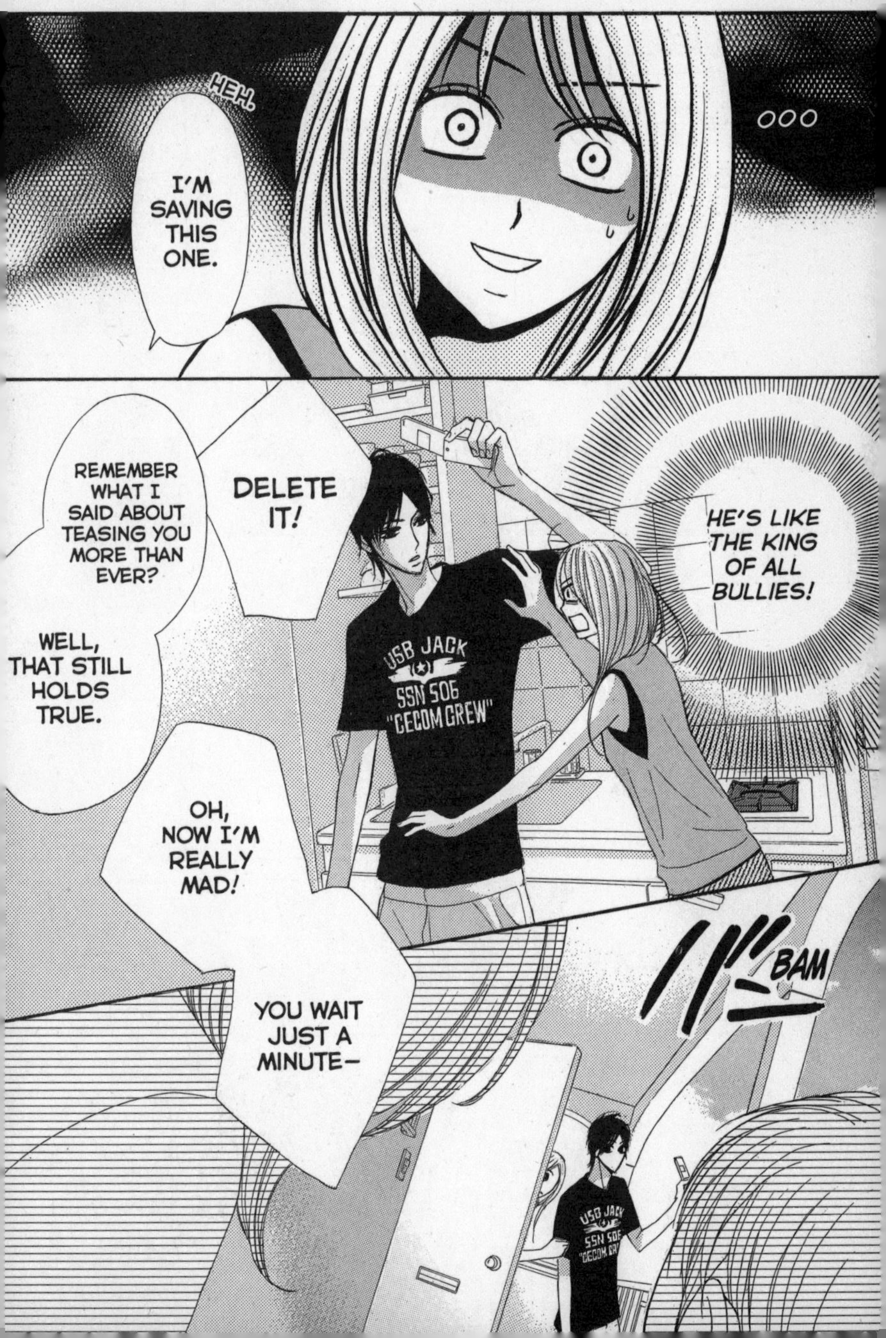
OOO
HEH.
I'M SAVING THIS ONE.
HE'S LIKE THE KING OF ALL BULLIES!
DELETE IT!
REMEMBER WHAT I SAID ABOUT TEASING YOU MORE THAN EVER?
USB JACK SSN 506 "CECOM GREW"
WELL, THAT STILL HOLDS TRUE.
OH, NOW I'M REALLY MAD!
BAM
YOU WAIT JUST A MINUTE—

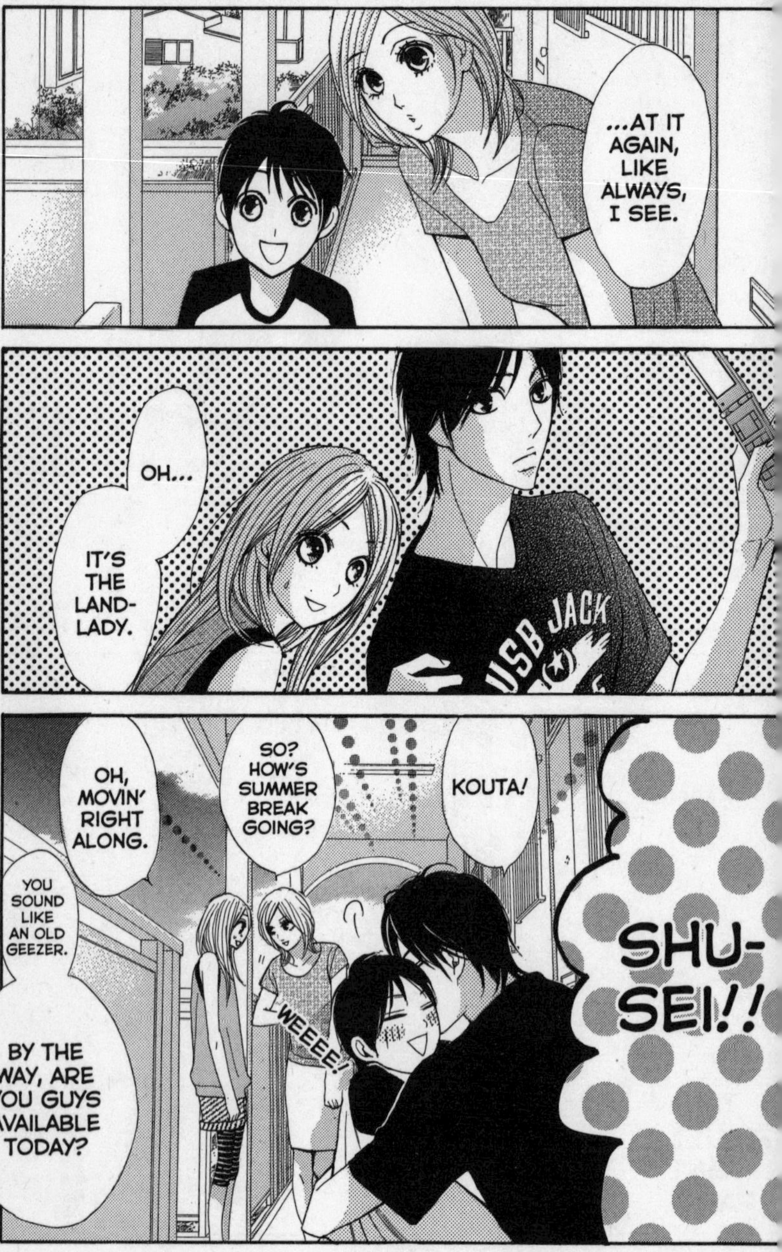
...AT IT AGAIN, LIKE ALWAYS, I SEE.
OH...
IT'S THE LANDLADY.
USB JACK
SHU-SEI!!
KOUTA!
SO? HOW'S SUMMER BREAK GOING?
OH, MOVIN' RIGHT ALONG.
WEEEEE!
YOU SOUND LIKE AN OLD GEEZER.
BY THE WAY, ARE YOU GUYS AVAILABLE TODAY?

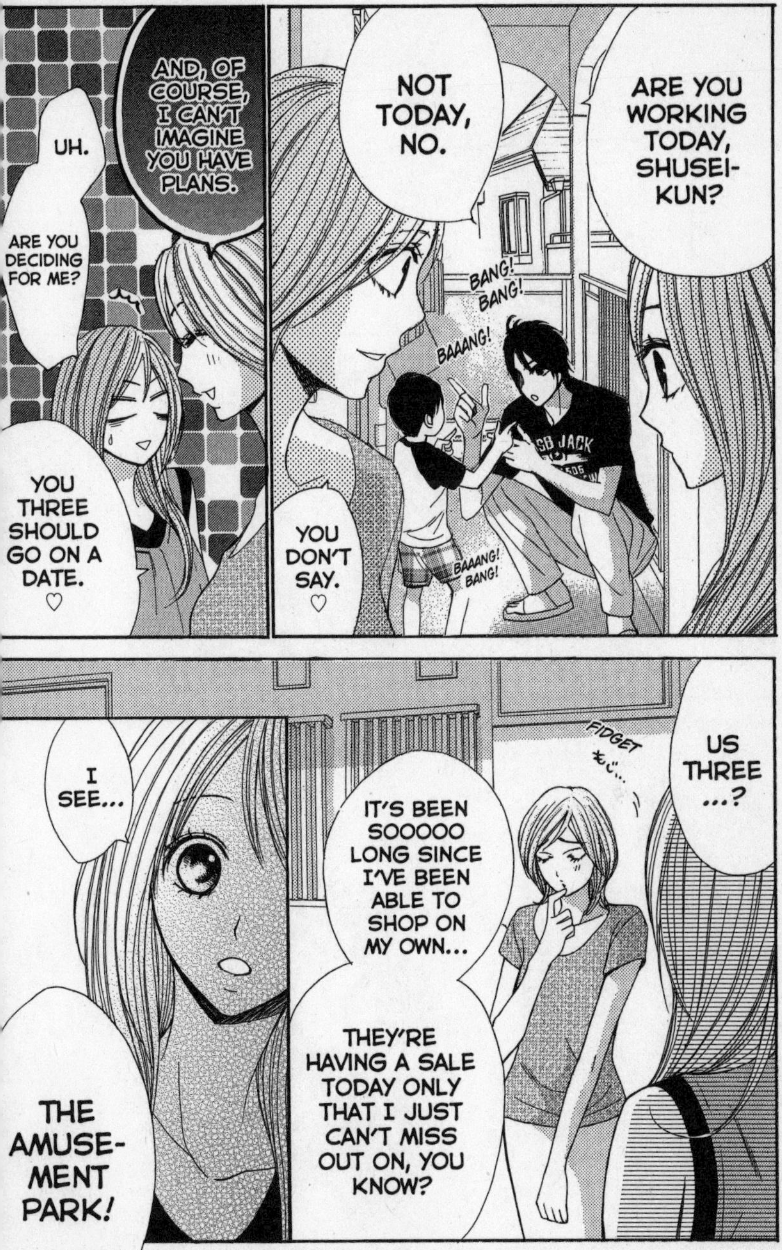
ARE YOU WORKING TODAY, SHUSEI-KUN?
NOT TODAY, NO.
BANG! BANG!
BAAANG!
BAAANG! BANG!
YOU DON'T SAY. ♡
AND, OF COURSE, I CAN'T IMAGINE YOU HAVE PLANS.
UH.
ARE YOU DECIDING FOR ME?
YOU THREE SHOULD GO ON A DATE. ♡
US THREE ...?
FIDGET
もじ…
IT'S BEEN SOOOOO LONG SINCE I'VE BEEN ABLE TO SHOP ON MY OWN...
THEY'RE HAVING A SALE TODAY ONLY THAT I JUST CAN'T MISS OUT ON, YOU KNOW?
I SEE...
THE AMUSEMENT-MENT PARK!

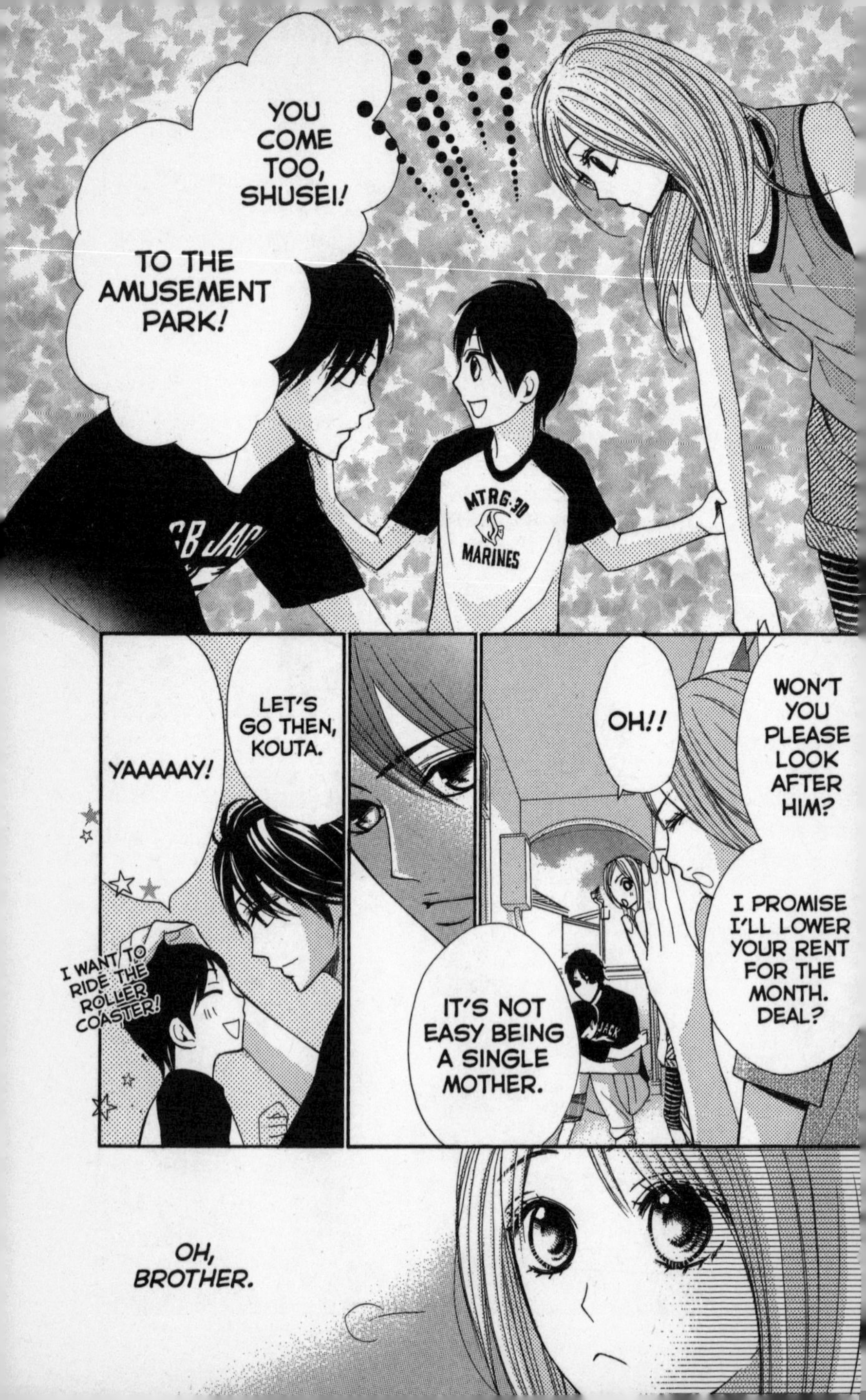
YOU COME TOO, SHUSEI!
TO THE AMUSEMENT PARK!
WON'T YOU PLEASE LOOK AFTER HIM?
OH!!
I PROMISE I'LL LOWER YOUR RENT FOR THE MONTH. DEAL?
IT'S NOT EASY BEING A SINGLE MOTHER.
LET'S GO THEN, KOUTA.
YAAAAAY!
I WANT TO RIDE THE ROLLER COASTER!
OH, BROTHER.

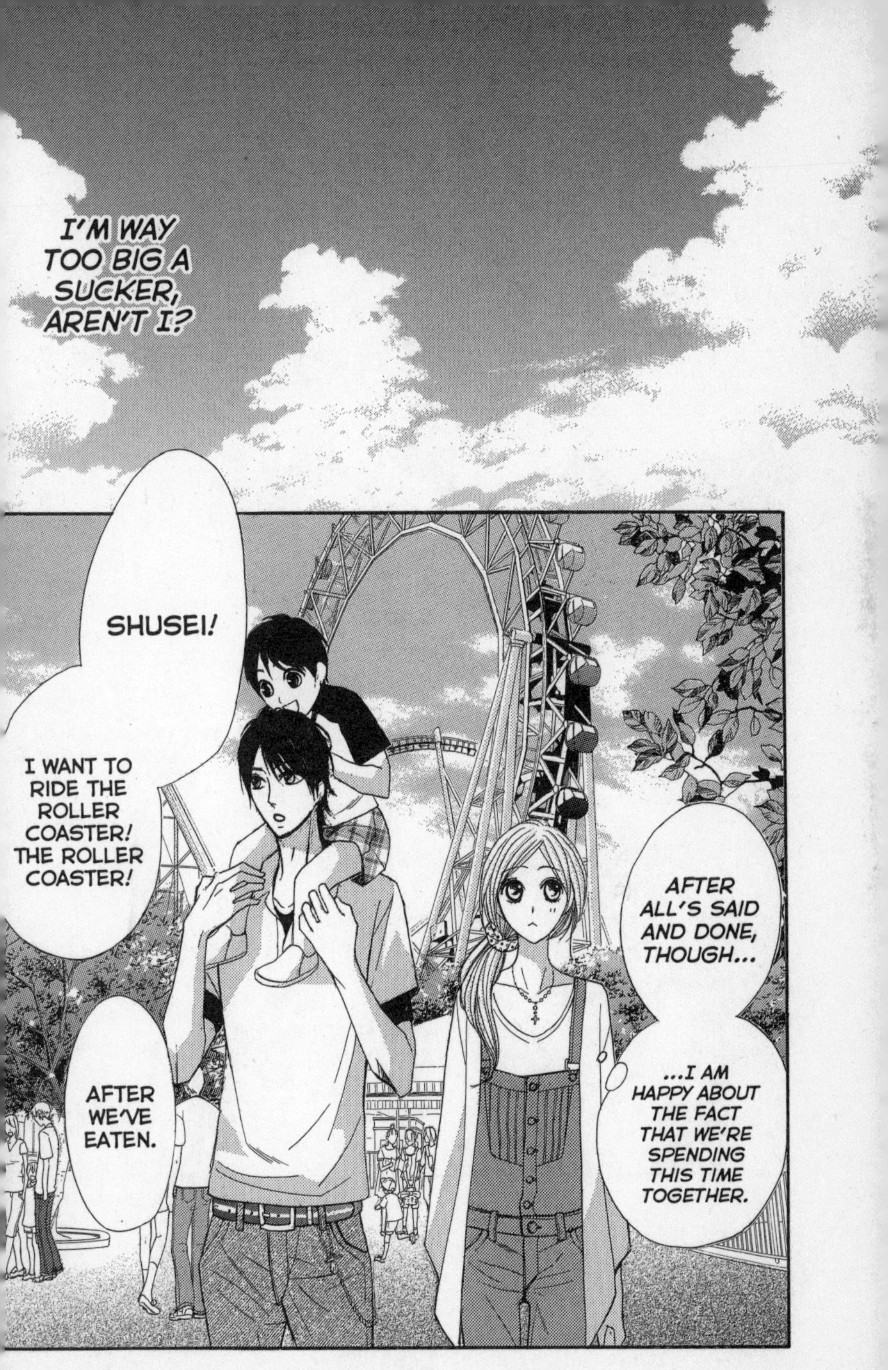
I'M WAY TOO BIG A SUCKER, AREN'T I?
SHUSEI!
I WANT TO RIDE THE ROLLER COASTER! THE ROLLER COASTER!
AFTER WE'VE EATEN.
AFTER ALL'S SAID AND DONE, THOUGH...
...I AM HAPPY ABOUT THE FACT THAT WE'RE SPENDING THIS TIME TOGETHER.

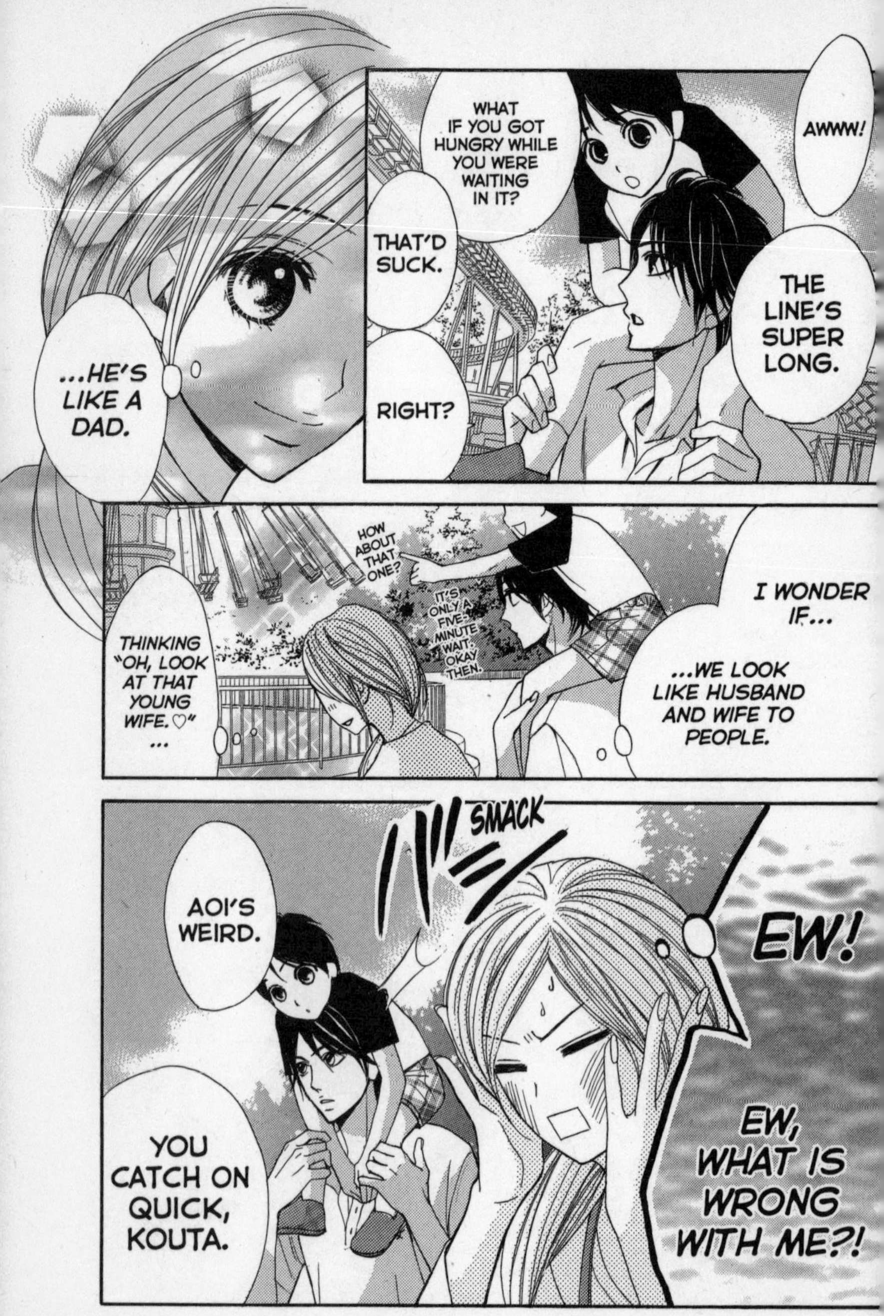
AWWW!
THE LINE'S SUPER LONG.
WHAT IF YOU GOT HUNGRY WHILE YOU WERE WAITING IN IT?
THAT'D SUCK.
RIGHT?
...HE'S LIKE A DAD.
I WONDER IF...
...WE LOOK LIKE HUSBAND AND WIFE TO PEOPLE.
HOW ABOUT THAT ONE?
IT'S ONLY A FIVE-MINUTE WAIT. OKAY THEN.
THINKING "OH, LOOK AT THAT YOUNG WIFE.♡" ...
SMACK
EW!
EW, WHAT IS WRONG WITH ME?!
AOI'S WEIRD.
YOU CATCH ON QUICK, KOUTA.

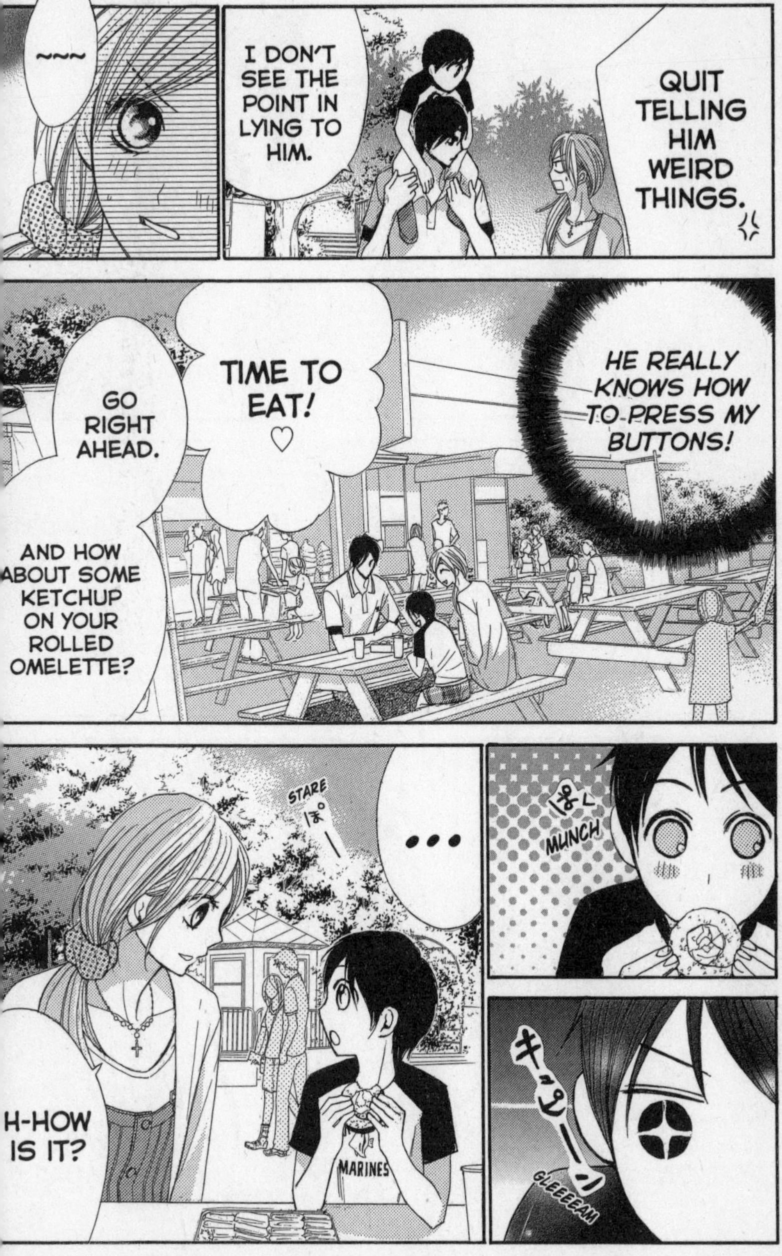
QUIT TELLING HIM WEIRD THINGS.
I DON'T SEE THE POINT IN LYING TO HIM.
~~~
HE REALLY KNOWS HOW TO PRESS MY BUTTONS!
TIME TO EAT! ♡
GO RIGHT AHEAD.
AND HOW ABOUT SOME KETCHUP ON YOUR ROLLED OMELETTE?
MUNCH
GLEEEEAM
...
STARE
MARINES
H-HOW IS IT?
~~~

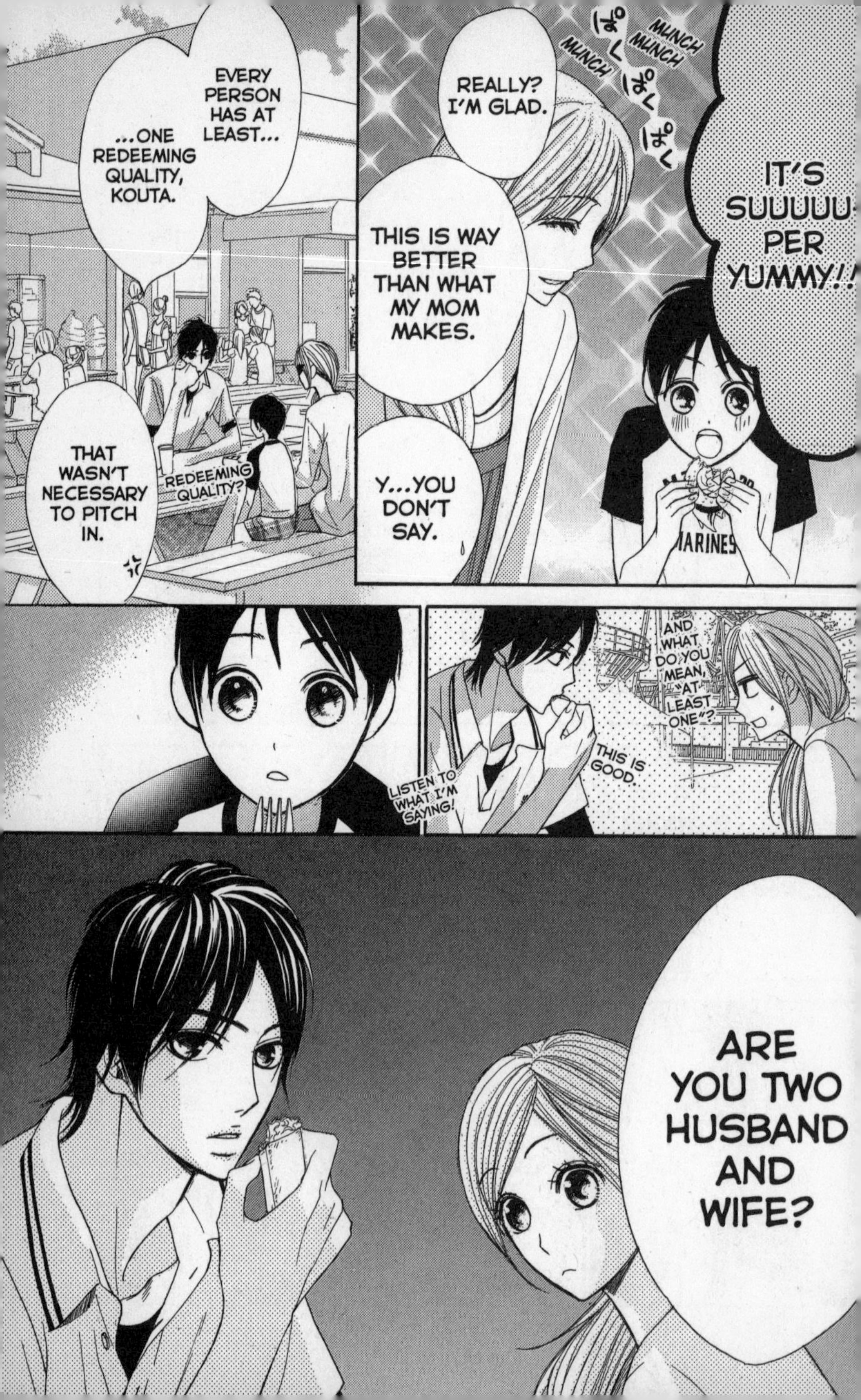
IT'S SUUUUU-PER YUMMY!!
ぱくぱくぱく
MUNCH MUNCH MUNCH
REALLY? I'M GLAD.
THIS IS WAY BETTER THAN WHAT MY MOM MAKES.
Y...YOU DON'T SAY.
EVERY PERSON HAS AT LEAST...
...ONE REDEEMING QUALITY, KOUTA.
REDEEMING QUALITY?
THAT WASN'T NECESSARY TO PITCH IN.
AND WHAT DO YOU MEAN, "AT LEAST ONE"?
THIS IS GOOD.
LISTEN TO WHAT I'M SAYING!
ARE YOU TWO HUSBAND AND WIFE?

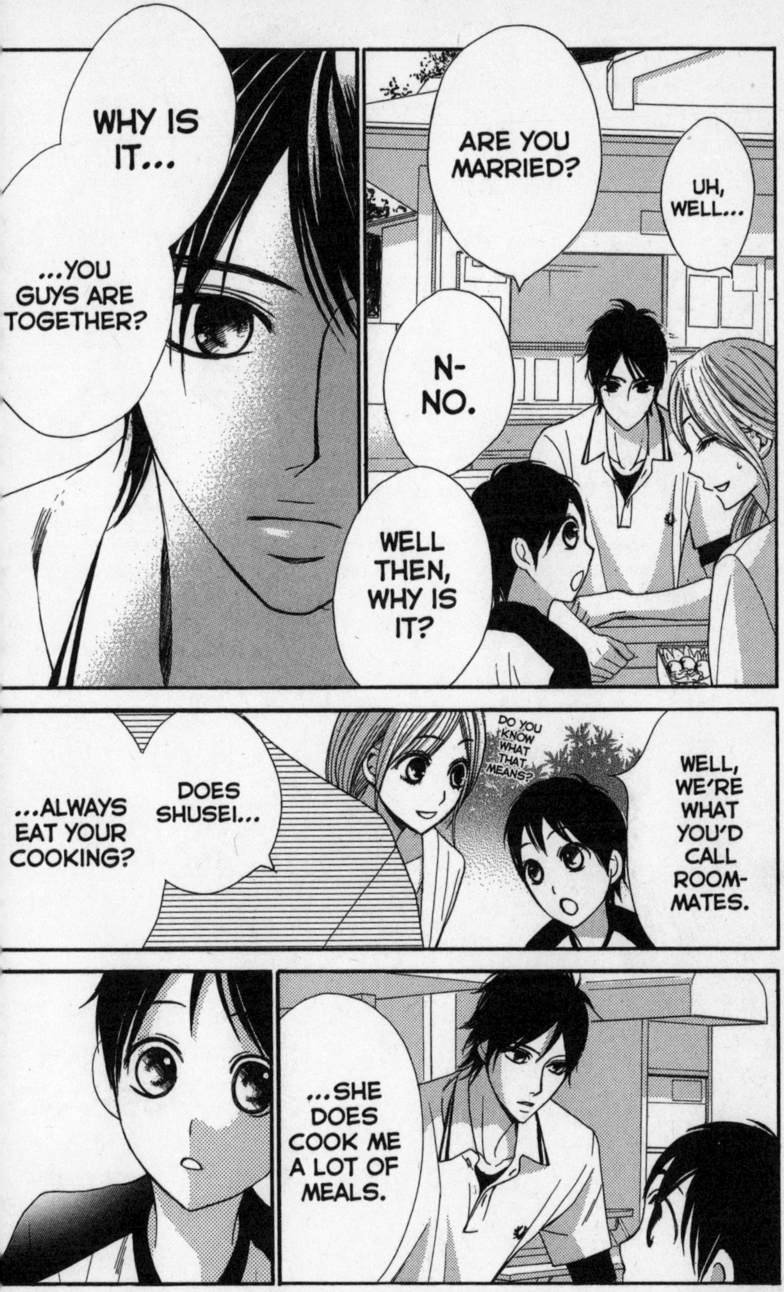
ARE YOU MARRIED?
UH, WELL...
N-NO.
WELL THEN, WHY IS IT?
WHY IS IT...
...YOU GUYS ARE TOGETHER?
WELL, WE'RE WHAT YOU'D CALL ROOMMATES.
DO YOU KNOW WHAT THAT MEANS?
DOES SHUSEI...
...ALWAYS EAT YOUR COOKING?
...SHE DOES COOK ME A LOT OF MEALS.

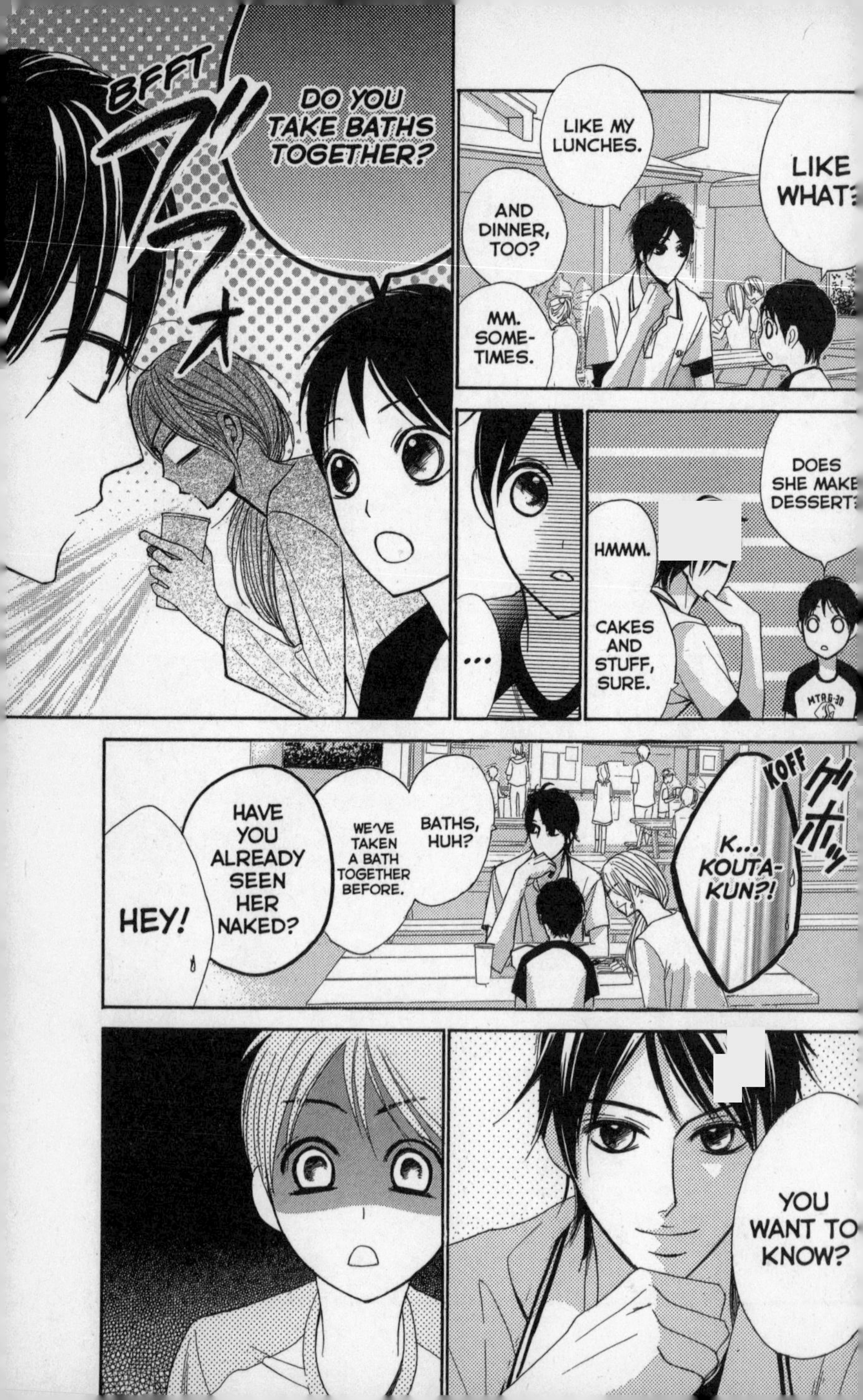
LIKE WHAT?
LIKE MY LUNCHES.
AND DINNER, TOO?
MM. SOME-TIMES.
DOES SHE MAKE DESSERT?
HMMM.
CAKES AND STUFF, SURE.
...
DO YOU TAKE BATHS TOGETHER?
BFFT
KOFF
K... KOUTA-KUN?!
BATHS, HUH?
WE'VE TAKEN A BATH TOGETHER BEFORE.
HAVE YOU ALREADY SEEN HER NAKED?
HEY!
YOU WANT TO KNOW?

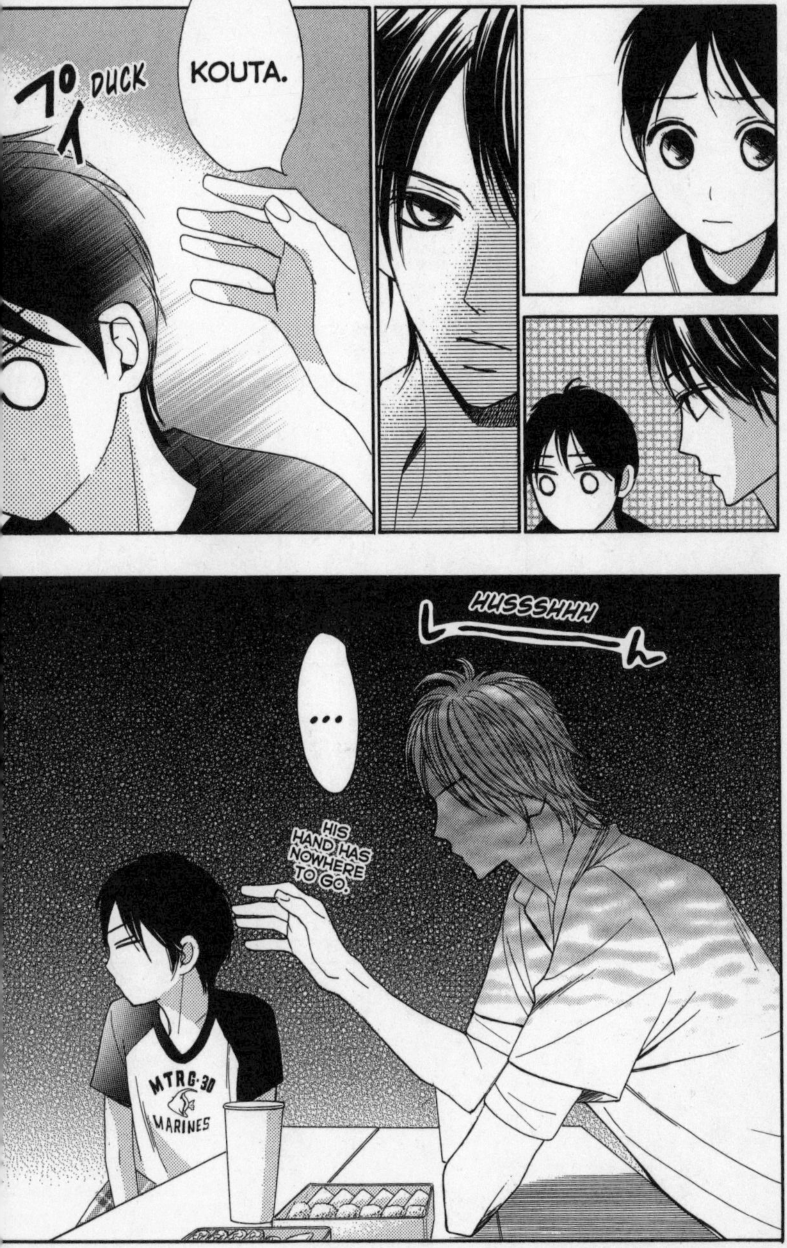
KOUTA.
DUCK
...
HUSSSHHH
HIS HAND HAS NOWHERE TO GO.
MTRG-30
MARINES

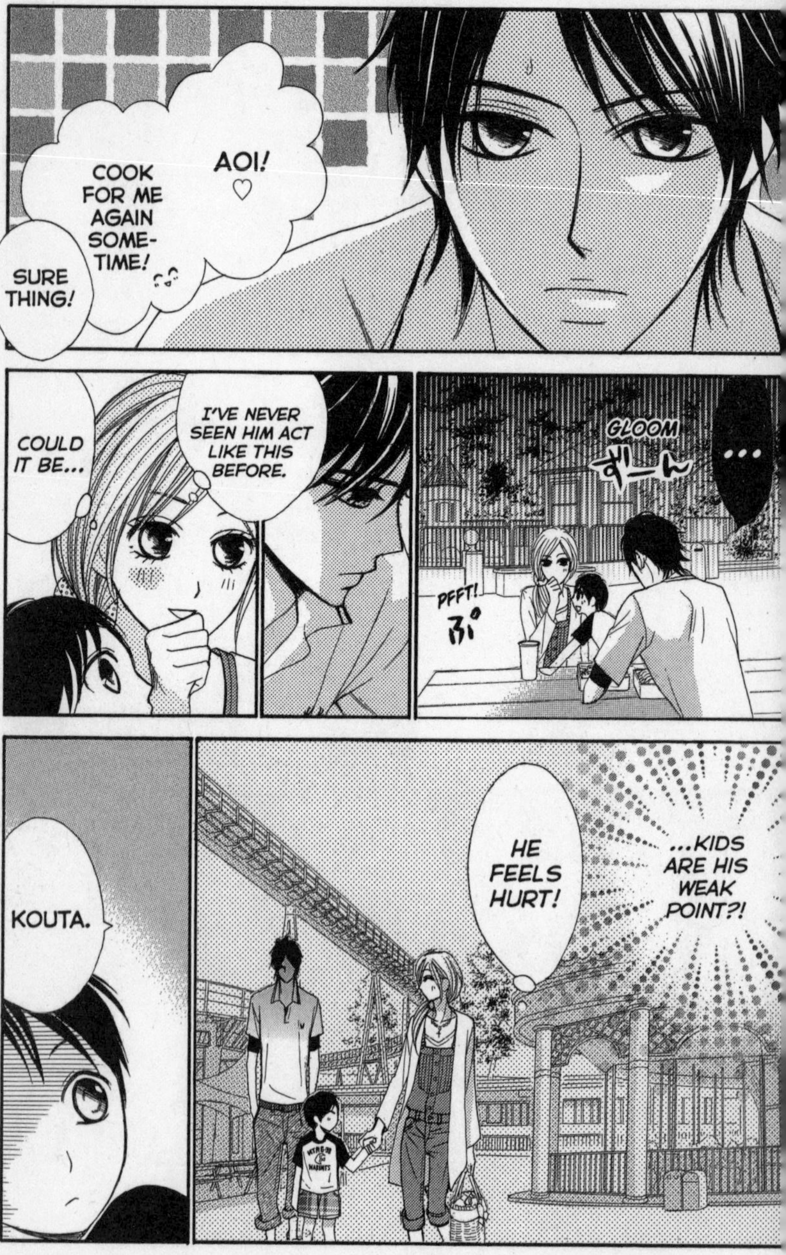
AOI! ♡
COOK FOR ME AGAIN SOMETIME!
SURE THING!
GLOOM
ずーん
...
PFFT!
ぷ
I'VE NEVER SEEN HIM ACT LIKE THIS BEFORE.
COULD IT BE...
...KIDS ARE HIS WEAK POINT?!
HE FEELS HURT!
KOUTA.

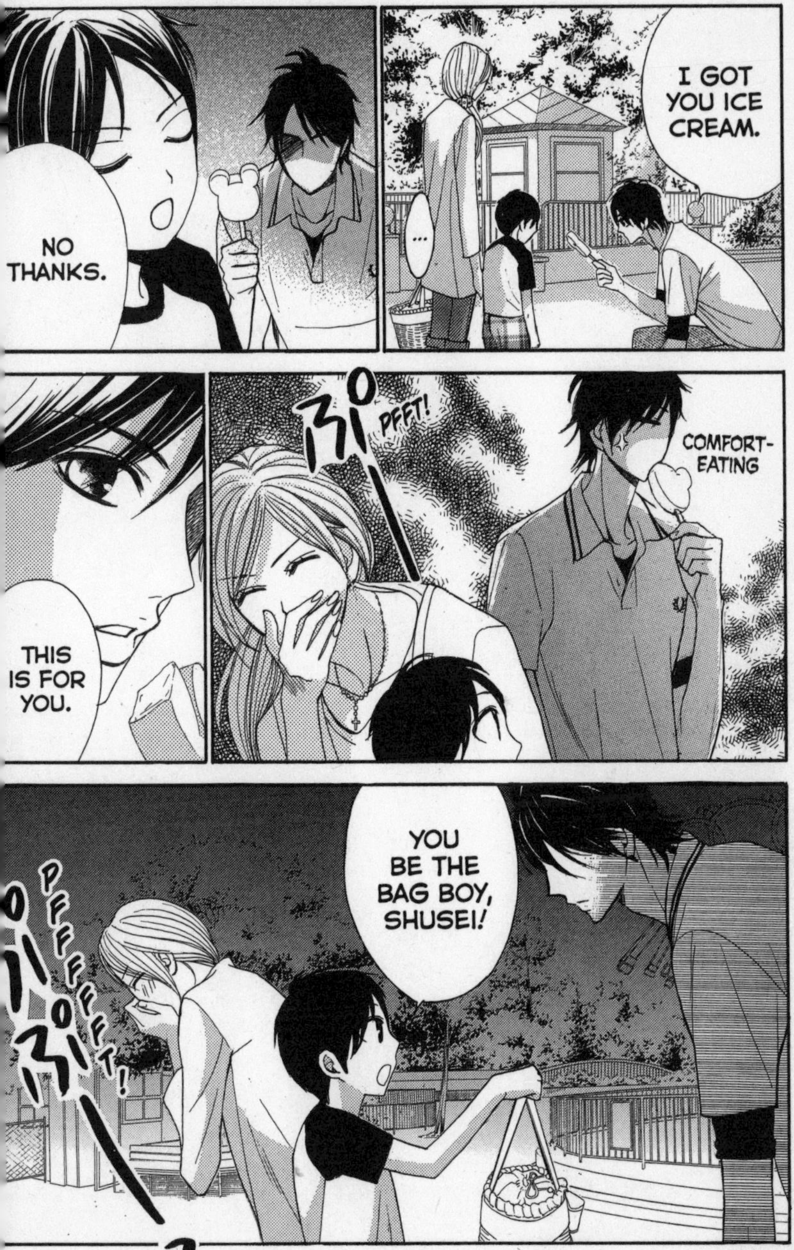
I GOT YOU ICE CREAM.
...
NO THANKS.
COMFORT-EATING
PFFT!
THIS IS FOR YOU.
YOU BE THE BAG BOY, SHUSEI!
PFFFFFFT!

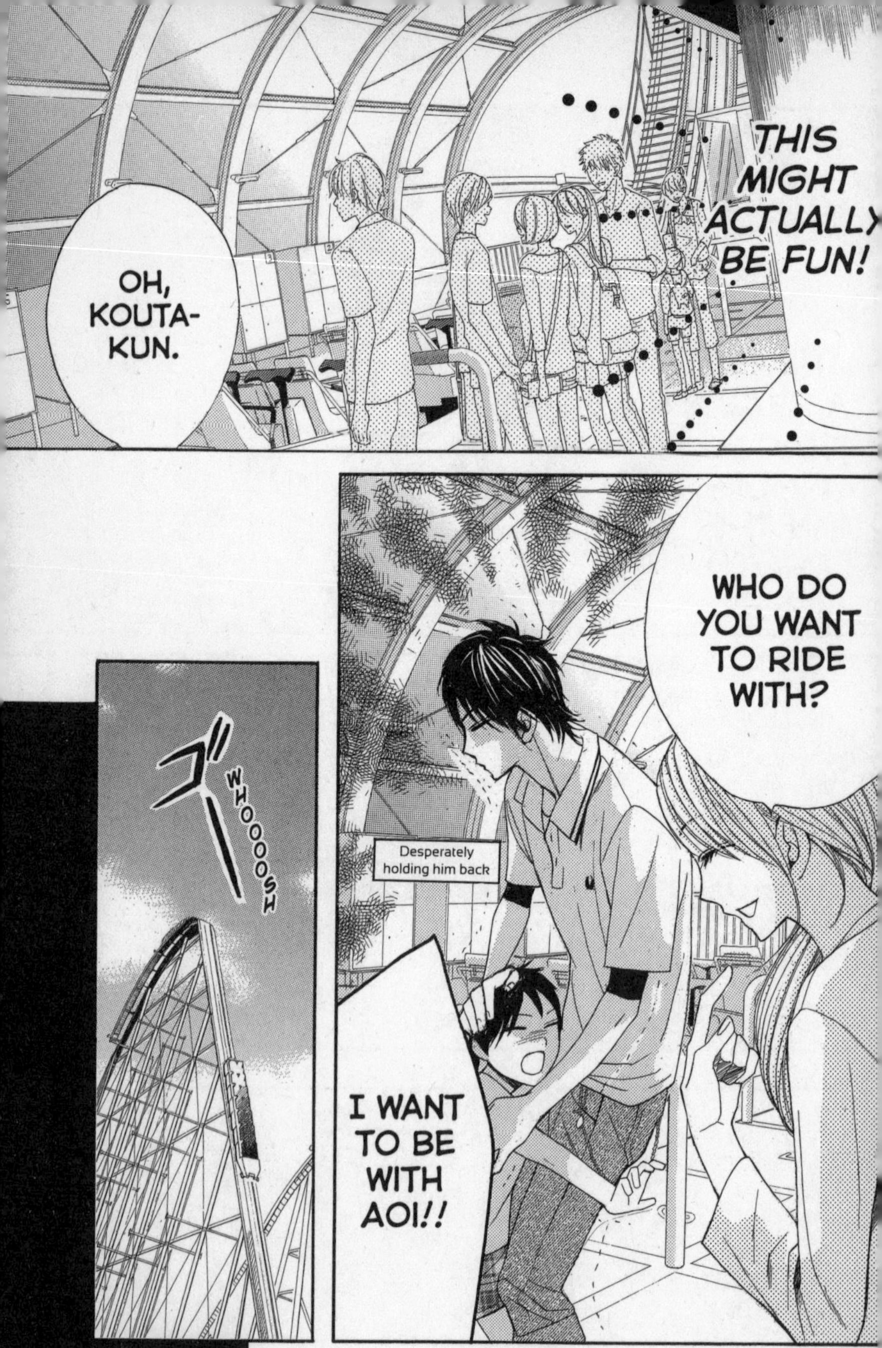
THIS MIGHT ACTUALLY BE FUN!
OH, KOUTA-KUN.
WHO DO YOU WANT TO RIDE WITH?
Desperately holding him back
I WANT TO BE WITH AOI!!
ゴー
WHOOOOSH

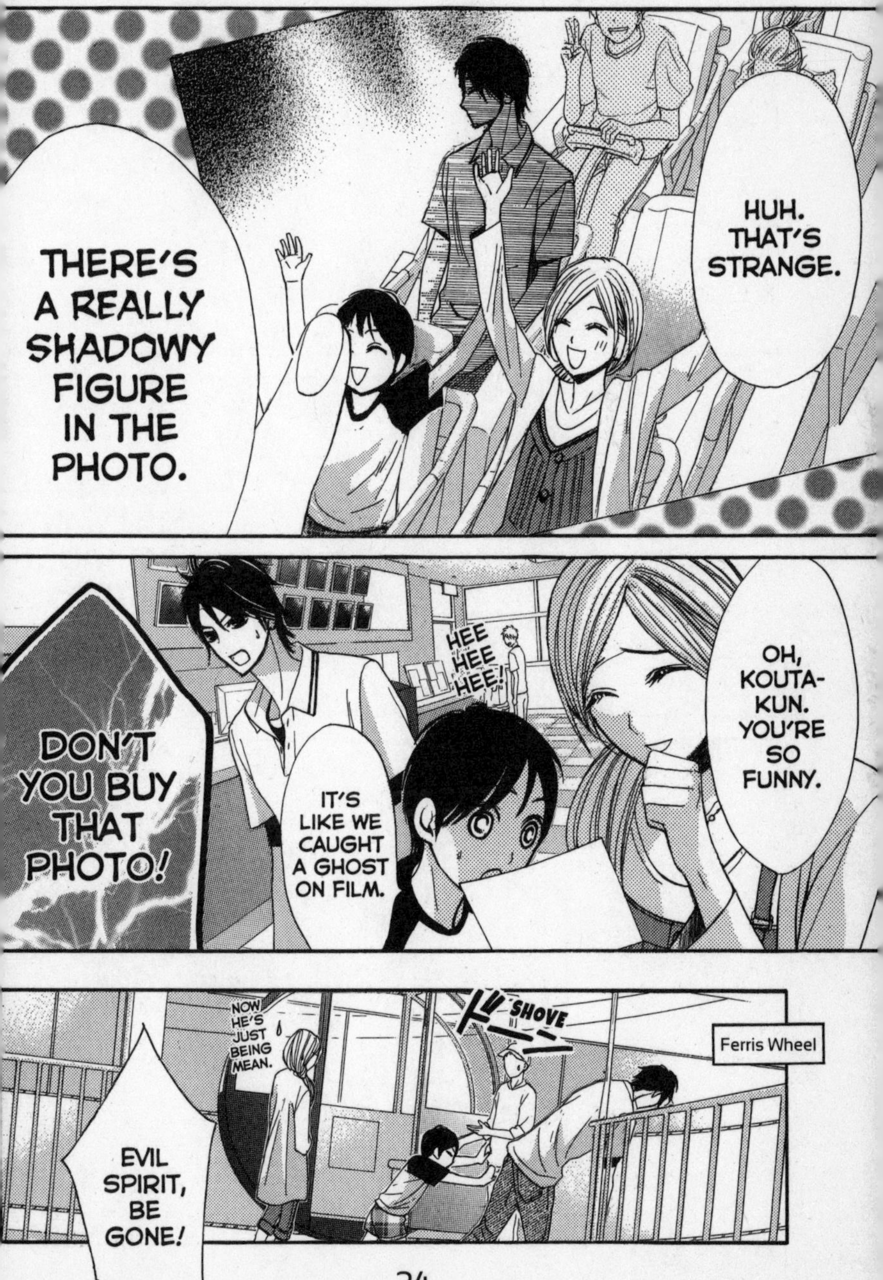
HUH. THAT'S STRANGE.
THERE'S A REALLY SHADOWY FIGURE IN THE PHOTO.
OH, KOUTA-KUN. YOU'RE SO FUNNY.
HEE HEE HEE!
IT'S LIKE WE CAUGHT A GHOST ON FILM.
DON'T YOU BUY THAT PHOTO!
Ferris Wheel
SHOVE
NOW HE'S JUST BEING MEAN.
EVIL SPIRIT, BE GONE!

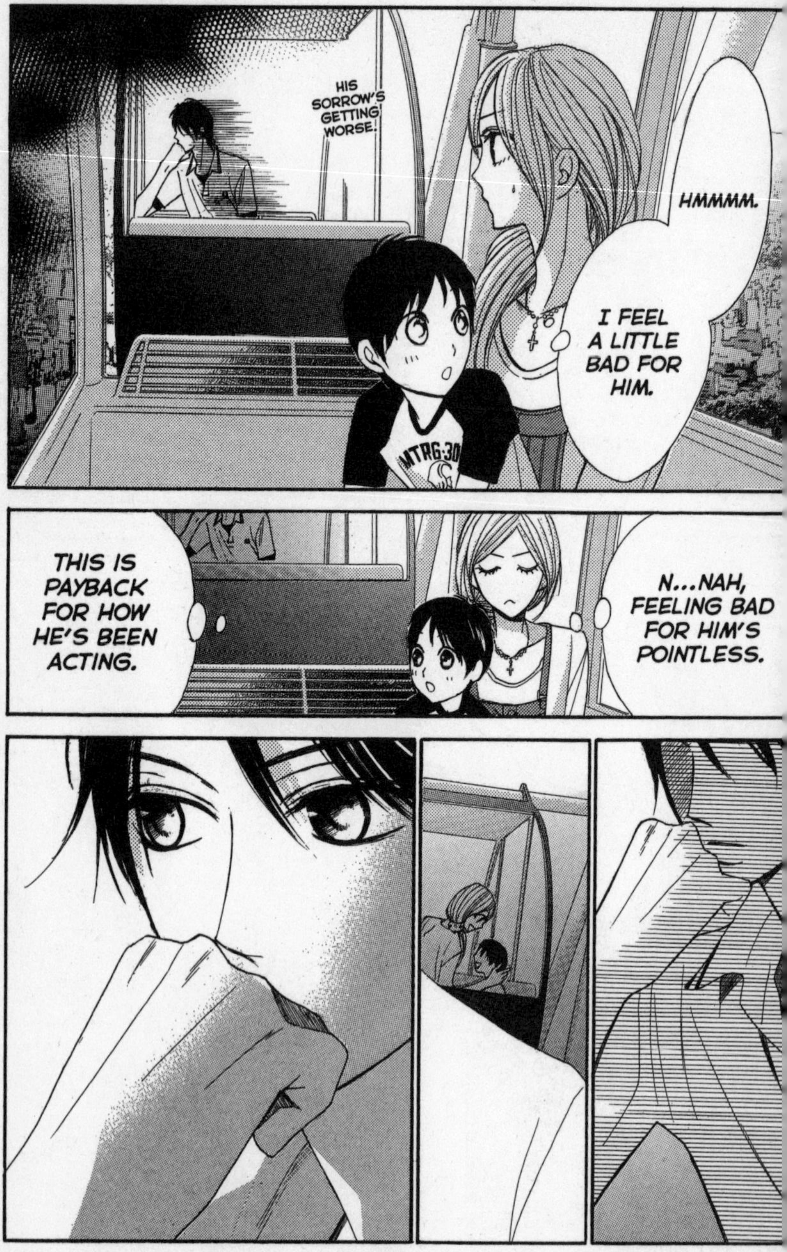
HMMMM.
I FEEL A LITTLE BAD FOR HIM.
HIS SORROW'S GETTING WORSE.
N...NAH, FEELING BAD FOR HIM'S POINTLESS.
THIS IS PAYBACK FOR HOW HE'S BEEN ACTING.

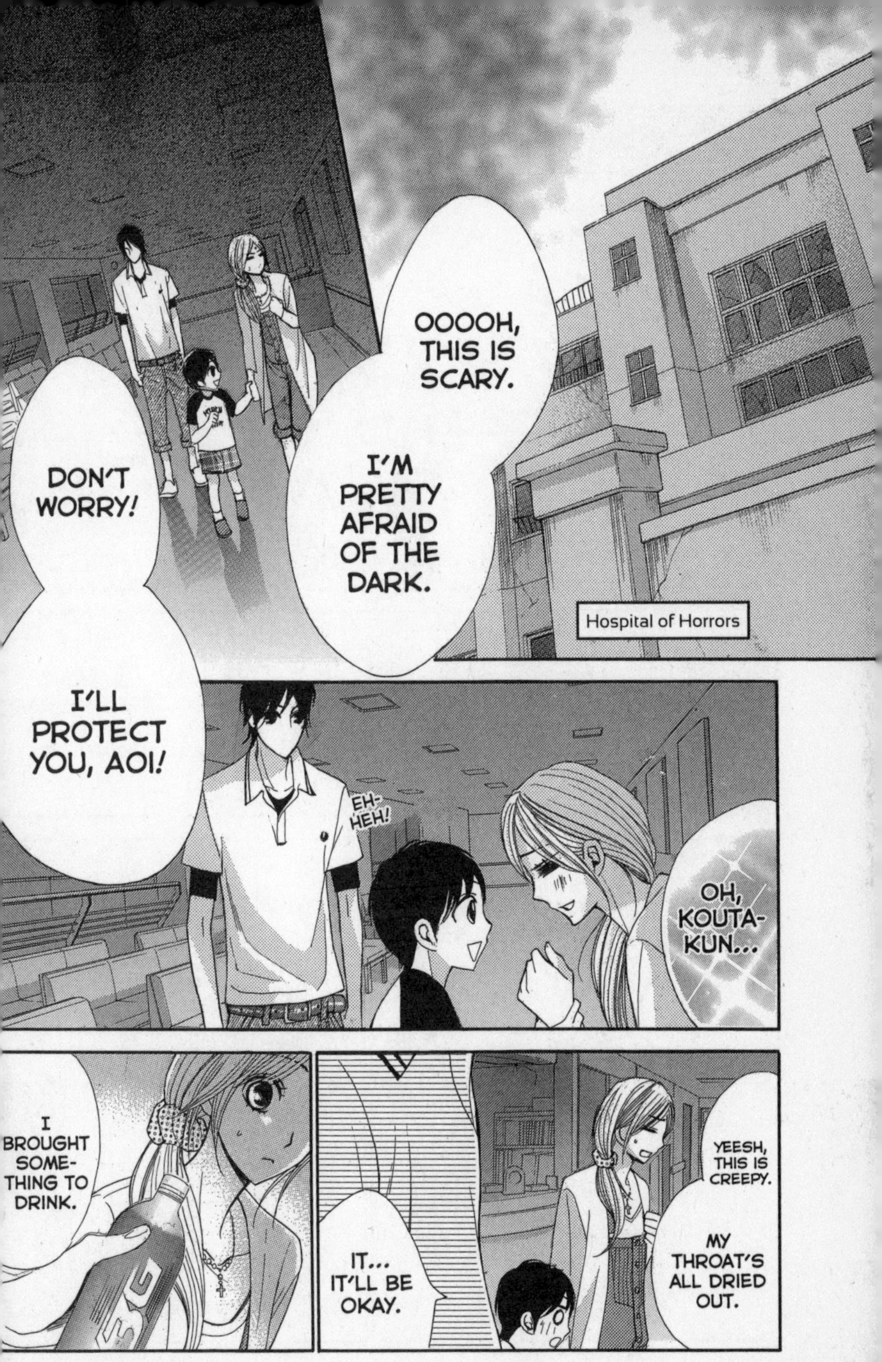
Hospital of Horrors
OOOOH, THIS IS SCARY.
I'M PRETTY AFRAID OF THE DARK.
DON'T WORRY!
I'LL PROTECT YOU, AOI!
OH, KOUTA-KUN...
EH-HEH!
YEESH, THIS IS CREEPY.
MY THROAT'S ALL DRIED OUT.
IT... IT'LL BE OKAY.
I BROUGHT SOME-THING TO DRINK.

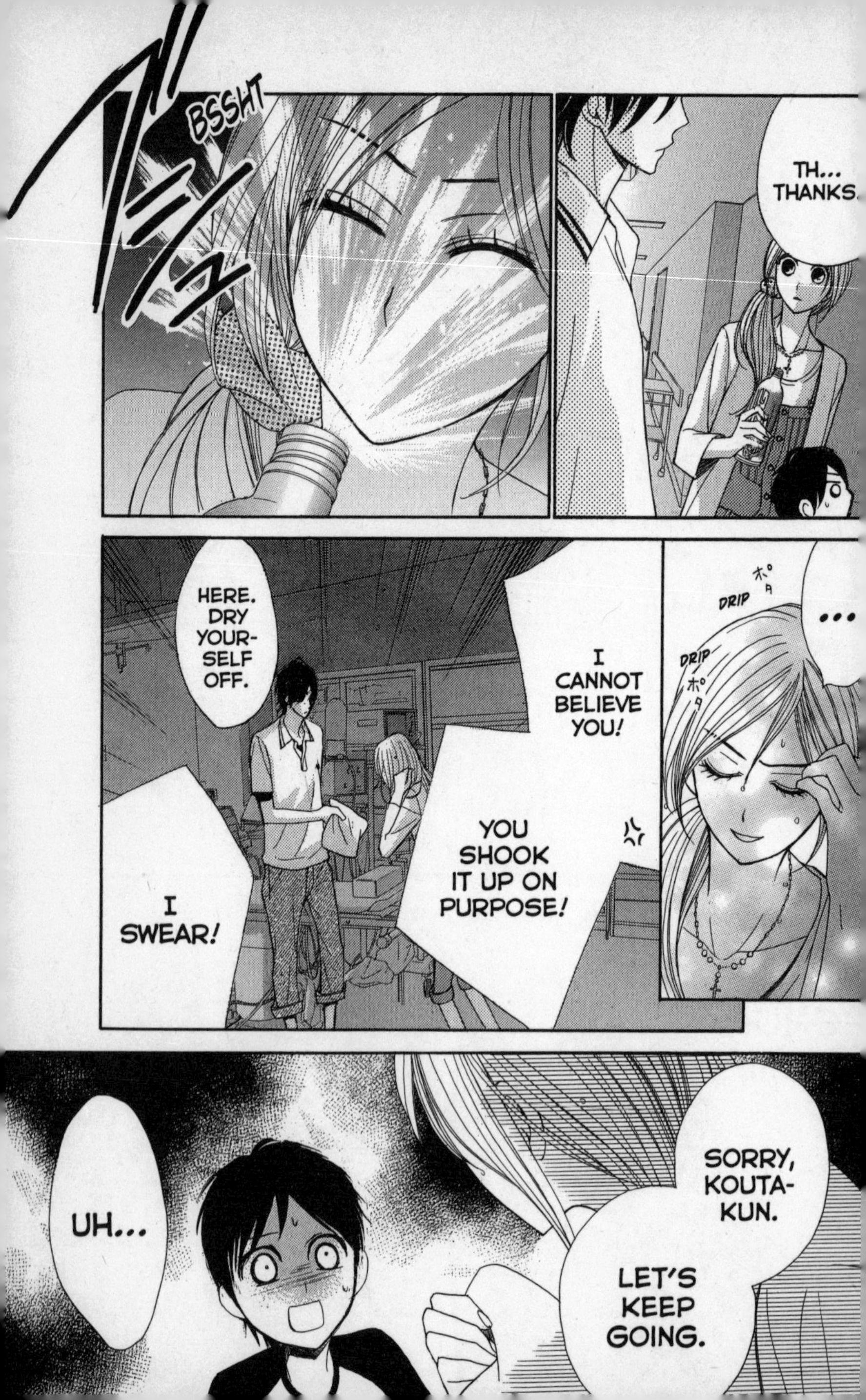
TH... THANKS.
BSSHT
...
DRIP
DRIP
I CANNOT BELIEVE YOU!
HERE. DRY YOUR-SELF OFF.
YOU SHOOK IT UP ON PURPOSE!
I SWEAR!
SORRY, KOUTA-KUN.
LET'S KEEP GOING.
UH...

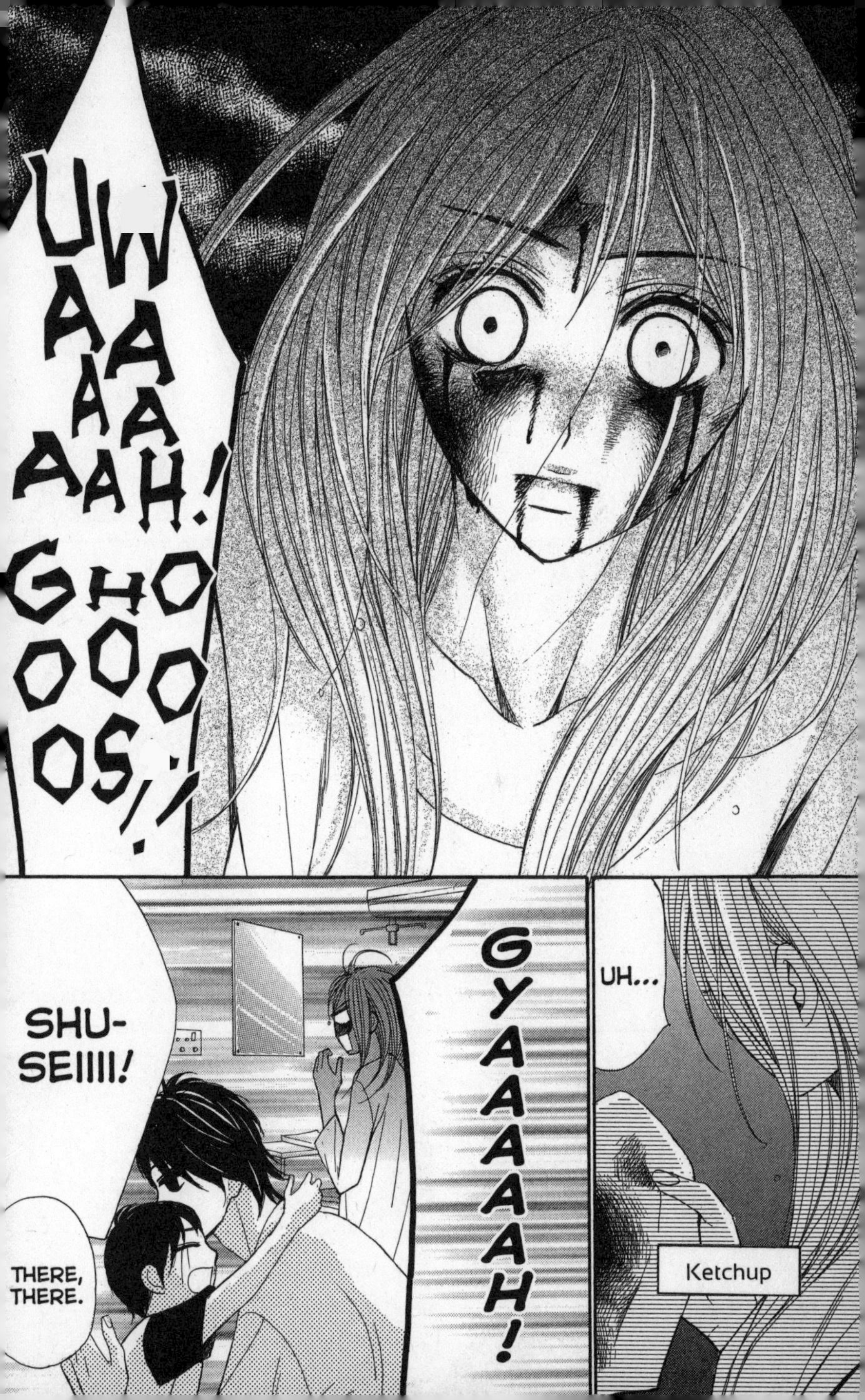
UWAAAAAAH! GHOOOOOS!!
UH...
Ketchup
GYAAAAAH!
SHU-SEIIIII!
THERE, THERE.

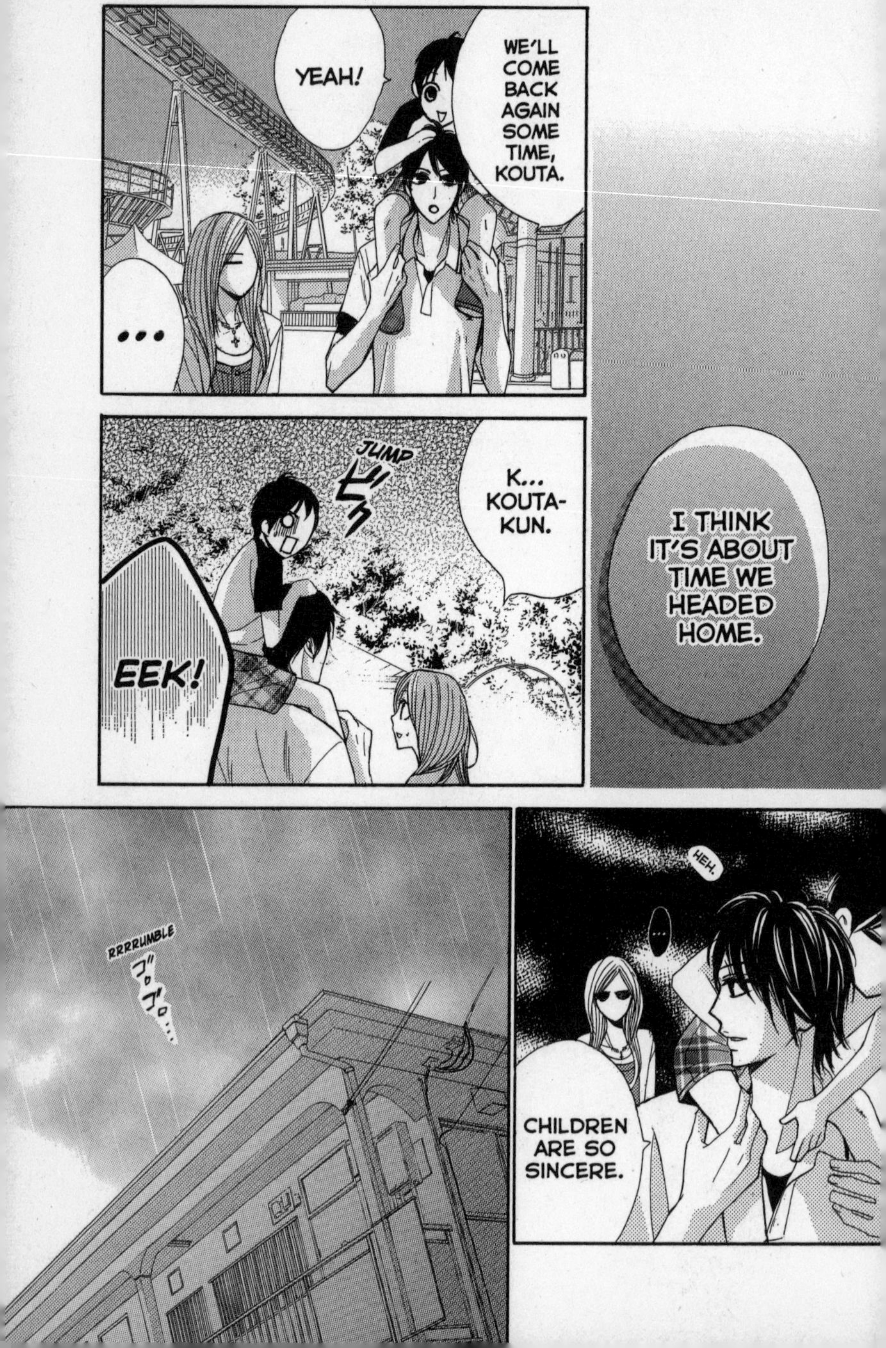
I THINK IT'S ABOUT TIME WE HEADED HOME.
WE'LL COME BACK AGAIN SOME TIME, KOUTA.
YEAH!
...
K... KOUTA-KUN.
JUMP
EEK!
HEH.
...
CHILDREN ARE SO SINCERE.
RRRRUMBLE

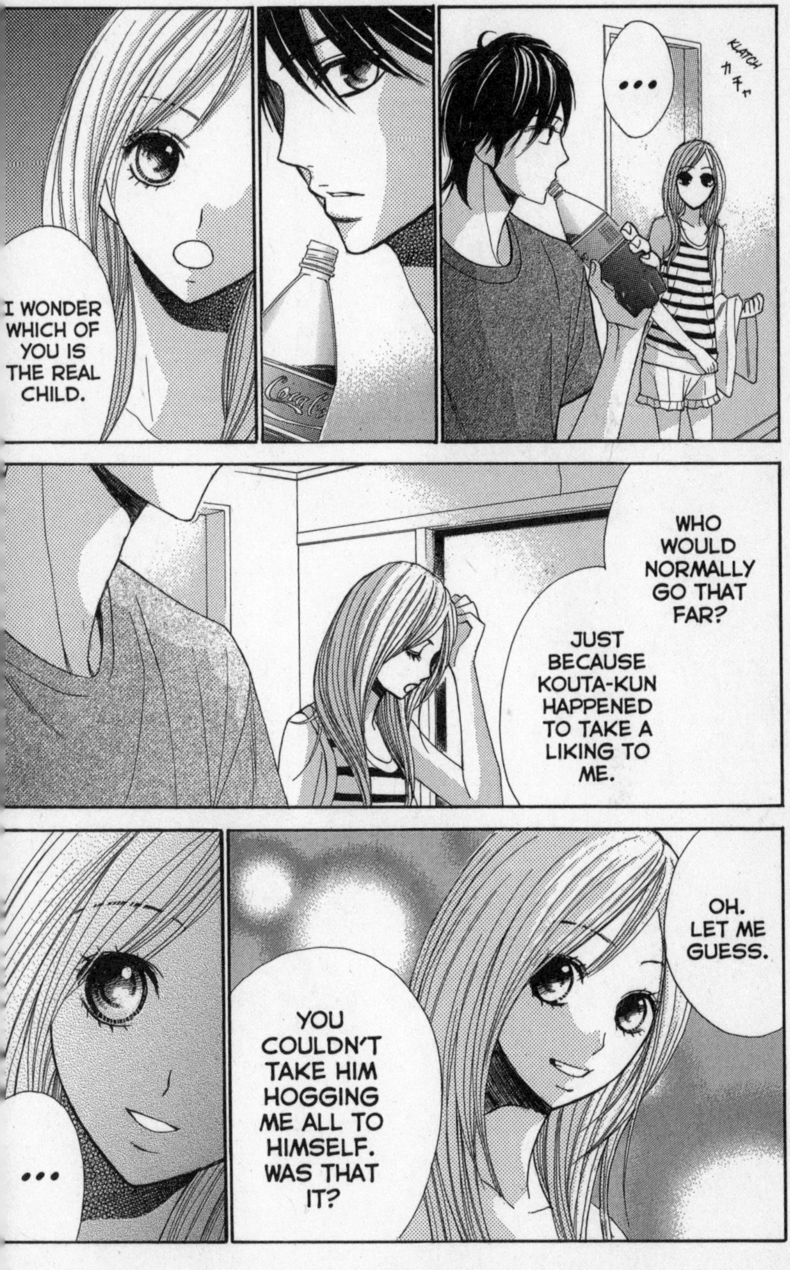
...
KLATCH
カチャ
I WONDER WHICH OF YOU IS THE REAL CHILD.
WHO WOULD NORMALLY GO THAT FAR?
JUST BECAUSE KOUTA-KUN HAPPENED TO TAKE A LIKING TO ME.
OH. LET ME GUESS.
YOU COULDN'T TAKE HIM HOGGING ME ALL TO HIMSELF. WAS THAT IT?
...

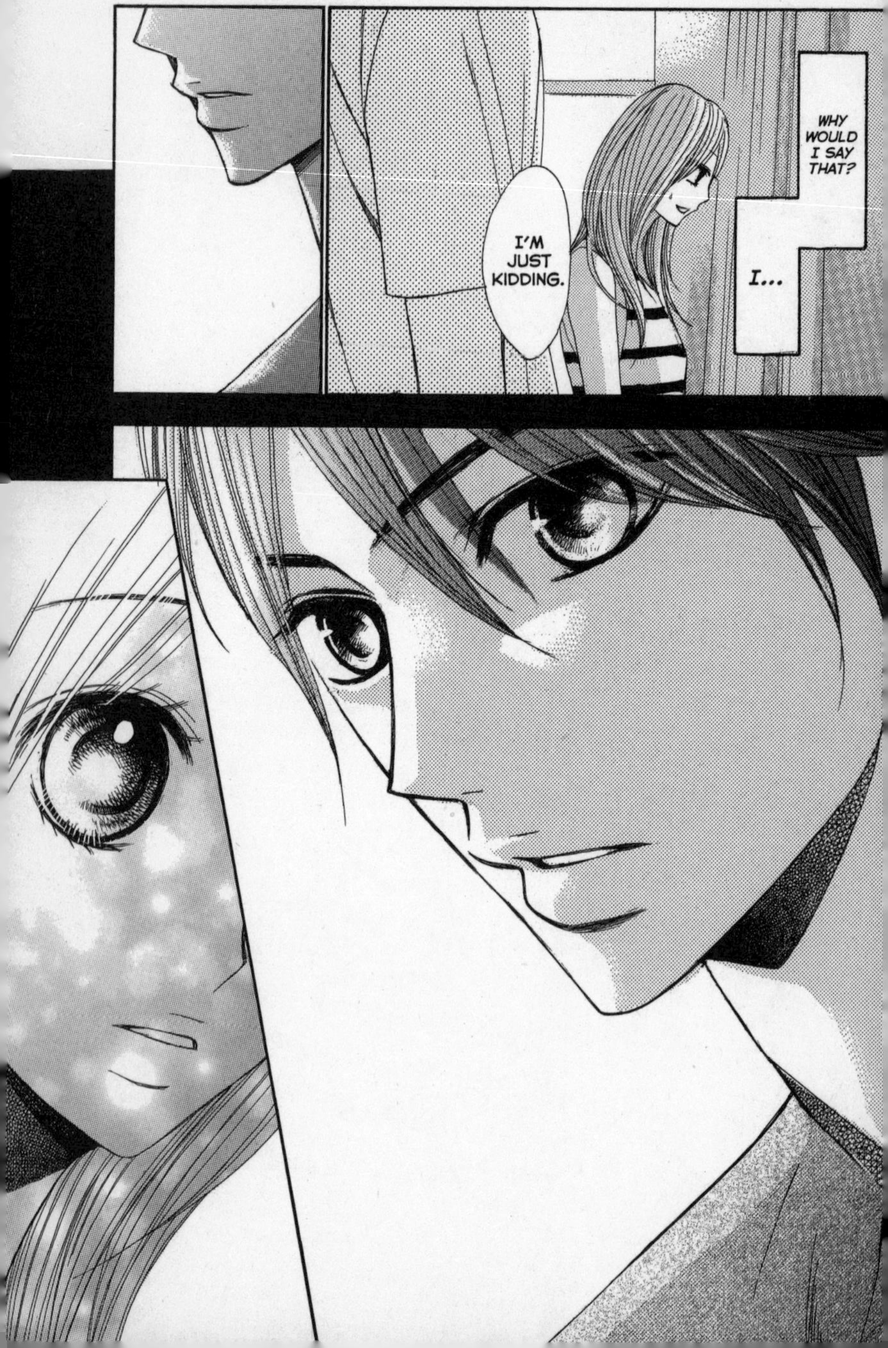
WHY WOULD I SAY THAT?
I...
I'M JUST KIDDING.

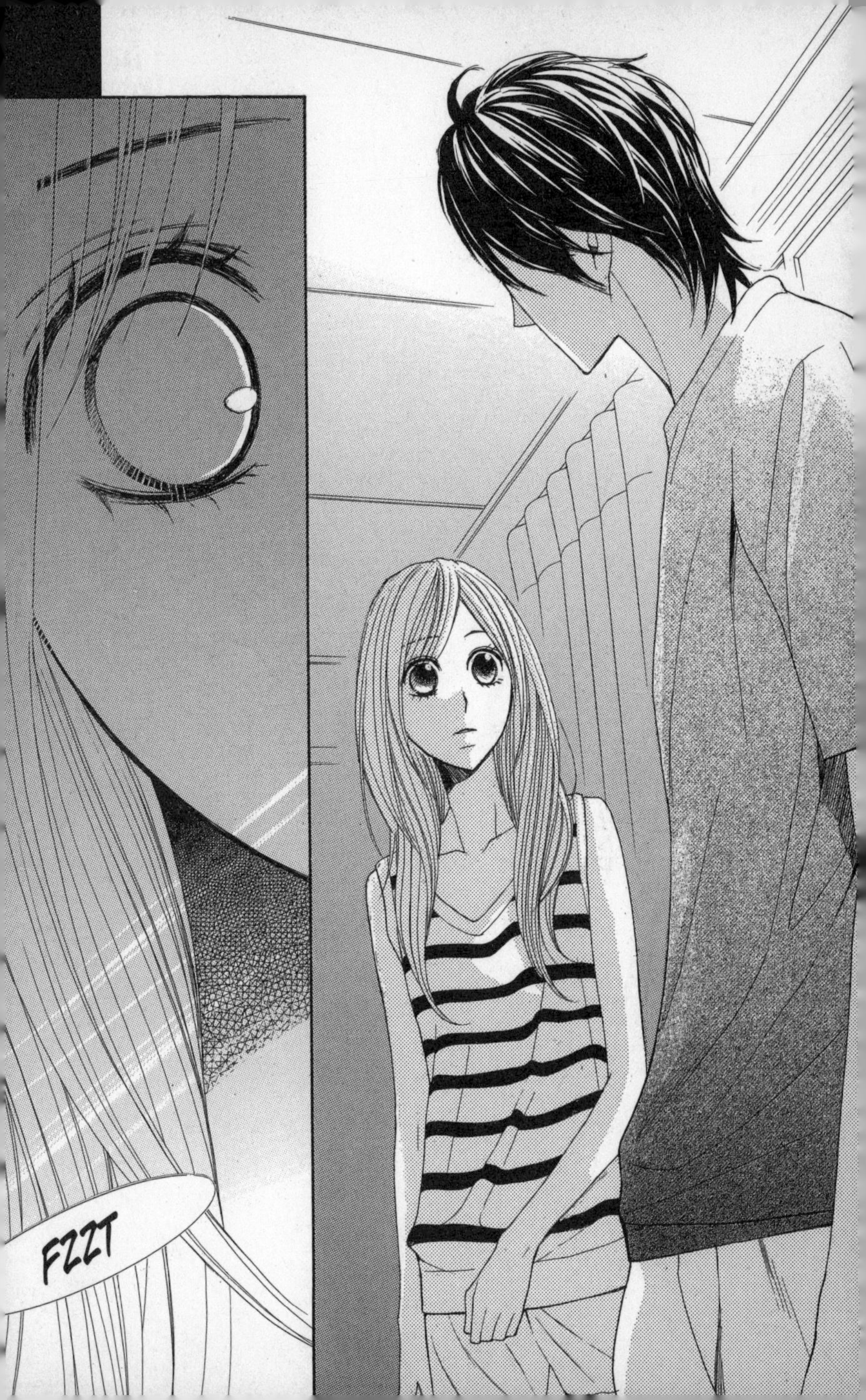
FZZT

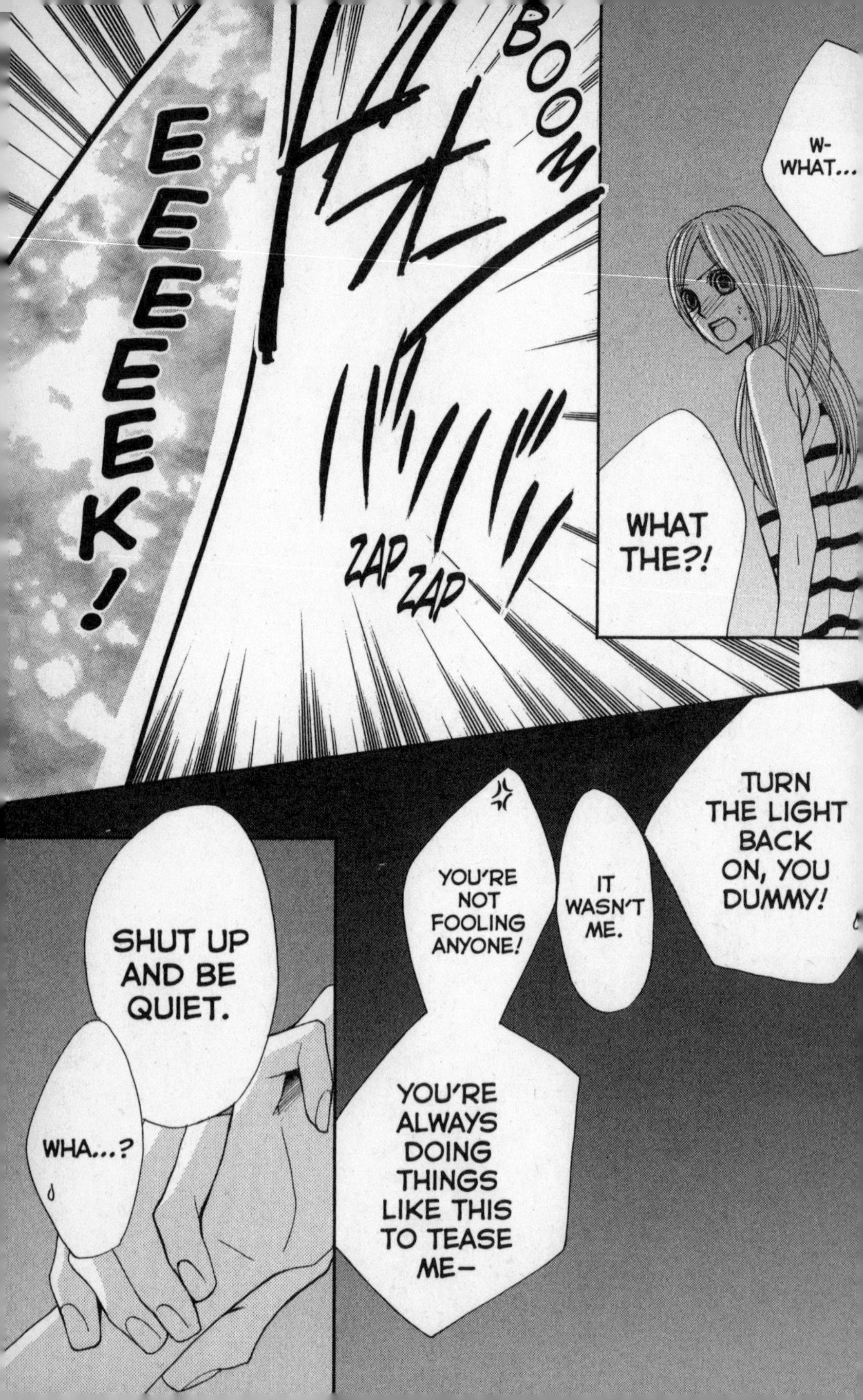
W-WHAT...
WHAT THE?!
BOOM
EEEEEK!
ZAP ZAP
TURN THE LIGHT BACK ON, YOU DUMMY!
IT WASN'T ME.
YOU'RE NOT FOOLING ANYONE!
YOU'RE ALWAYS DOING THINGS LIKE THIS TO TEASE ME—
SHUT UP AND BE QUIET.
WHA...?

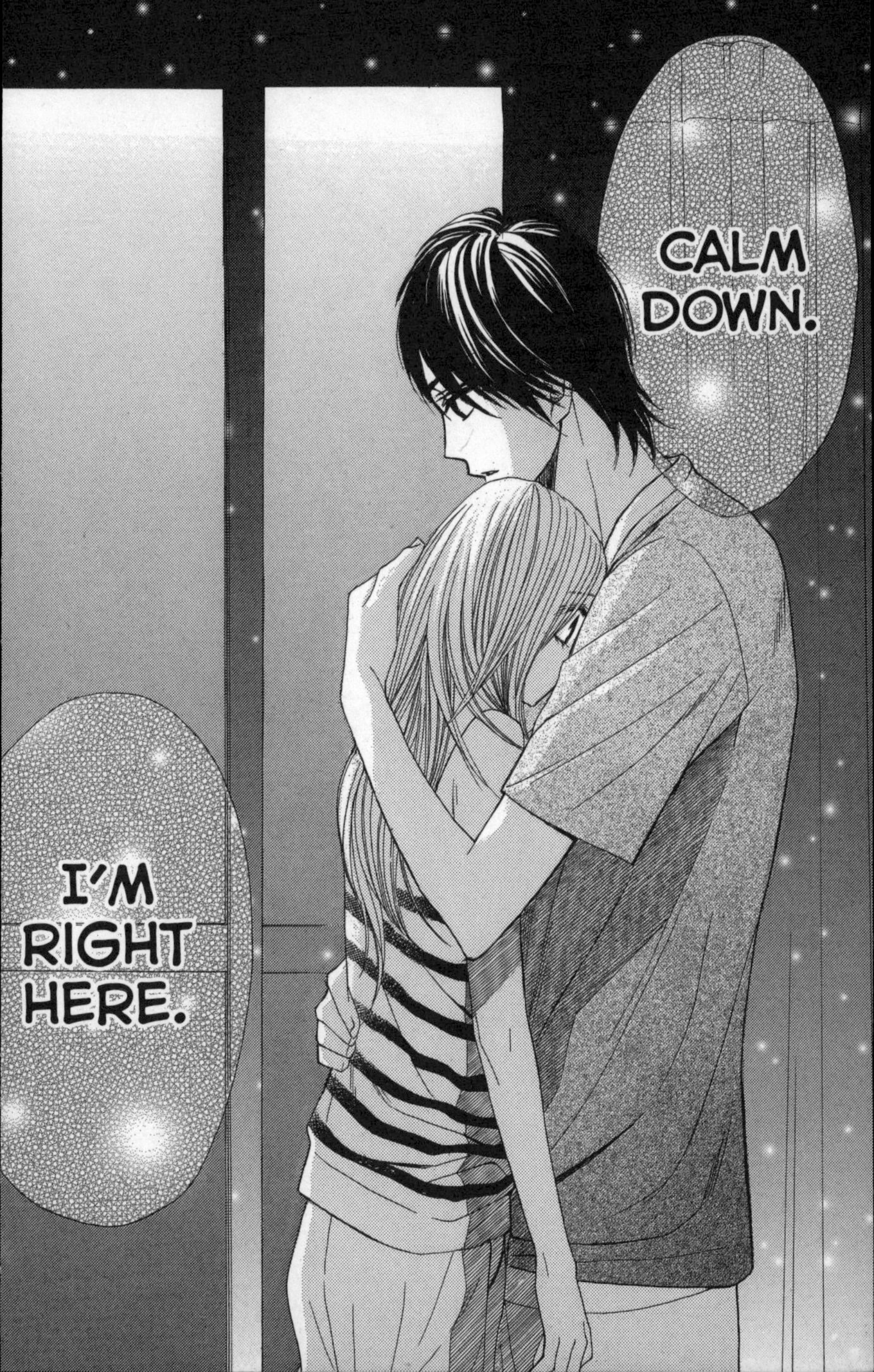
CALM DOWN.
I'M RIGHT HERE.

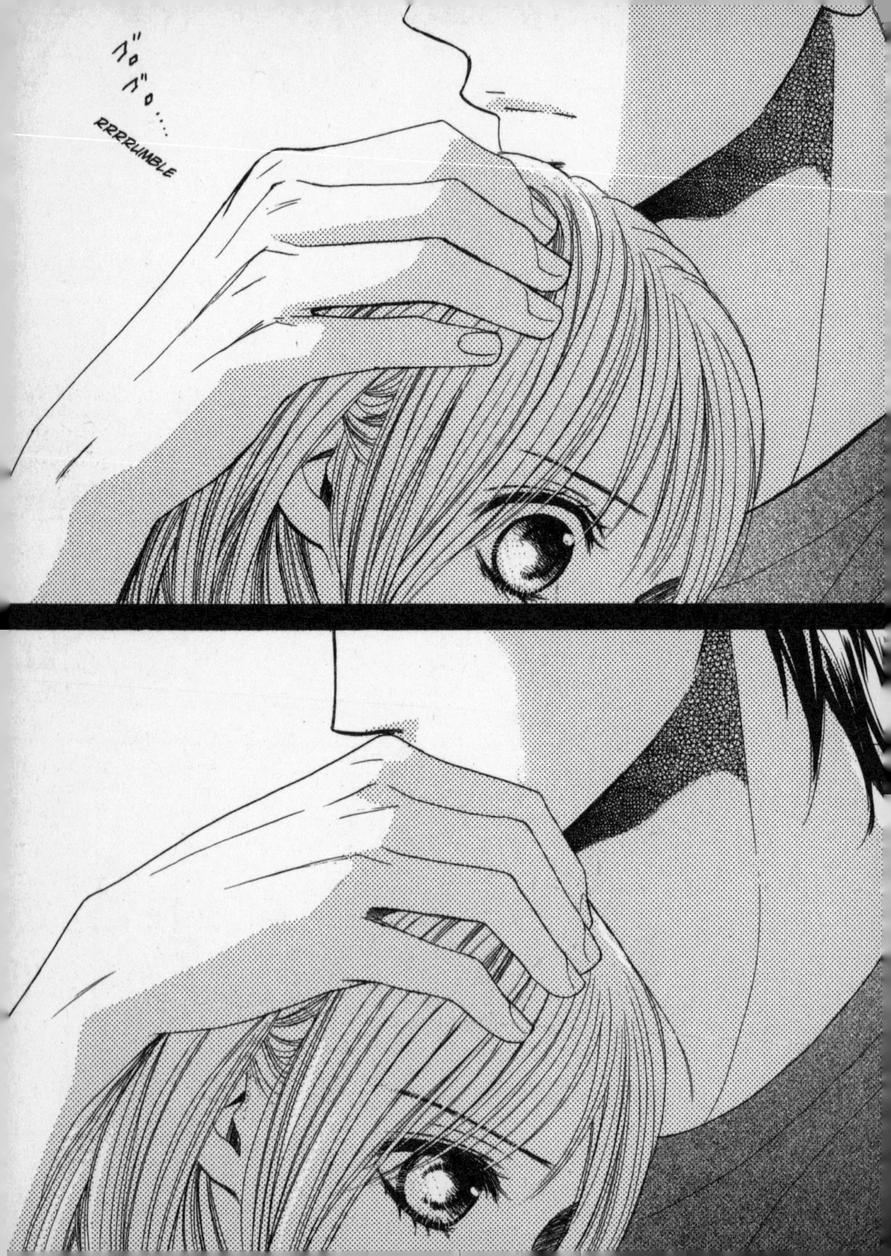
ゴロゴロ…
RRRRUMBLE

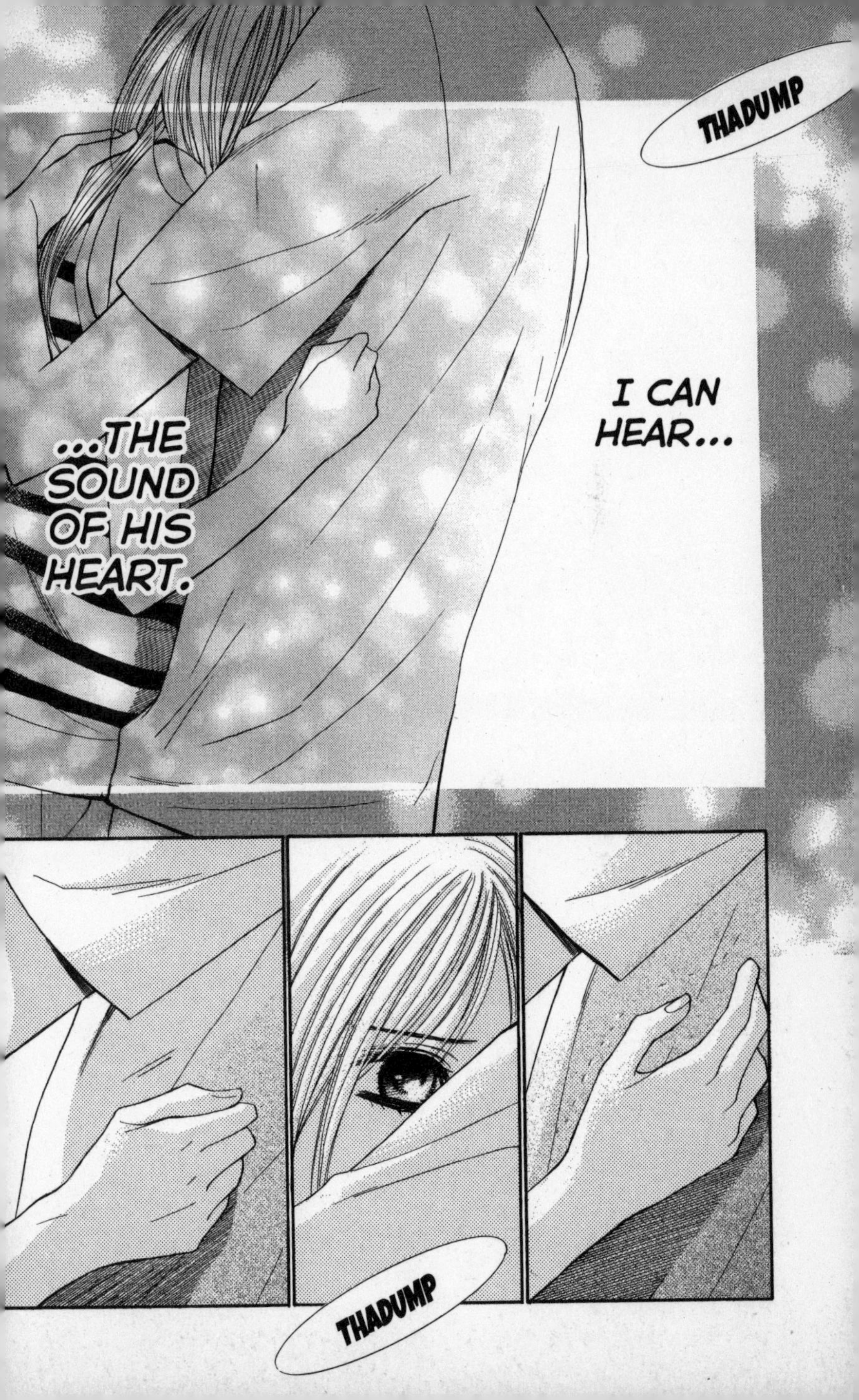
THADUMP
I CAN HEAR...
...THE SOUND OF HIS HEART.
THADUMP

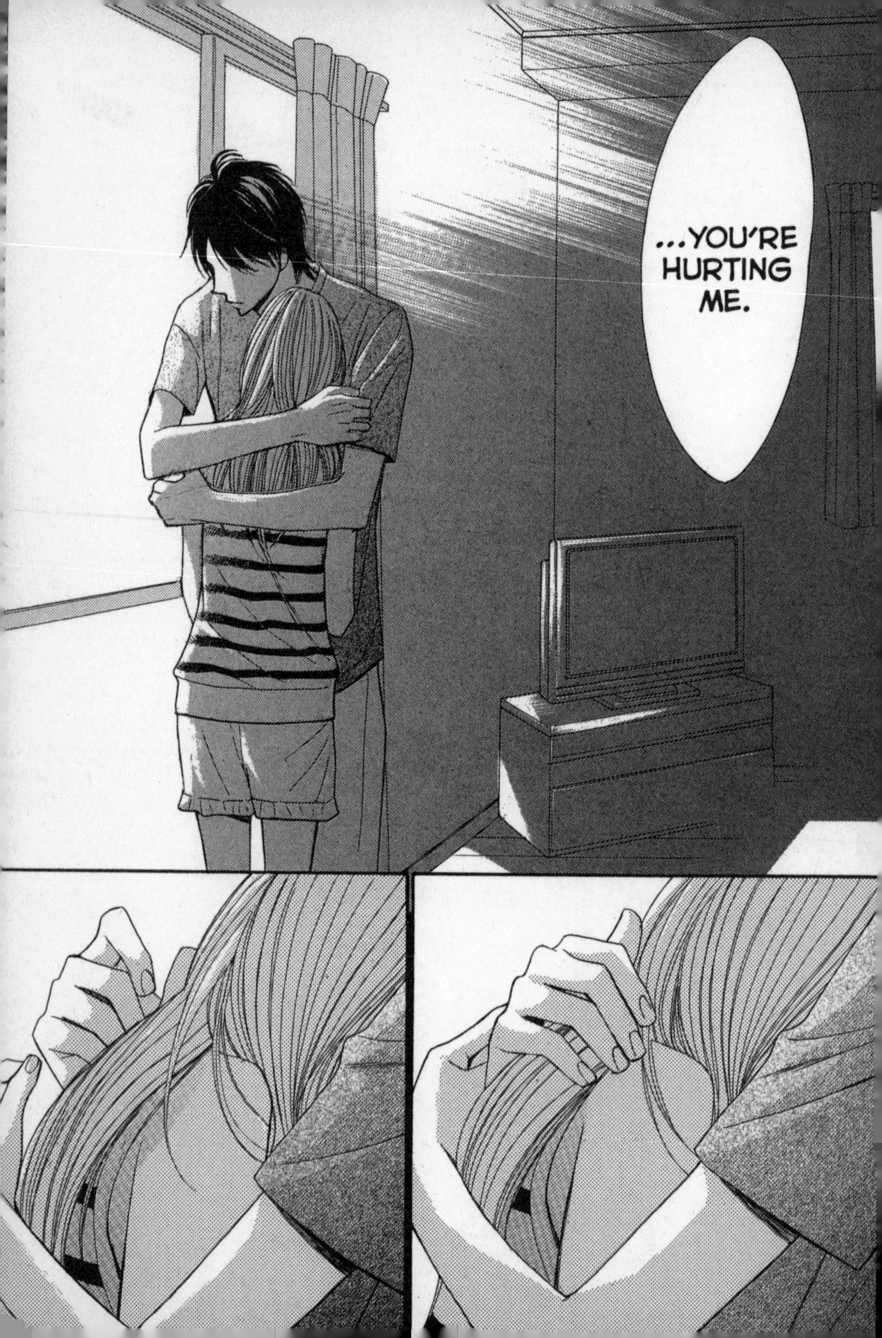
...YOU'RE HURTING ME.

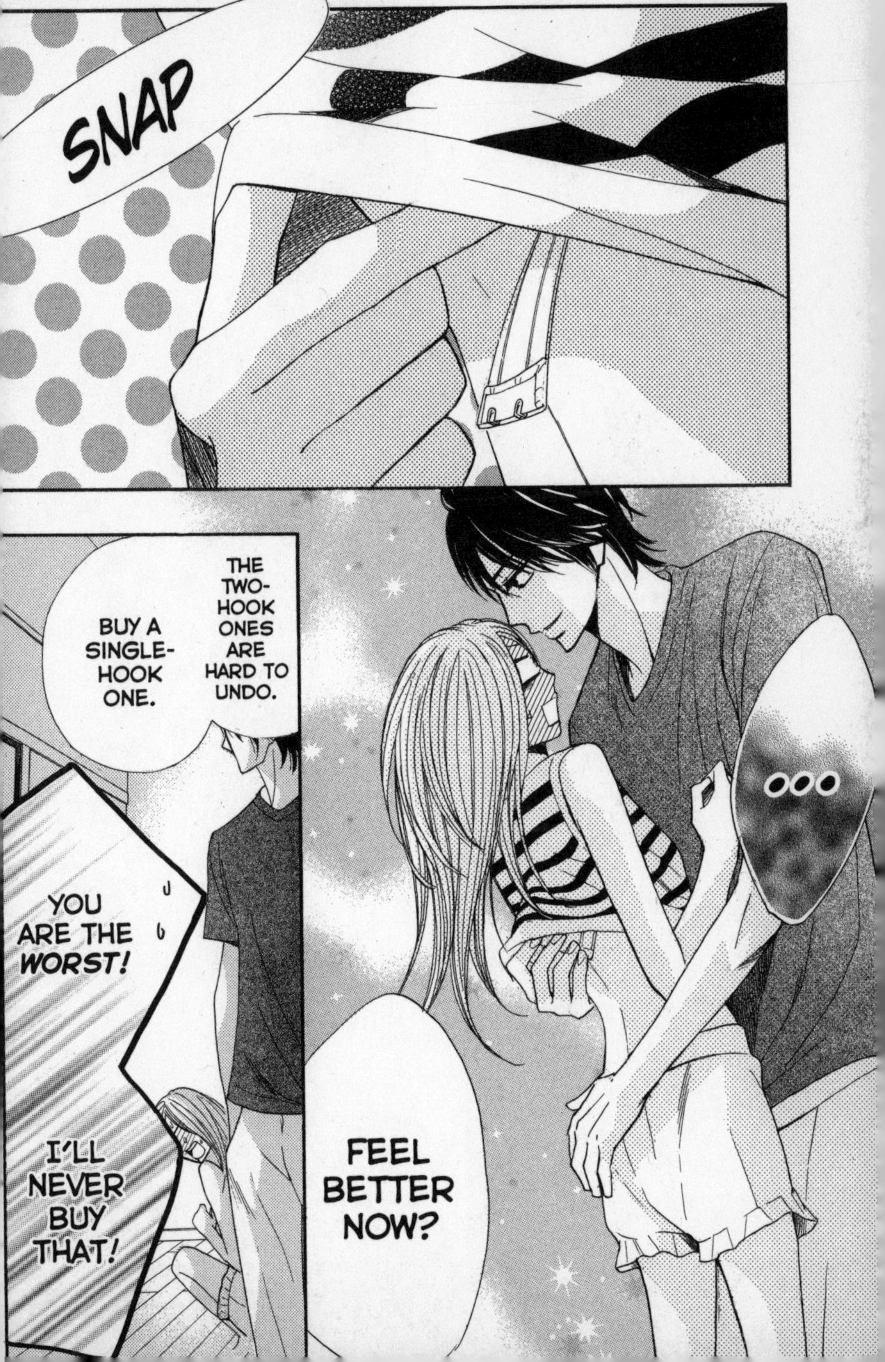
SNAP
...
FEEL BETTER NOW?
THE TWO-HOOK ONES ARE HARD TO UNDO.
BUY A SINGLE-HOOK ONE.
YOU ARE THE *WORST!*
I'LL NEVER BUY THAT!

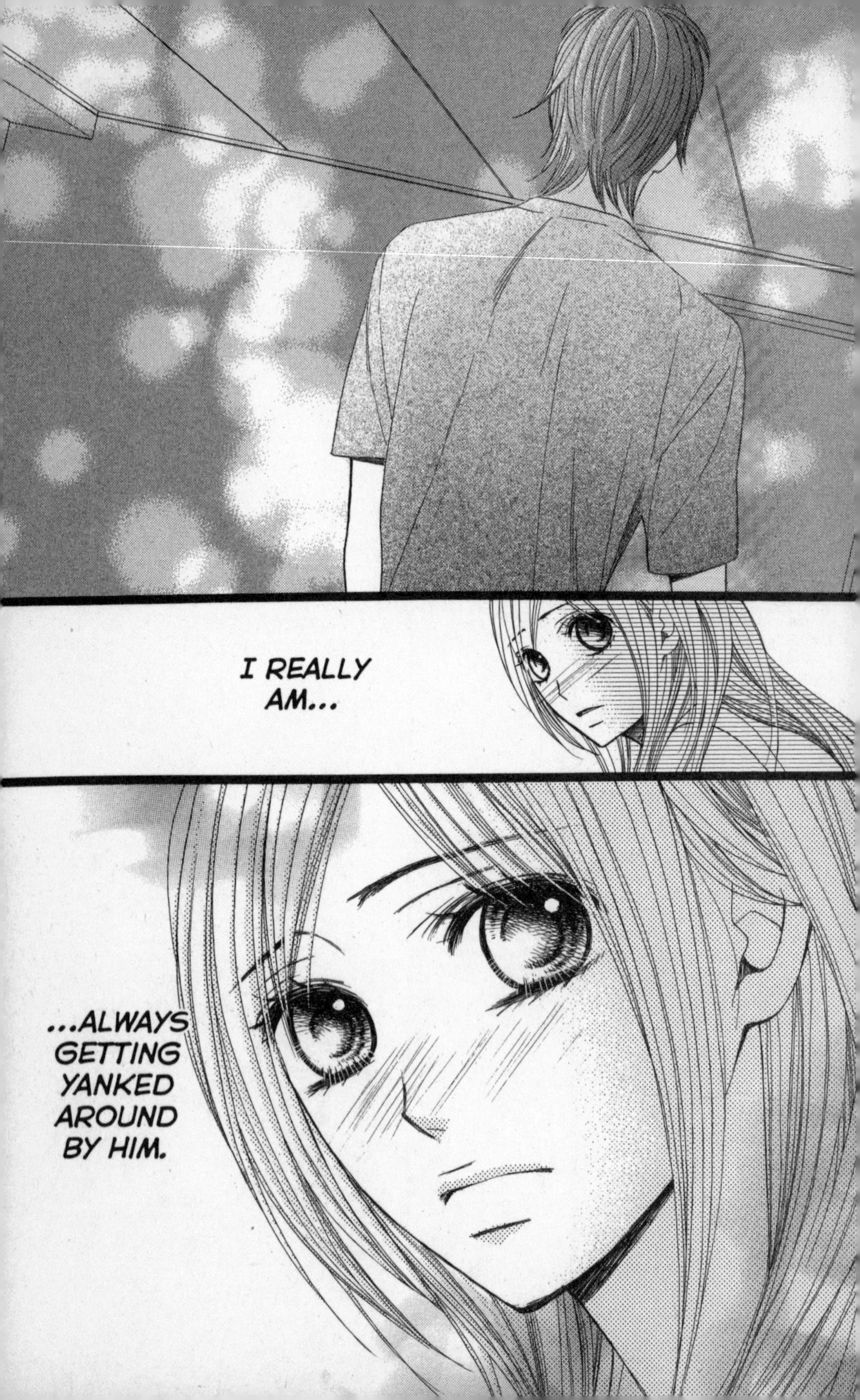
I REALLY AM...
...ALWAYS GETTING YANKED AROUND BY HIM.

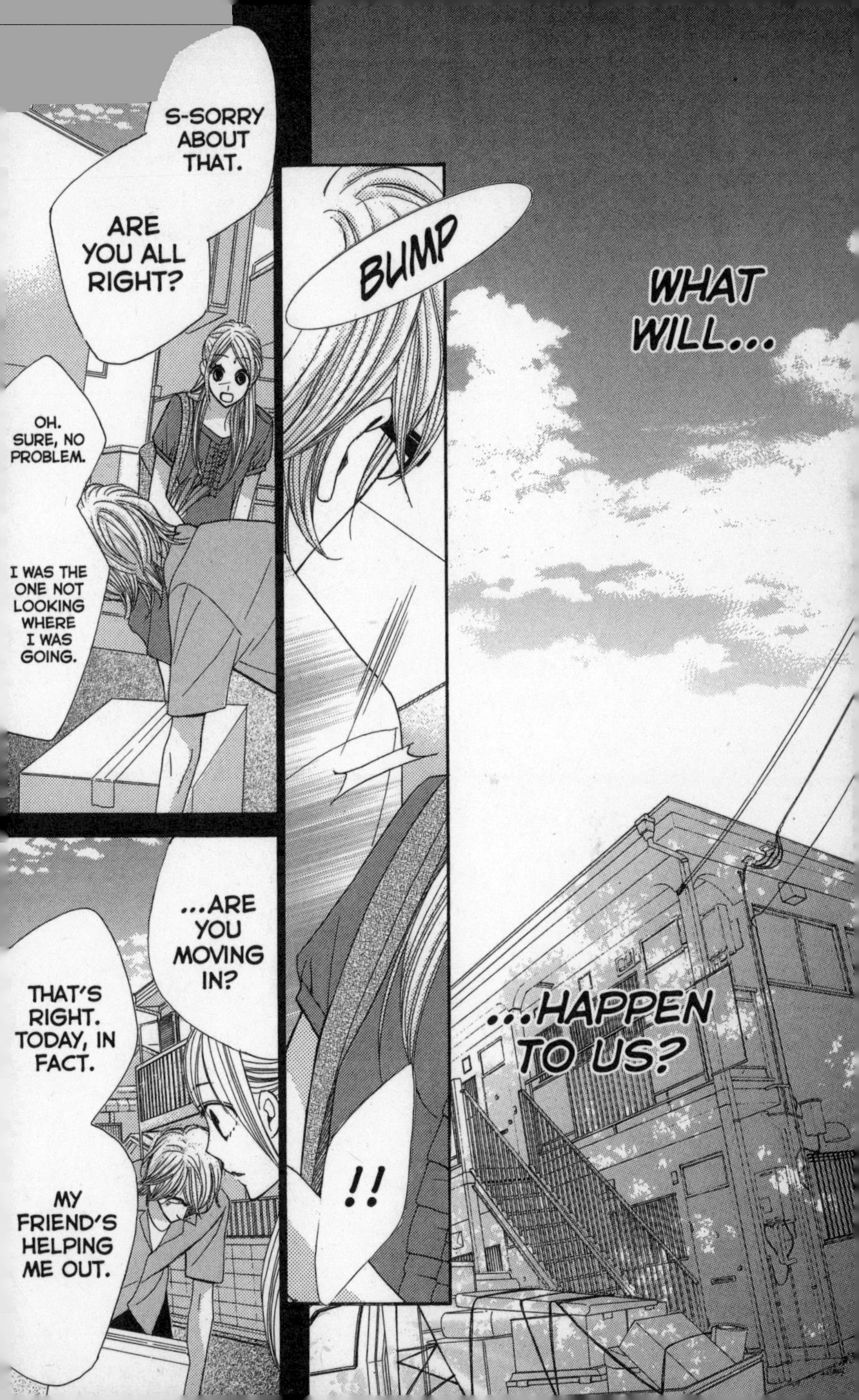
WHAT WILL...
...HAPPEN TO US?
BUMP
!!
S-SORRY ABOUT THAT.
ARE YOU ALL RIGHT?
OH. SURE, NO PROBLEM.
I WAS THE ONE NOT LOOKING WHERE I WAS GOING.
...ARE YOU MOVING IN?
THAT'S RIGHT. TODAY, IN FACT.
MY FRIEND'S HELPING ME OUT.

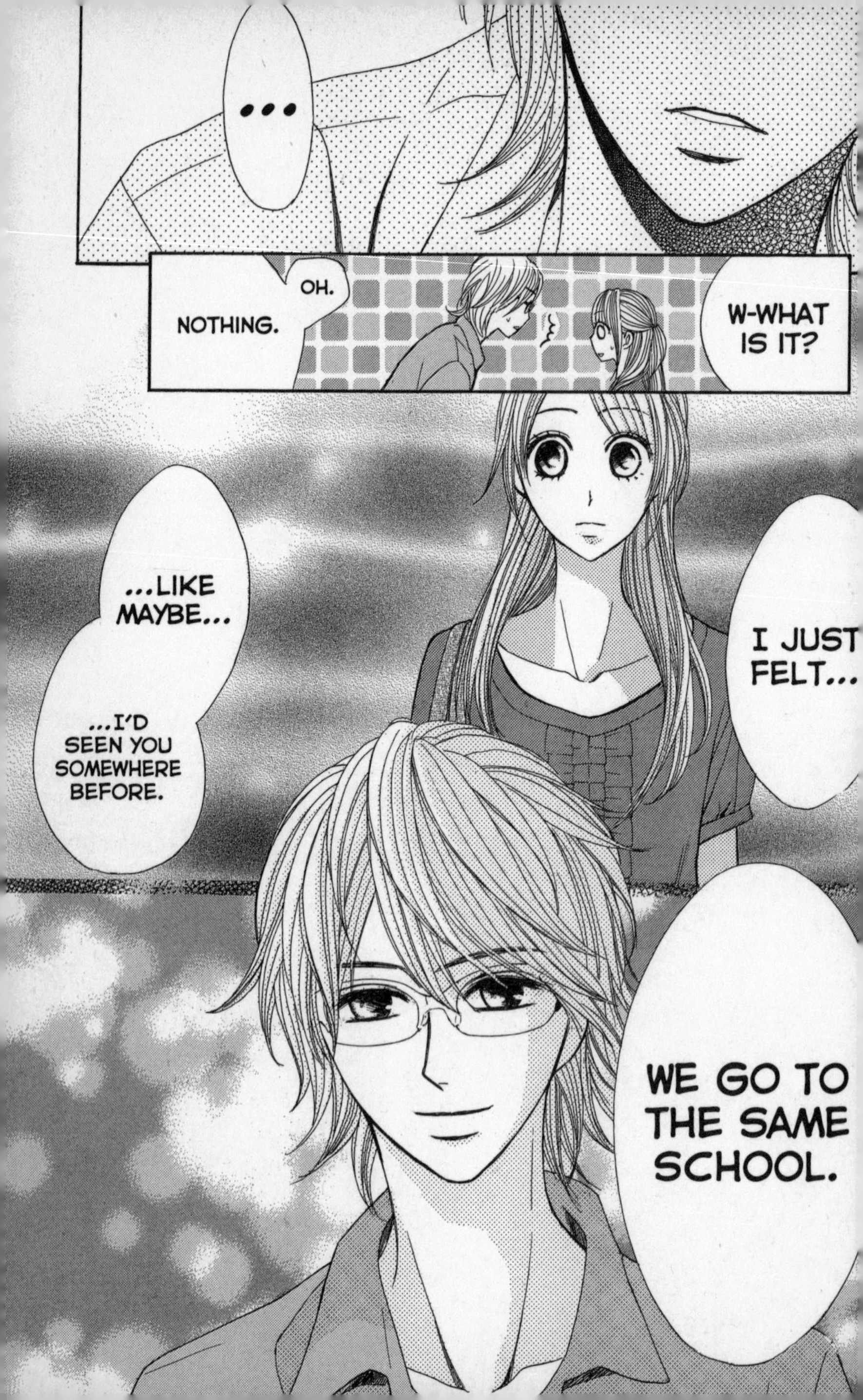
...
W-WHAT IS IT?
OH.
NOTHING.
I JUST FELT...
...LIKE MAYBE...
...I'D SEEN YOU SOMEWHERE BEFORE.
WE GO TO THE SAME SCHOOL.

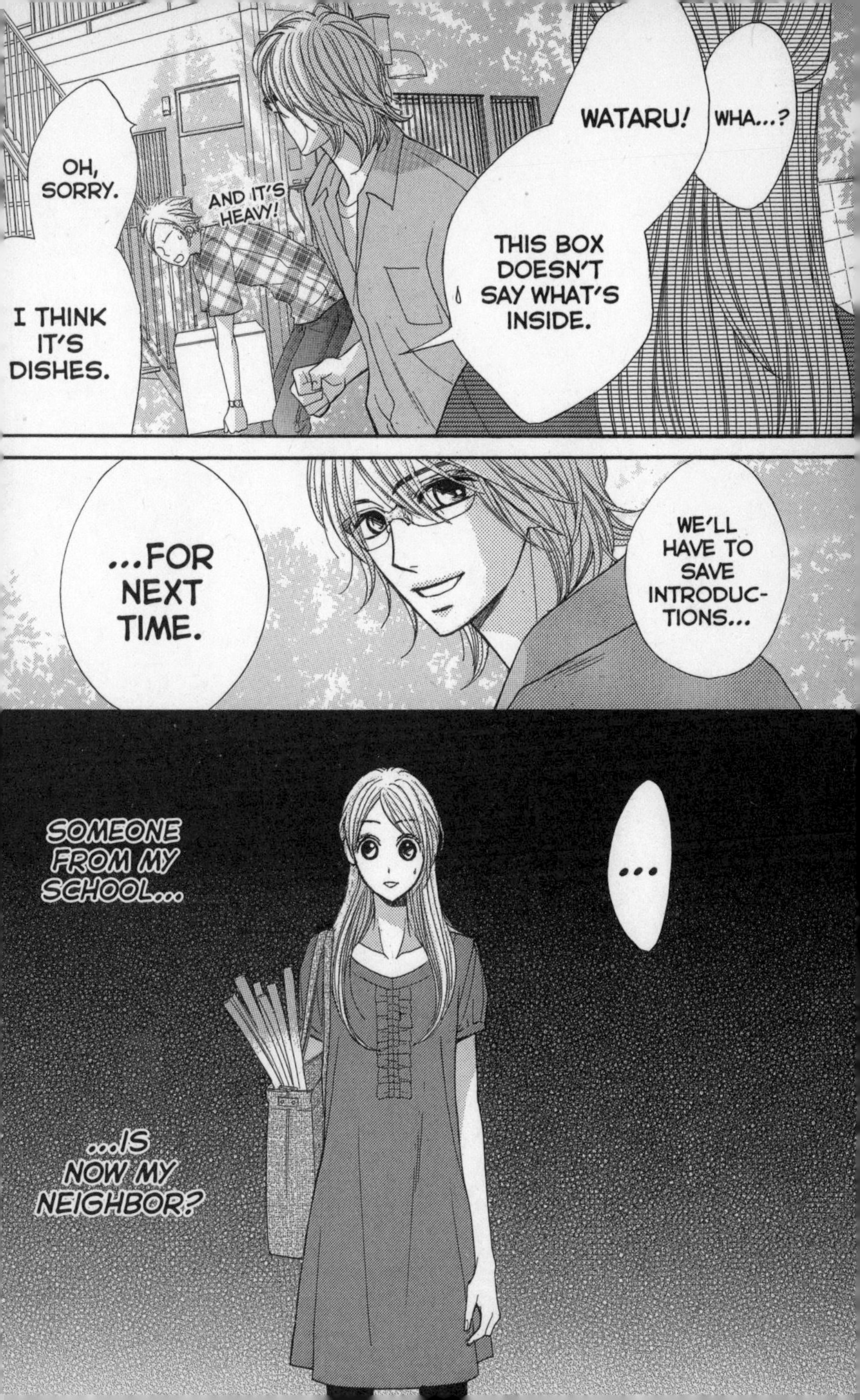
WHA...?
WATARU!
THIS BOX DOESN'T SAY WHAT'S INSIDE.
AND IT'S HEAVY!
OH, SORRY.
I THINK IT'S DISHES.
WE'LL HAVE TO SAVE INTRODUC-TIONS...
...FOR NEXT TIME.
...
SOMEONE FROM MY SCHOOL...
...IS NOW MY NEIGHBOR?

L♥DK

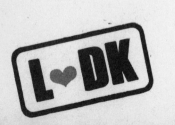

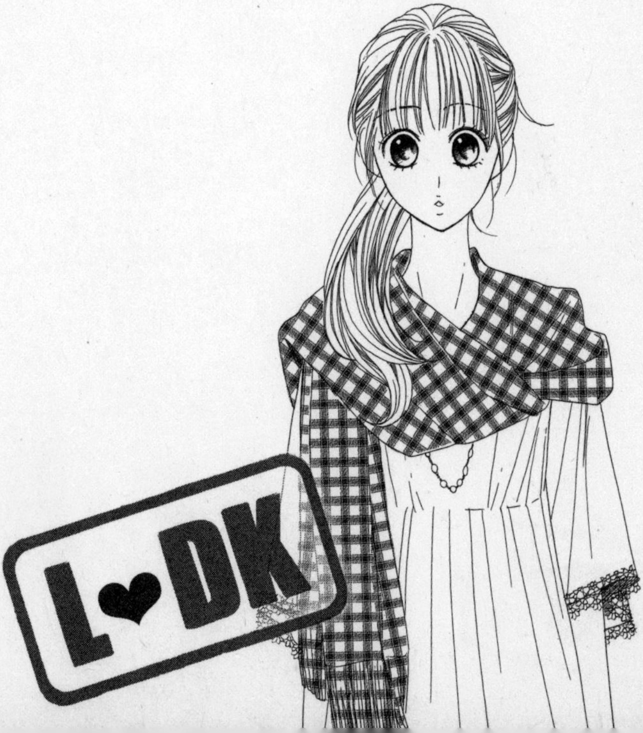
L♥DK

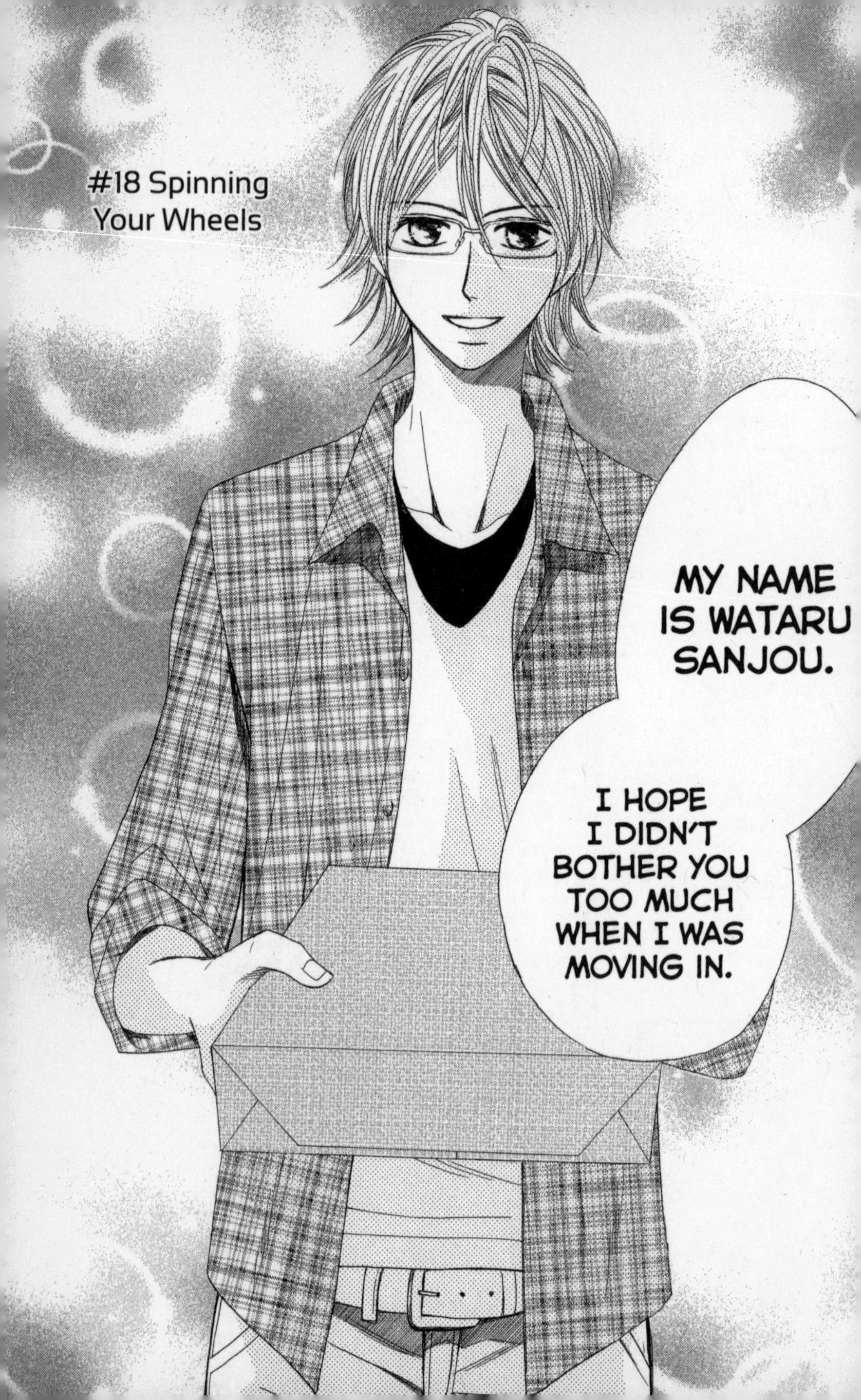
#18 Spinning Your Wheels
MY NAME IS WATARU SANJOU.
I HOPE I DIDN'T BOTHER YOU TOO MUCH WHEN I WAS MOVING IN.

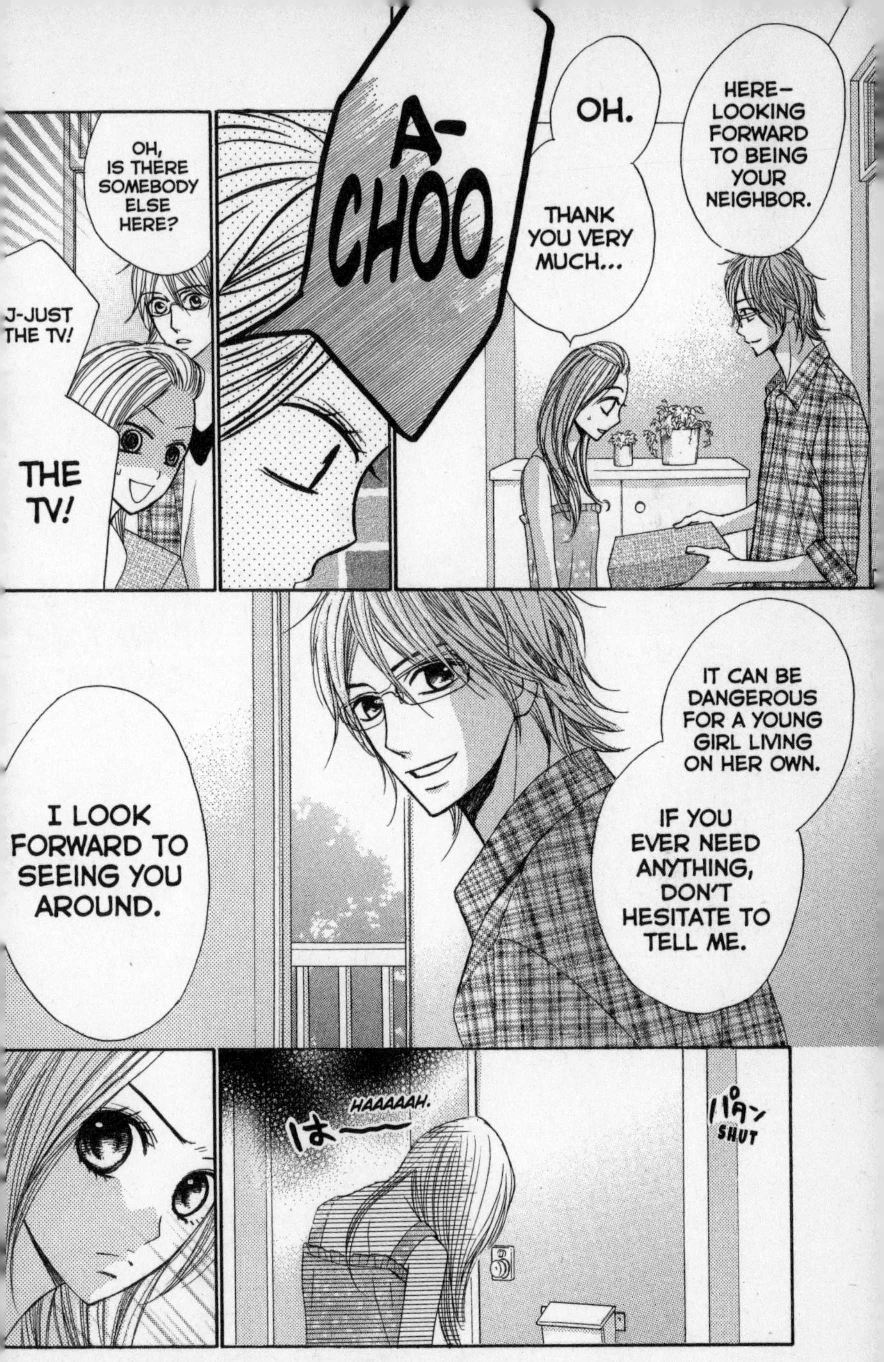
HERE— LOOKING FORWARD TO BEING YOUR NEIGHBOR.
OH.
THANK YOU VERY MUCH...
A-CHOO
OH, IS THERE SOMEBODY ELSE HERE?
J-JUST THE TV!
THE TV!
IT CAN BE DANGEROUS FOR A YOUNG GIRL LIVING ON HER OWN.
IF YOU EVER NEED ANYTHING, DON'T HESITATE TO TELL ME.
I LOOK FORWARD TO SEEING YOU AROUND.
パタン
SHUT
は──
HAAAAAH.

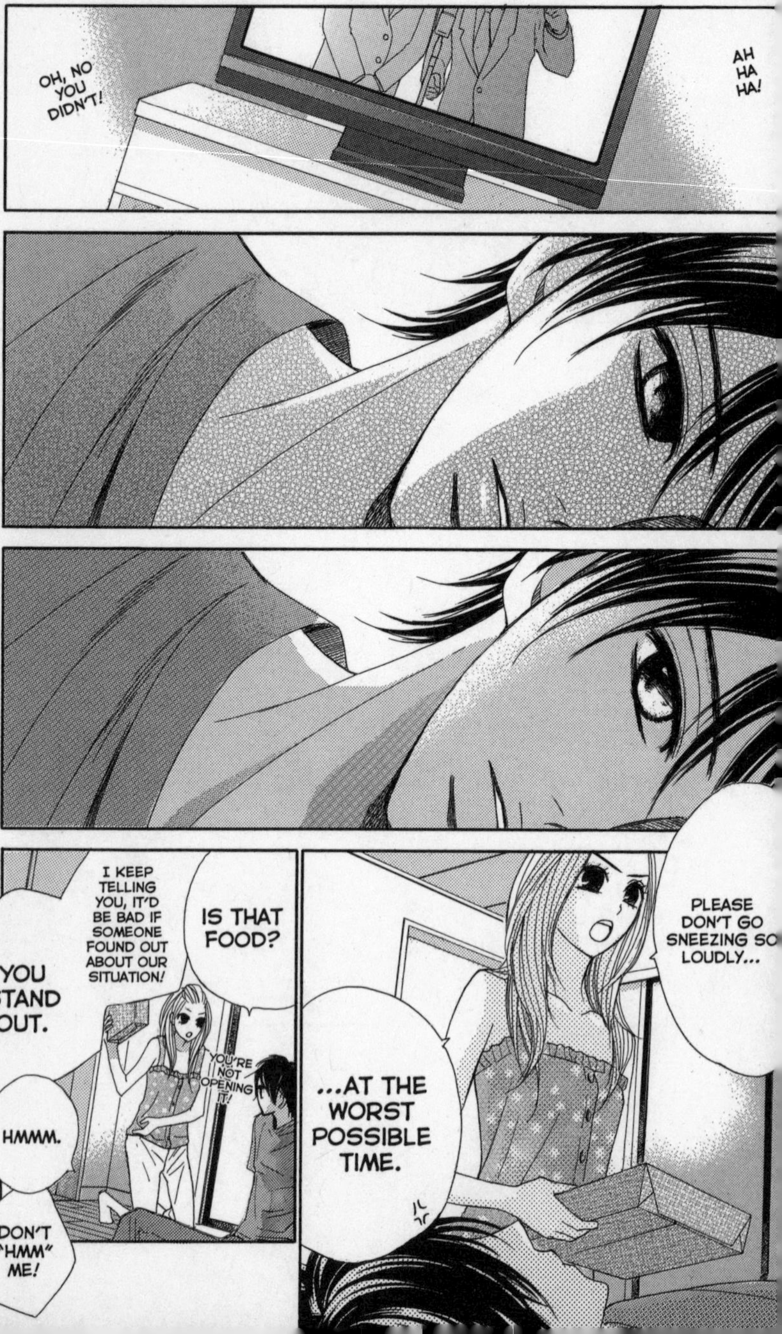
AH HA HA!
OH, NO YOU DIDN'T!
PLEASE DON'T GO SNEEZING SO LOUDLY...
...AT THE WORST POSSIBLE TIME.
IS THAT FOOD?
I KEEP TELLING YOU, IT'D BE BAD IF SOMEONE FOUND OUT ABOUT OUR SITUATION!
YOU STAND OUT.
YOU'RE NOT OPENING IT!
HMMM.
DON'T "HMM" ME!

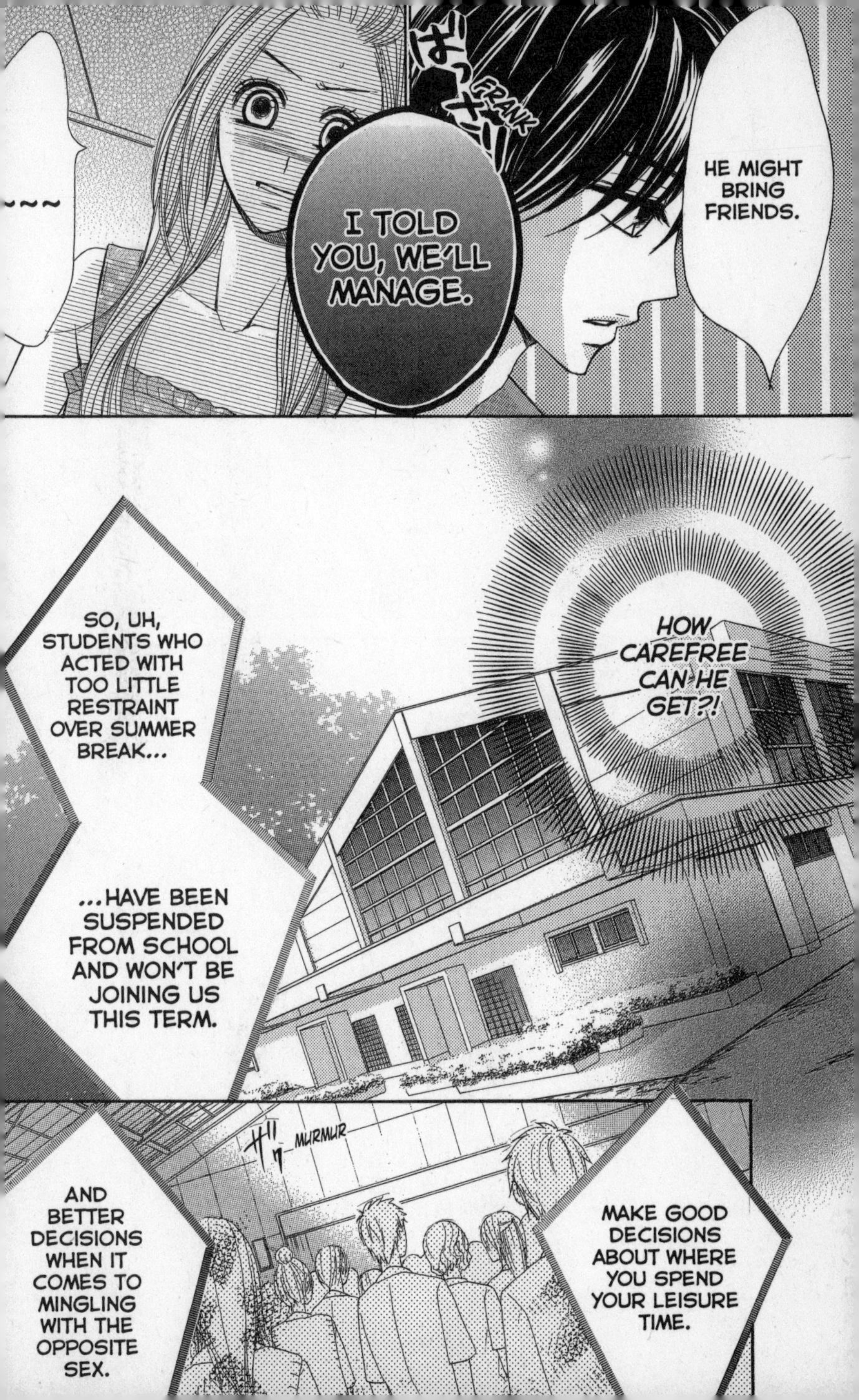
HE MIGHT BRING FRIENDS.
FRANK
I TOLD YOU, WE'LL MANAGE.
~~~
HOW CAREFREE CAN HE GET?!
SO, UH, STUDENTS WHO ACTED WITH TOO LITTLE RESTRAINT OVER SUMMER BREAK...
...HAVE BEEN SUSPENDED FROM SCHOOL AND WON'T BE JOINING US THIS TERM.
MAKE GOOD DECISIONS ABOUT WHERE YOU SPEND YOUR LEISURE TIME.
MURMUR
AND BETTER DECISIONS WHEN IT COMES TO MINGLING WITH THE OPPOSITE SEX.
~~~

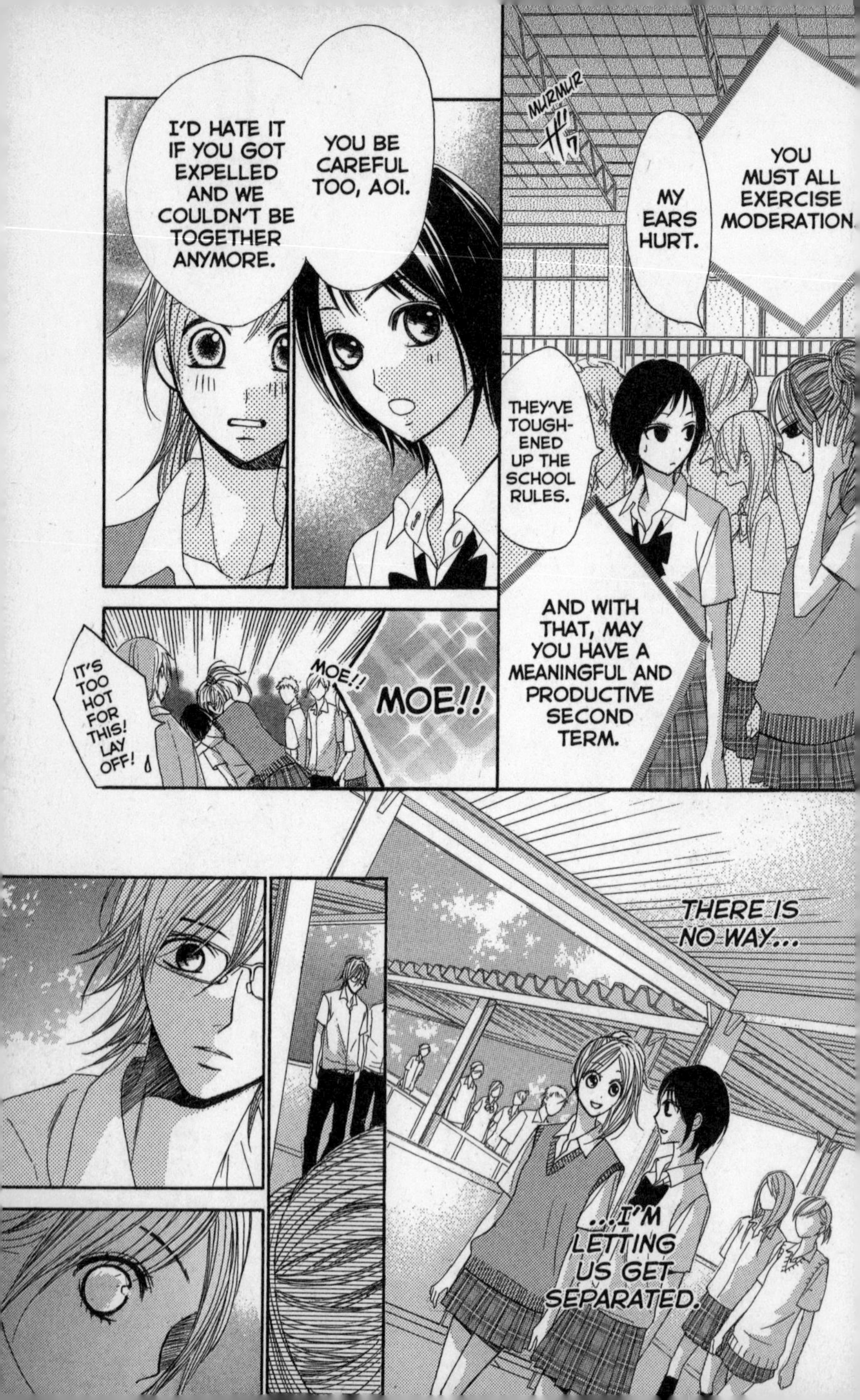
MURMUR
YOU MUST ALL EXERCISE MODERATION.
MY EARS HURT.
THEY'VE TOUGHENED UP THE SCHOOL RULES.
AND WITH THAT, MAY YOU HAVE A MEANINGFUL AND PRODUCTIVE SECOND TERM.
YOU BE CAREFUL TOO, AOI.
I'D HATE IT IF YOU GOT EXPELLED AND WE COULDN'T BE TOGETHER ANYMORE.
MOE!!
MOE!!
IT'S TOO HOT FOR THIS! LAY OFF!
THERE IS NO WAY...
...I'M LETTING US GET SEPARATED.

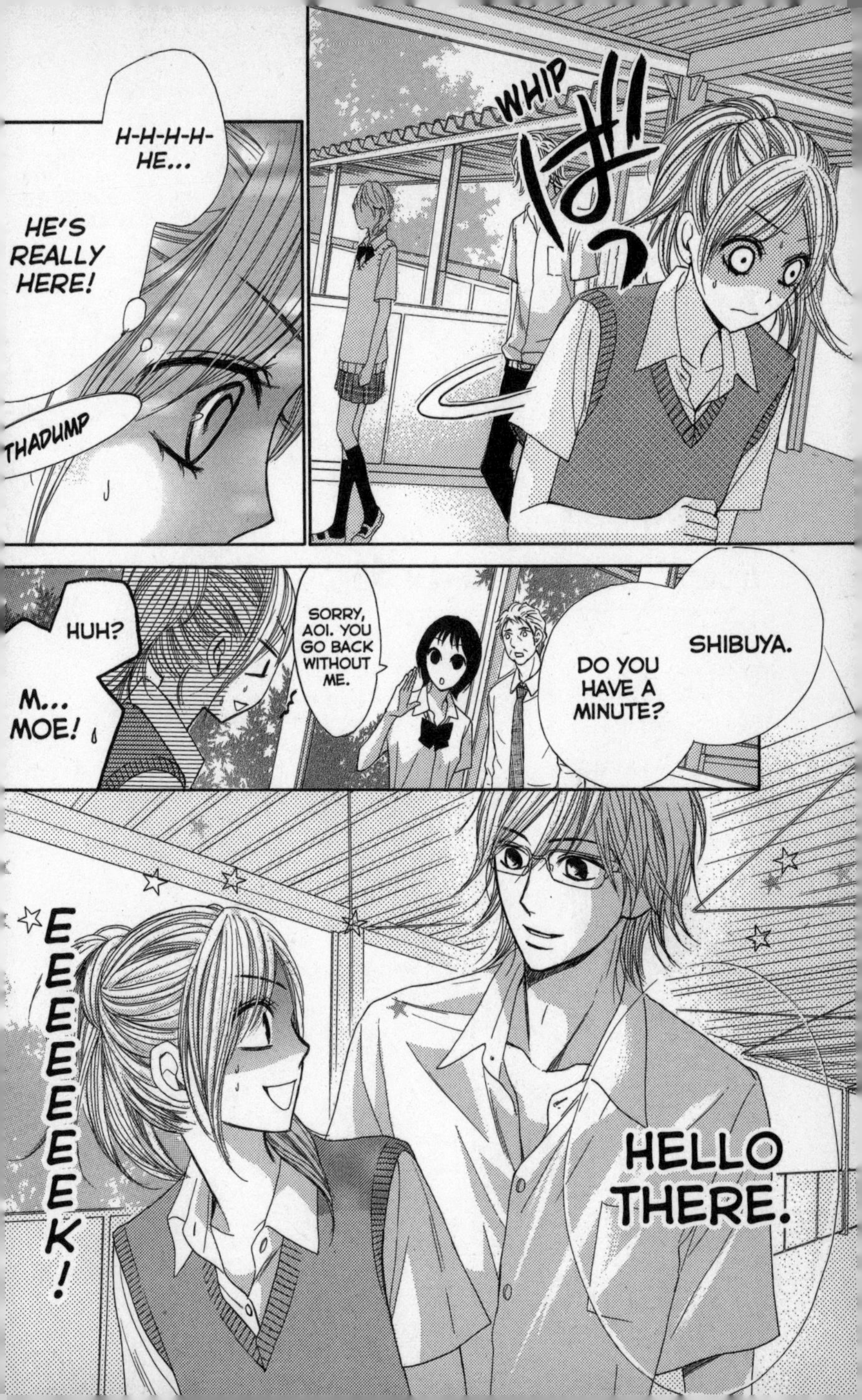
WHIP
H-H-H-H-HE...
HE'S REALLY HERE!
THADUMP
SHIBUYA.
DO YOU HAVE A MINUTE?
SORRY, AOI. YOU GO BACK WITHOUT ME.
HUH?
M... MOE!
HELLO THERE.
EEEEEEEEEK!

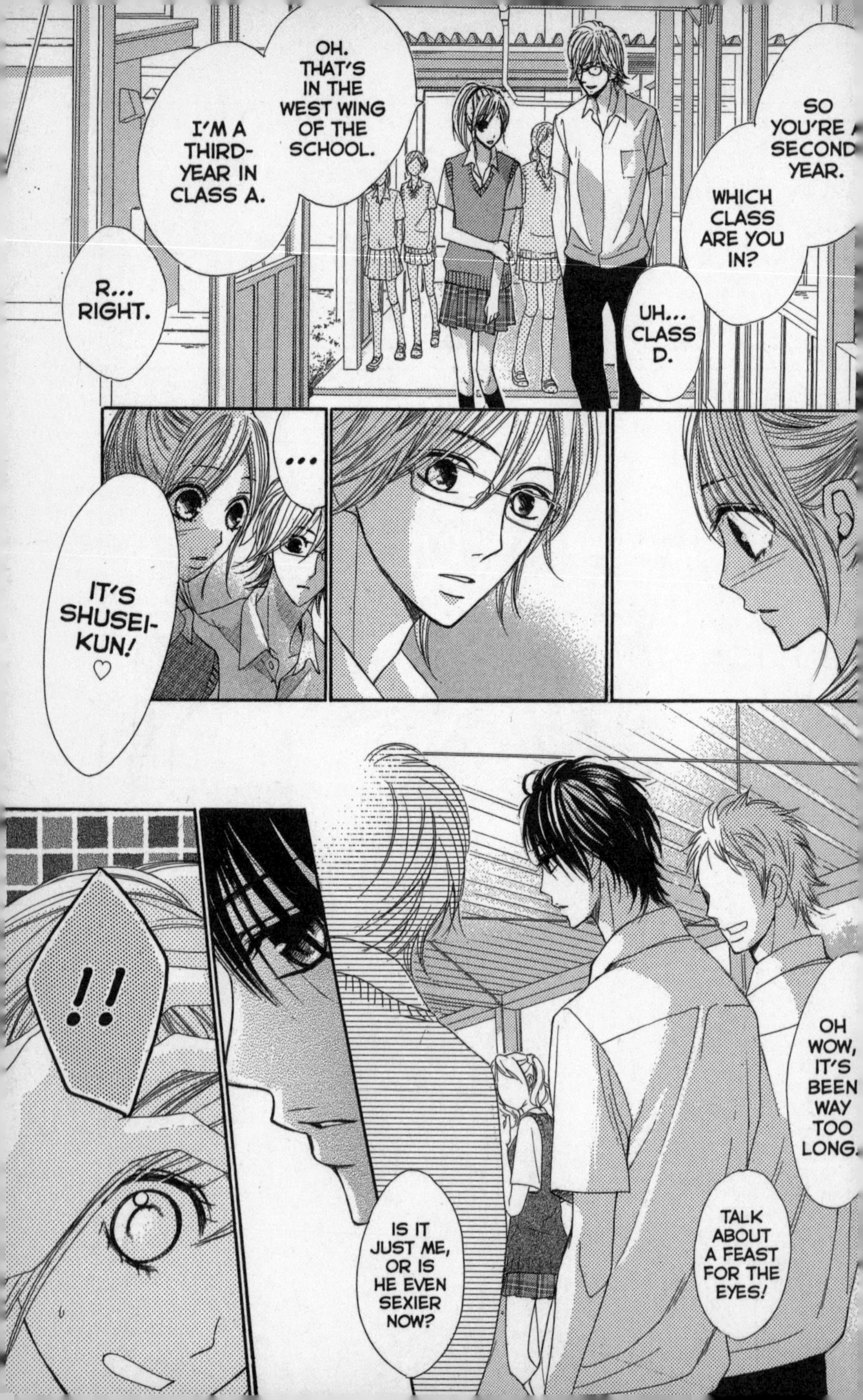
SO YOU'RE A SECOND YEAR.
WHICH CLASS ARE YOU IN?
UH... CLASS D.
OH. THAT'S IN THE WEST WING OF THE SCHOOL.
I'M A THIRD-YEAR IN CLASS A.
R... RIGHT.
...
IT'S SHUSEI-KUN! ♡
OH WOW, IT'S BEEN WAY TOO LONG.
TALK ABOUT A FEAST FOR THE EYES!
IS IT JUST ME, OR IS HE EVEN SEXIER NOW?
!!

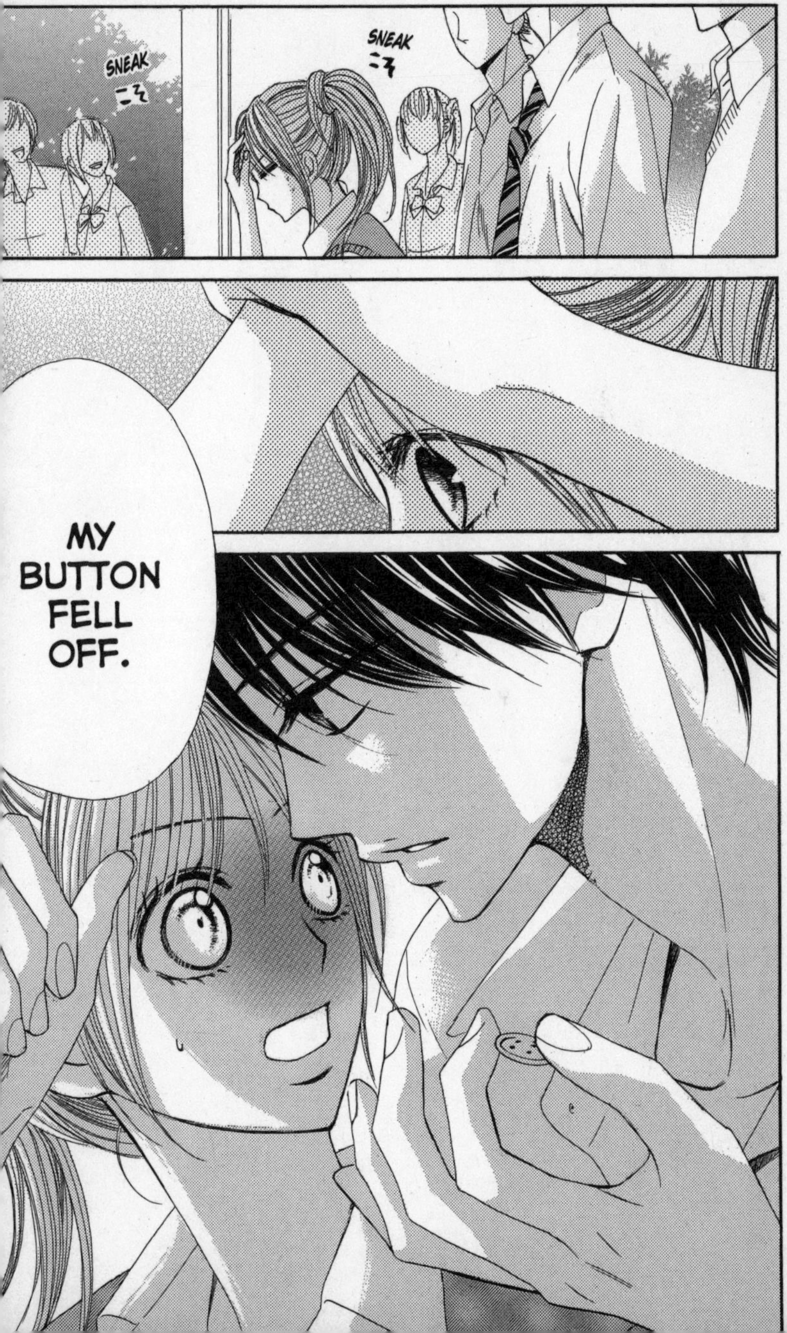
SNEAK
こそ
SNEAK
こそ
MY BUTTON FELL OFF.

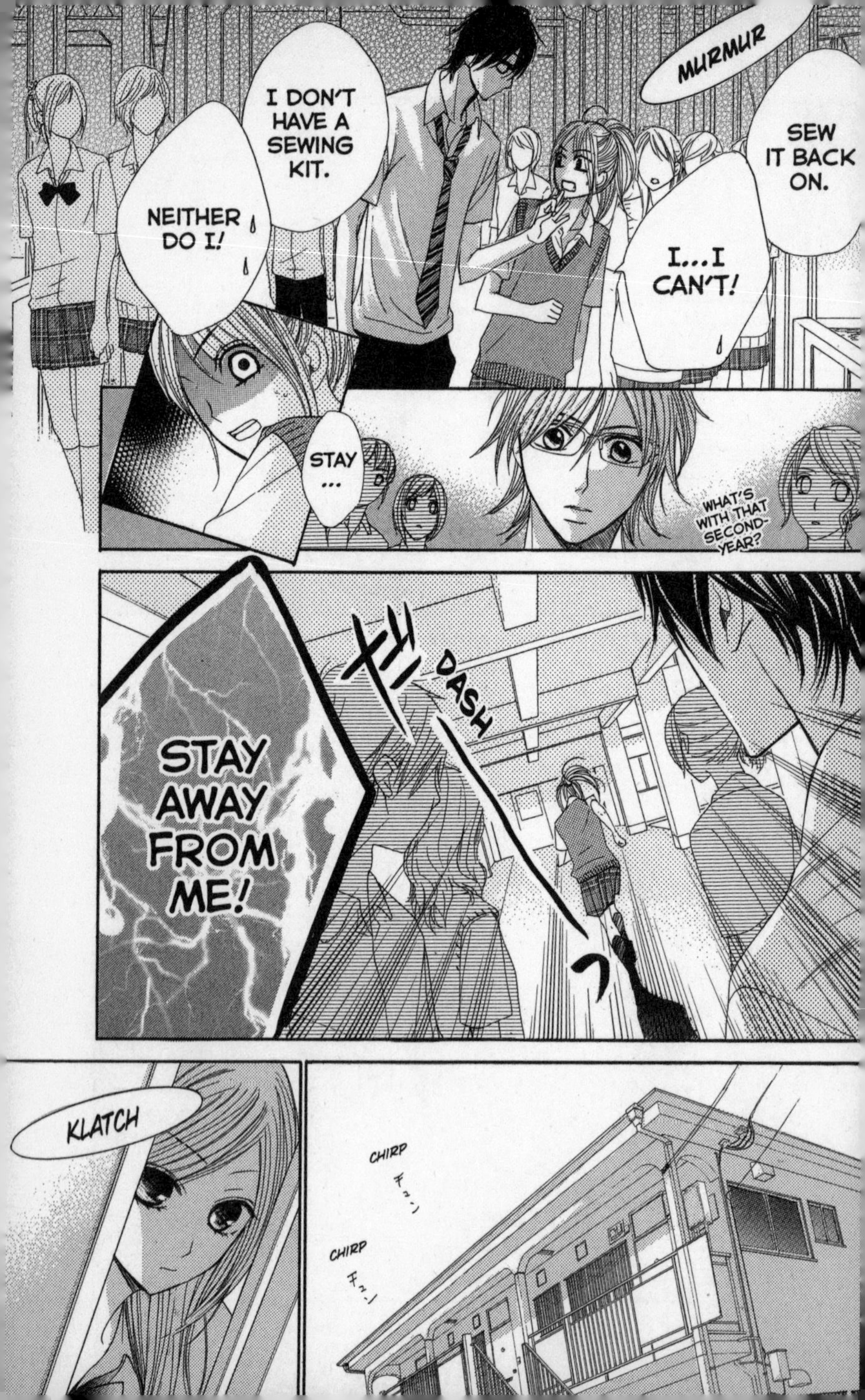
MURMUR
SEW IT BACK ON.
I...I CAN'T!
I DON'T HAVE A SEWING KIT.
NEITHER DO I!
WHAT'S WITH THAT SECOND-YEAR?
STAY ...
DASH
STAY AWAY FROM ME!
CHIRP
CHIRP
KLATCH

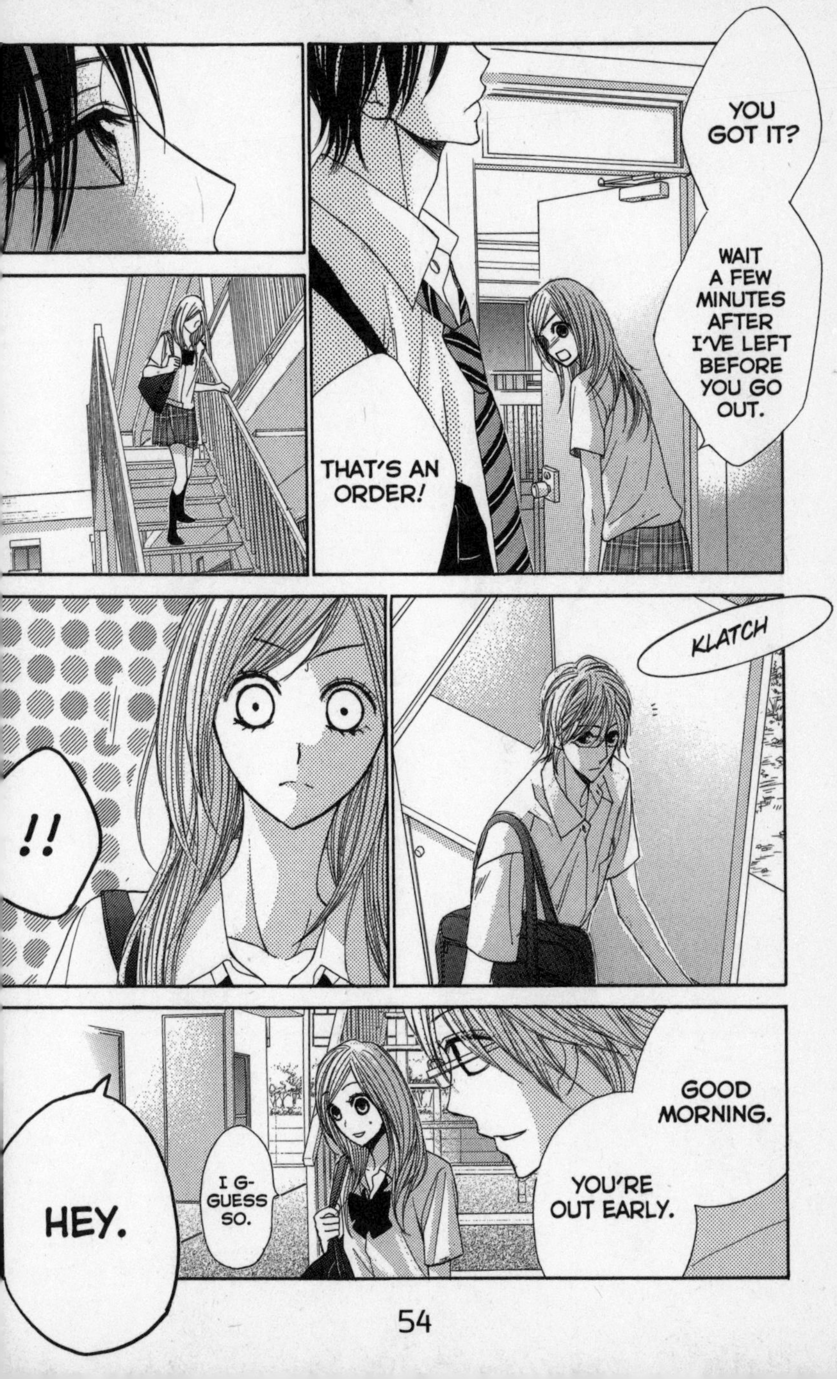
YOU GOT IT?
WAIT A FEW MINUTES AFTER I'VE LEFT BEFORE YOU GO OUT.
THAT'S AN ORDER!
KLATCH
!!
GOOD MORNING.
YOU'RE OUT EARLY.
I G-GUESS SO.
HEY.

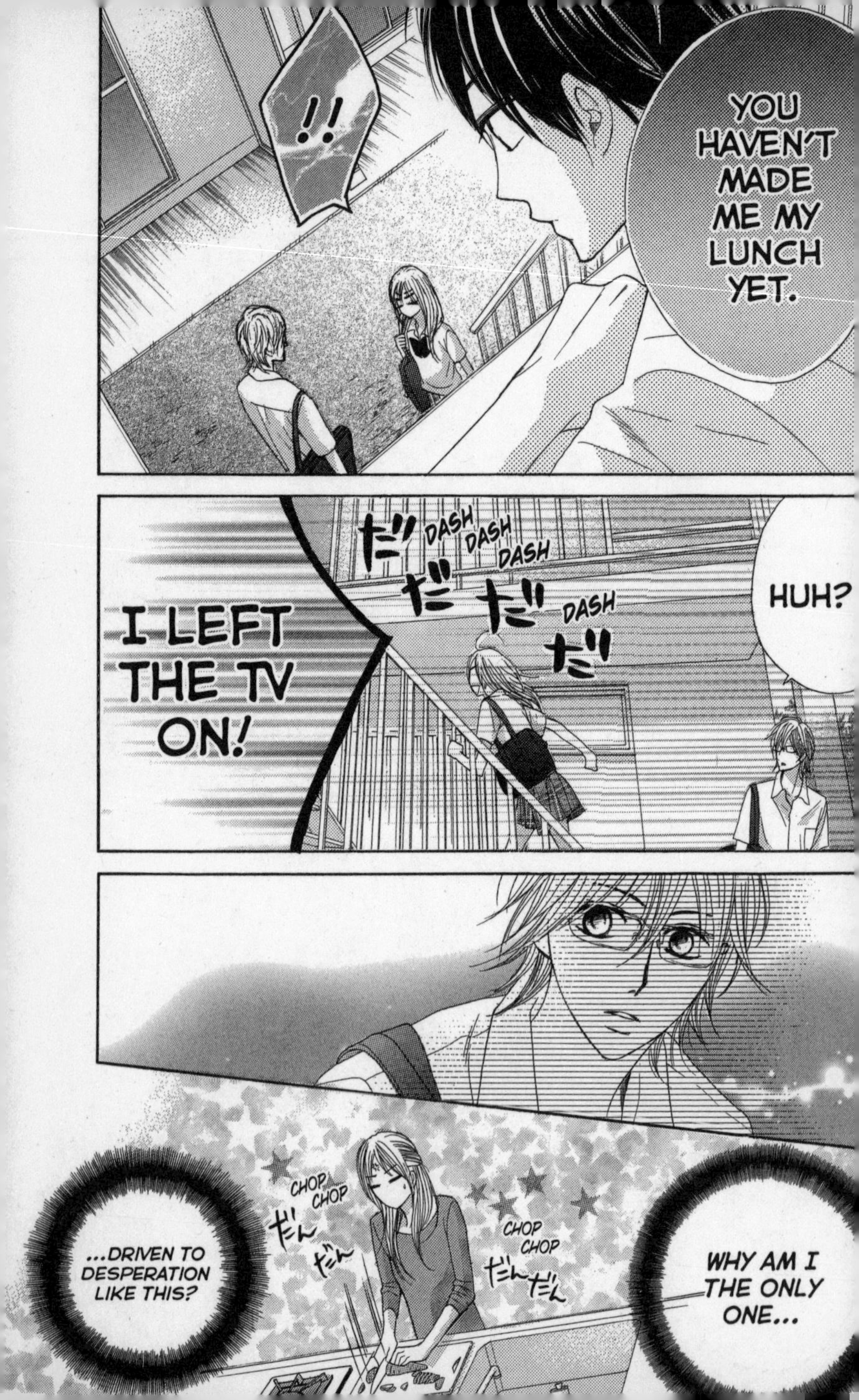
YOU HAVEN'T MADE ME MY LUNCH YET.
!!
HUH?
だ DASH
だ DASH
だ DASH
だ DASH
I LEFT THE TV ON!
WHY AM I THE ONLY ONE...
だん CHOP
だん CHOP
だん CHOP
だん CHOP
...DRIVEN TO DESPERATION LIKE THIS?

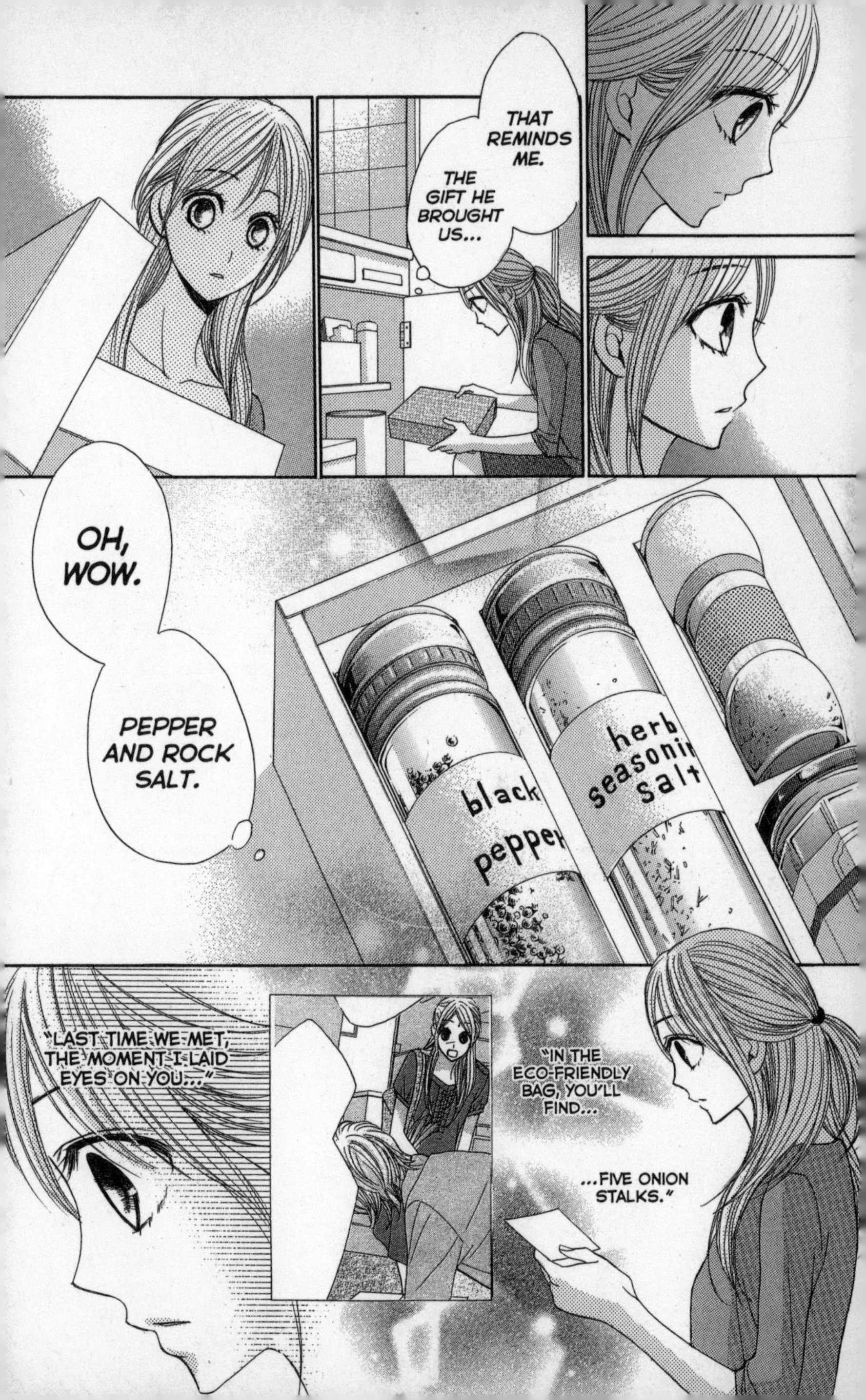
THAT REMINDS ME.
THE GIFT HE BROUGHT US...
OH, WOW.
PEPPER AND ROCK SALT.
black
herb
salt
"IN THE ECO-FRIENDLY BAG, YOU'LL FIND...
...FIVE ONION STALKS."
"LAST TIME WE MET, THE MOMENT I LAID EYES ON YOU..."

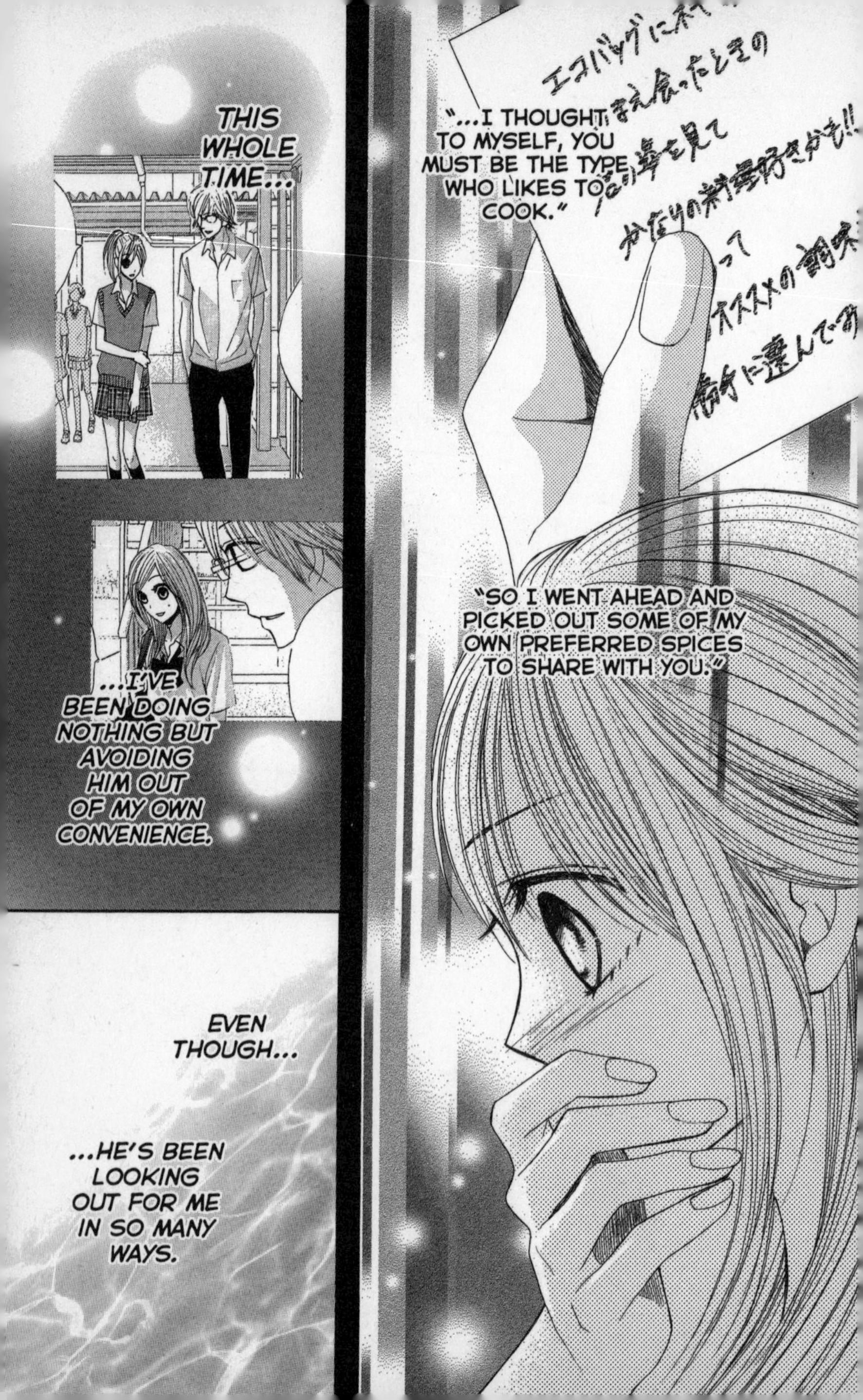
"...I THOUGHT TO MYSELF, YOU MUST BE THE TYPE WHO LIKES TO COOK."
"SO I WENT AHEAD AND PICKED OUT SOME OF MY OWN PREFERRED SPICES TO SHARE WITH YOU."
THIS WHOLE TIME...
...I'VE BEEN DOING NOTHING BUT AVOIDING HIM OUT OF MY OWN CONVENIENCE.
EVEN THOUGH...
...HE'S BEEN LOOKING OUT FOR ME IN SO MANY WAYS.

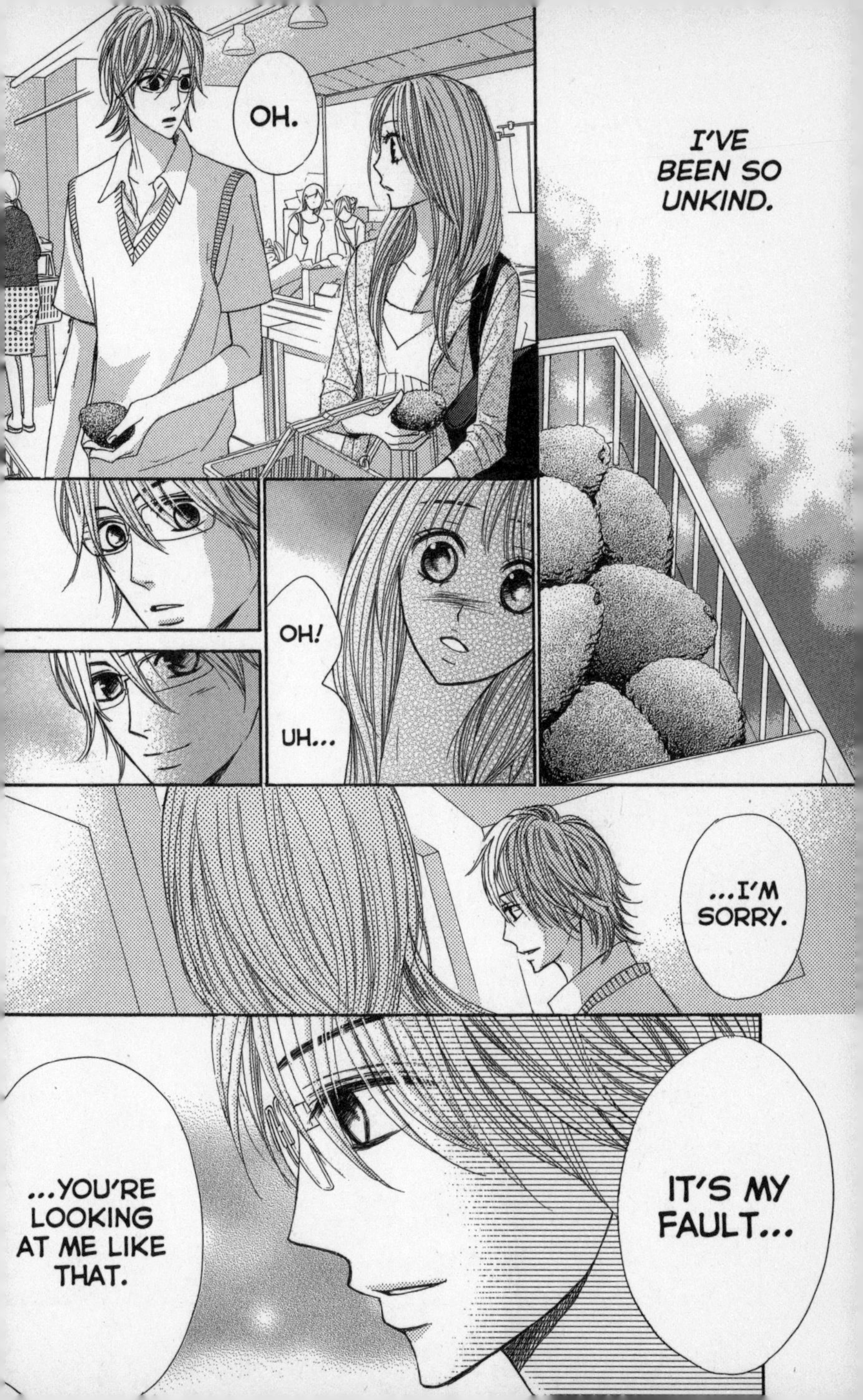
I'VE BEEN SO UNKIND.
OH.
OH!
UH...
...I'M SORRY.
IT'S MY FAULT...
...YOU'RE LOOKING AT ME LIKE THAT.

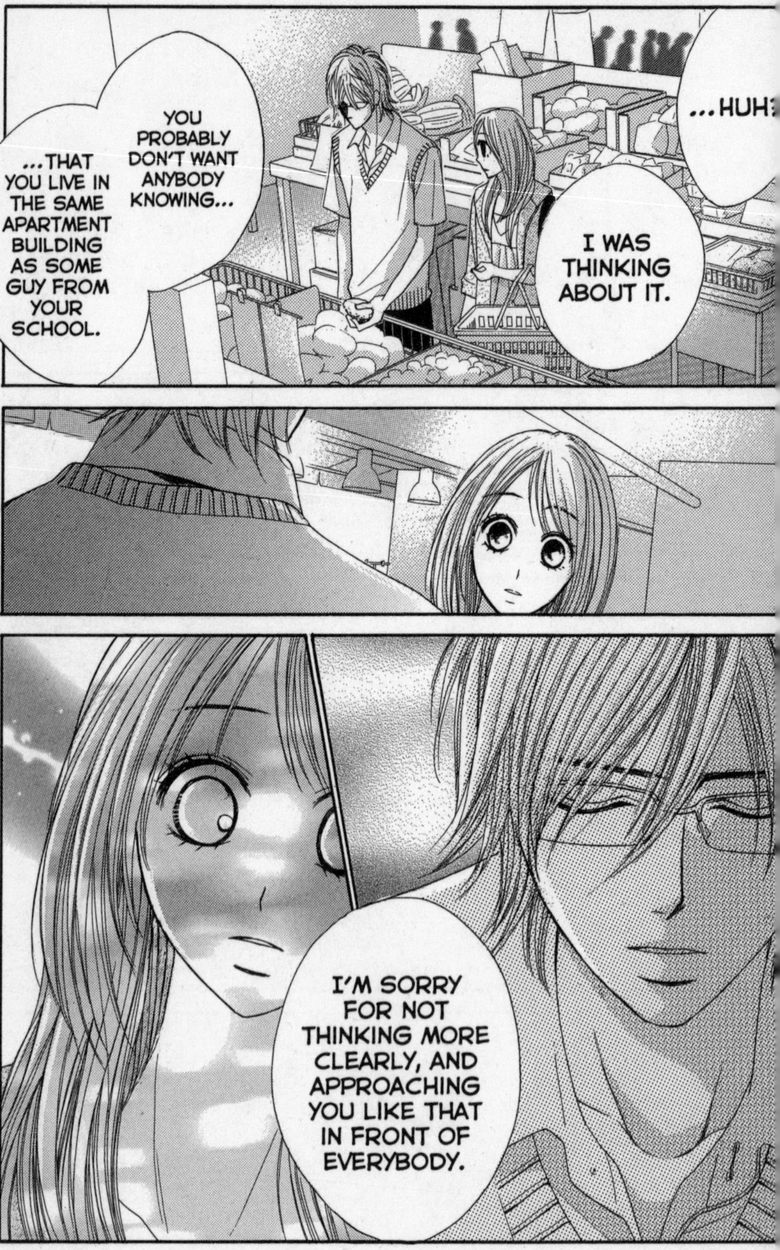
...HUH
I WAS THINKING ABOUT IT.
YOU PROBABLY DON'T WANT ANYBODY KNOWING...
...THAT YOU LIVE IN THE SAME APARTMENT BUILDING AS SOME GUY FROM YOUR SCHOOL.
I'M SORRY FOR NOT THINKING MORE CLEARLY, AND APPROACHING YOU LIKE THAT IN FRONT OF EVERYBODY.

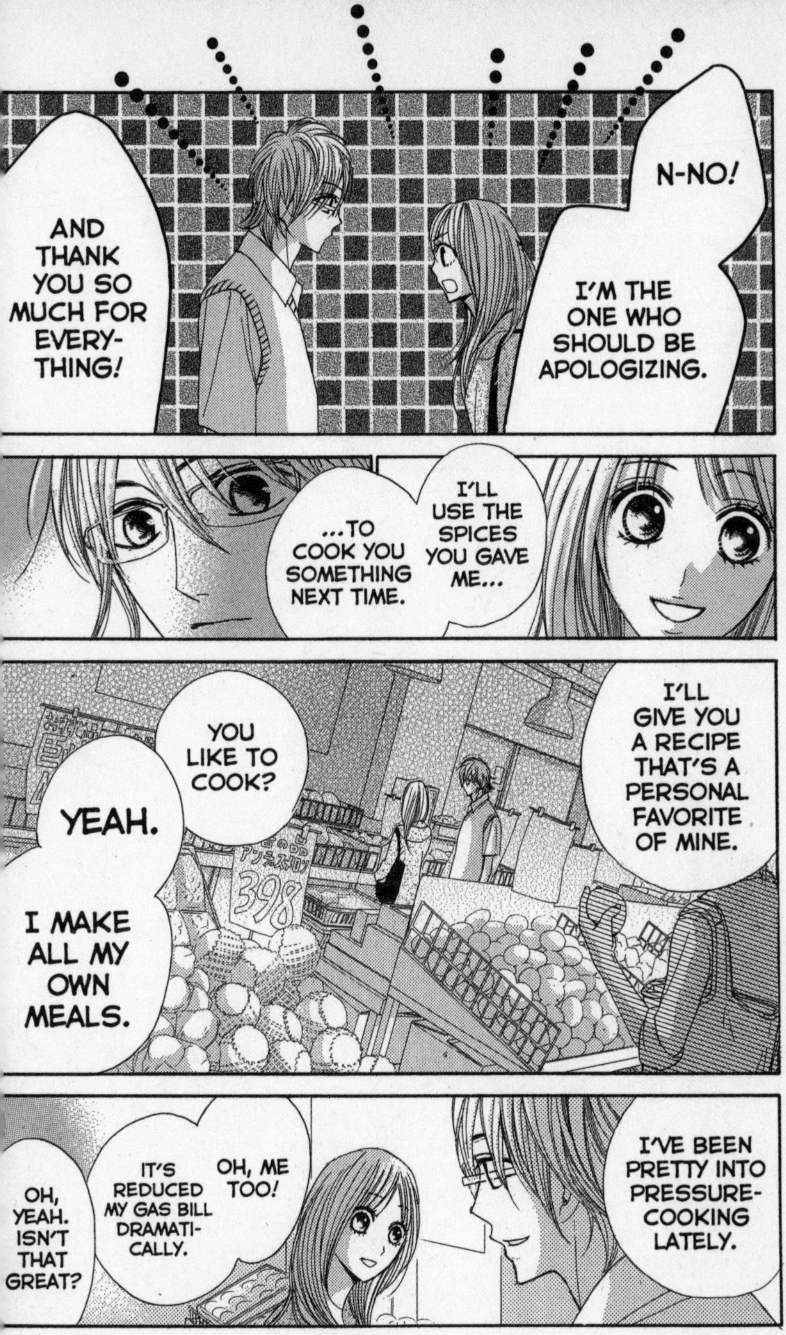
N-NO!
I'M THE ONE WHO SHOULD BE APOLOGIZING.
AND THANK YOU SO MUCH FOR EVERYTHING!
I'LL USE THE SPICES YOU GAVE ME...
...TO COOK YOU SOMETHING NEXT TIME.
I'LL GIVE YOU A RECIPE THAT'S A PERSONAL FAVORITE OF MINE.
YOU LIKE TO COOK?
YEAH.
I MAKE ALL MY OWN MEALS.
398
I'VE BEEN PRETTY INTO PRESSURE-COOKING LATELY.
OH, ME TOO!
IT'S REDUCED MY GAS BILL DRAMATICALLY.
OH, YEAH. ISN'T THAT GREAT?

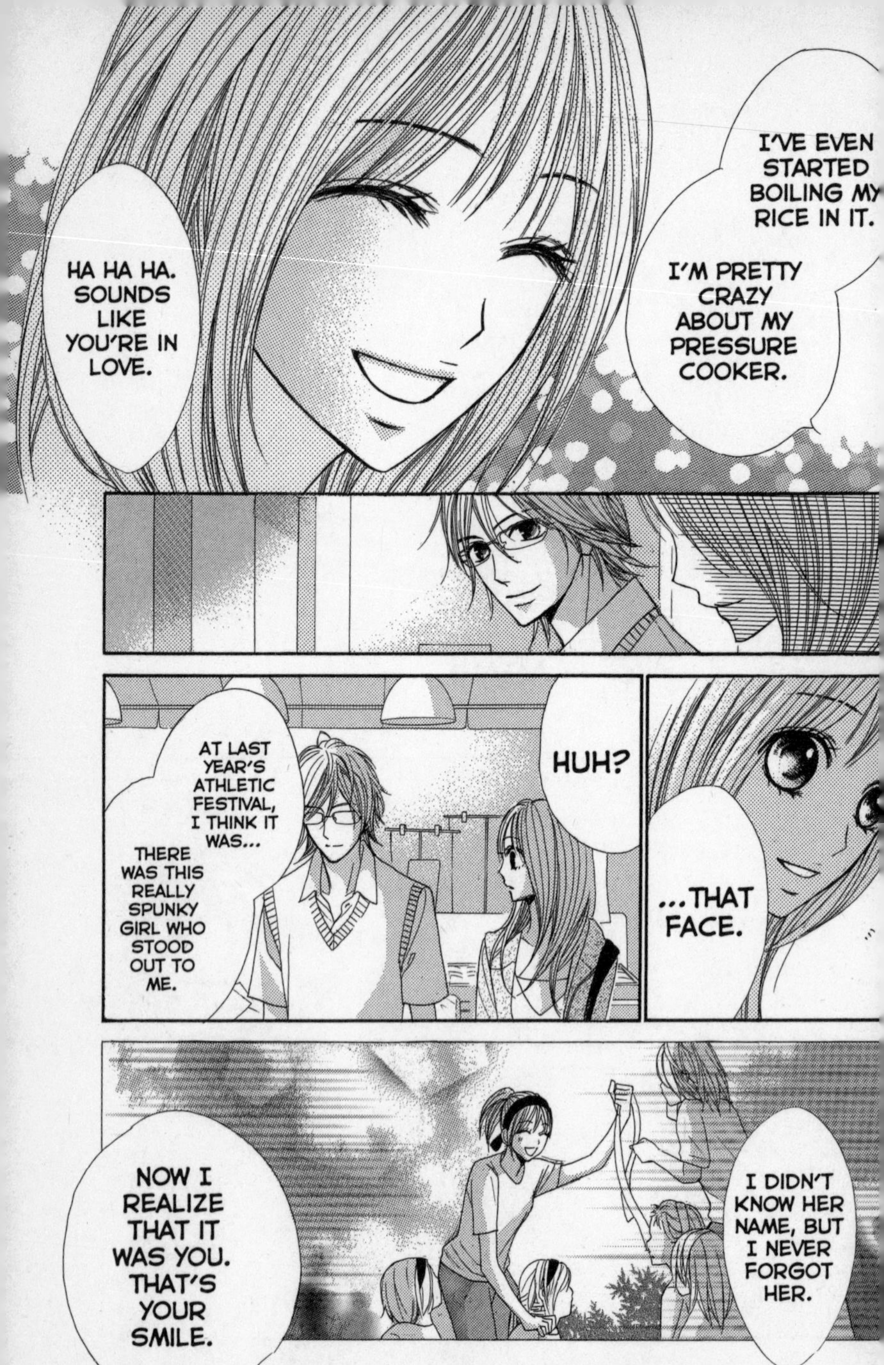
I'VE EVEN STARTED BOILING MY RICE IN IT.
I'M PRETTY CRAZY ABOUT MY PRESSURE COOKER.
HA HA HA. SOUNDS LIKE YOU'RE IN LOVE.
...THAT FACE.
HUH?
AT LAST YEAR'S ATHLETIC FESTIVAL, I THINK IT WAS...
THERE WAS THIS REALLY SPUNKY GIRL WHO STOOD OUT TO ME.
I DIDN'T KNOW HER NAME, BUT I NEVER FORGOT HER.
NOW I REALIZE THAT IT WAS YOU. THAT'S YOUR SMILE.

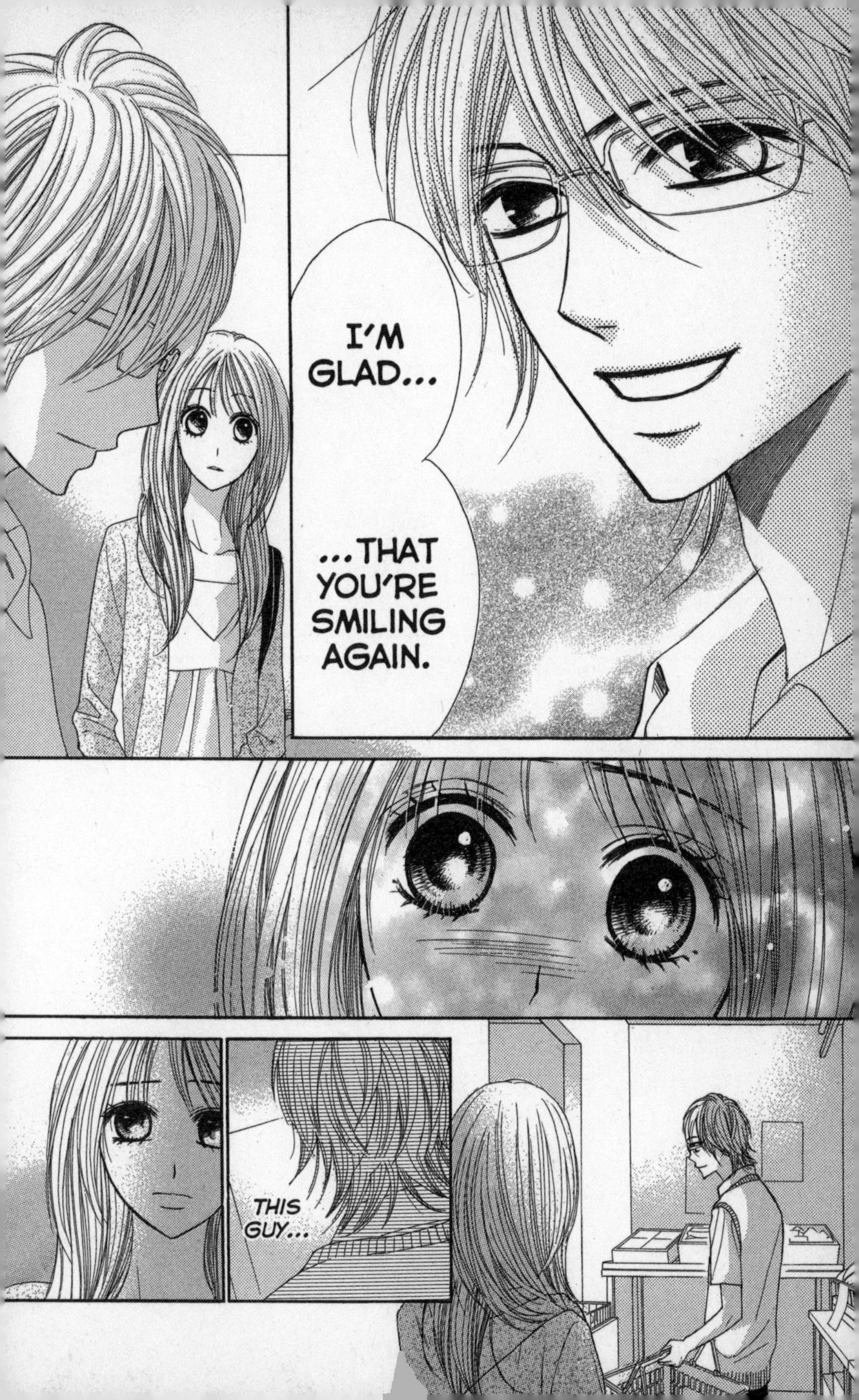
I'M GLAD...
...THAT YOU'RE SMILING AGAIN.
THIS GUY...

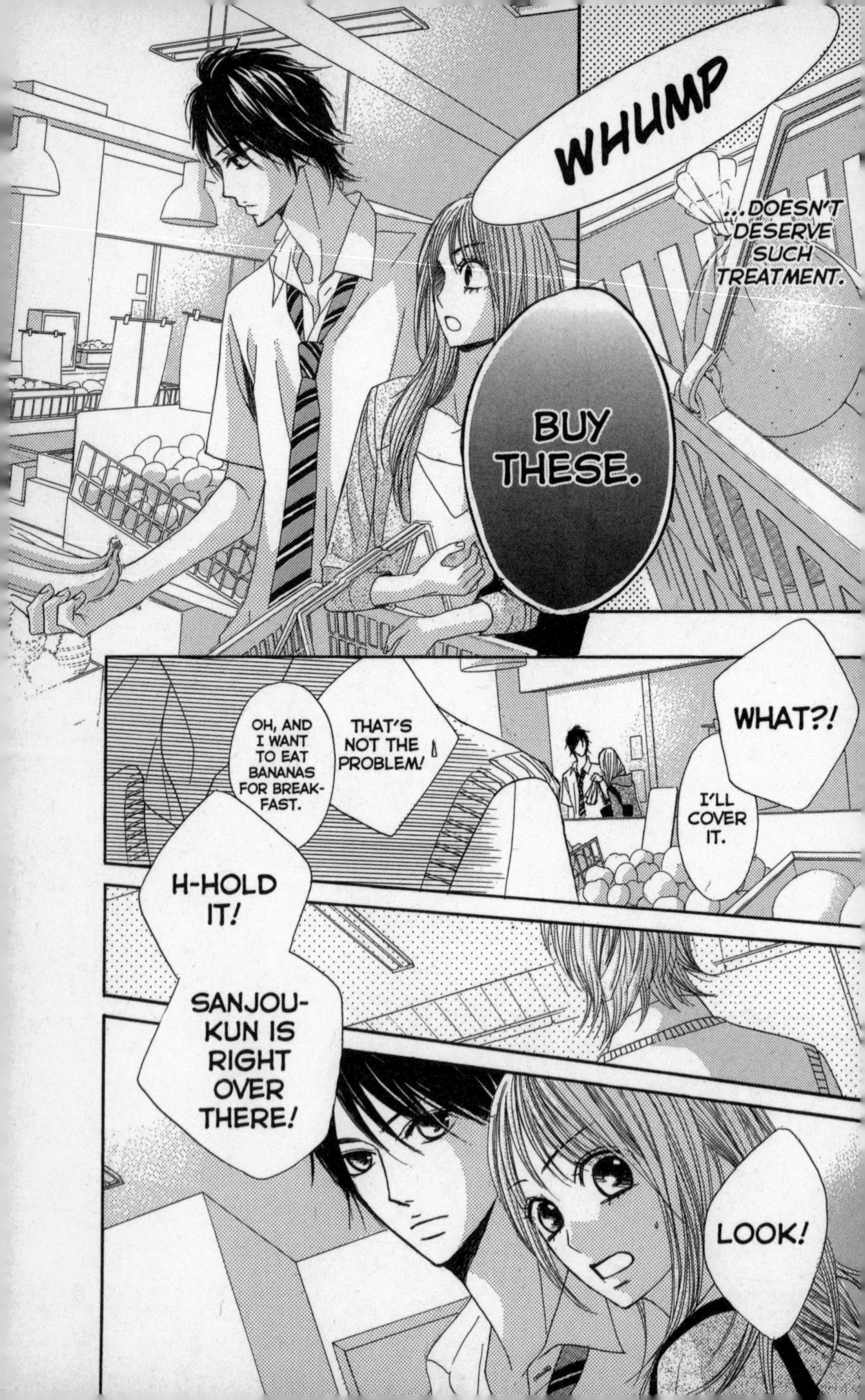
WHUMP
...DOESN'T DESERVE SUCH TREATMENT.
BUY THESE.
WHAT?!
I'LL COVER IT.
THAT'S NOT THE PROBLEM!
OH, AND I WANT TO EAT BANANAS FOR BREAK-FAST.
H-HOLD IT!
SANJOU-KUN IS RIGHT OVER THERE!
LOOK!

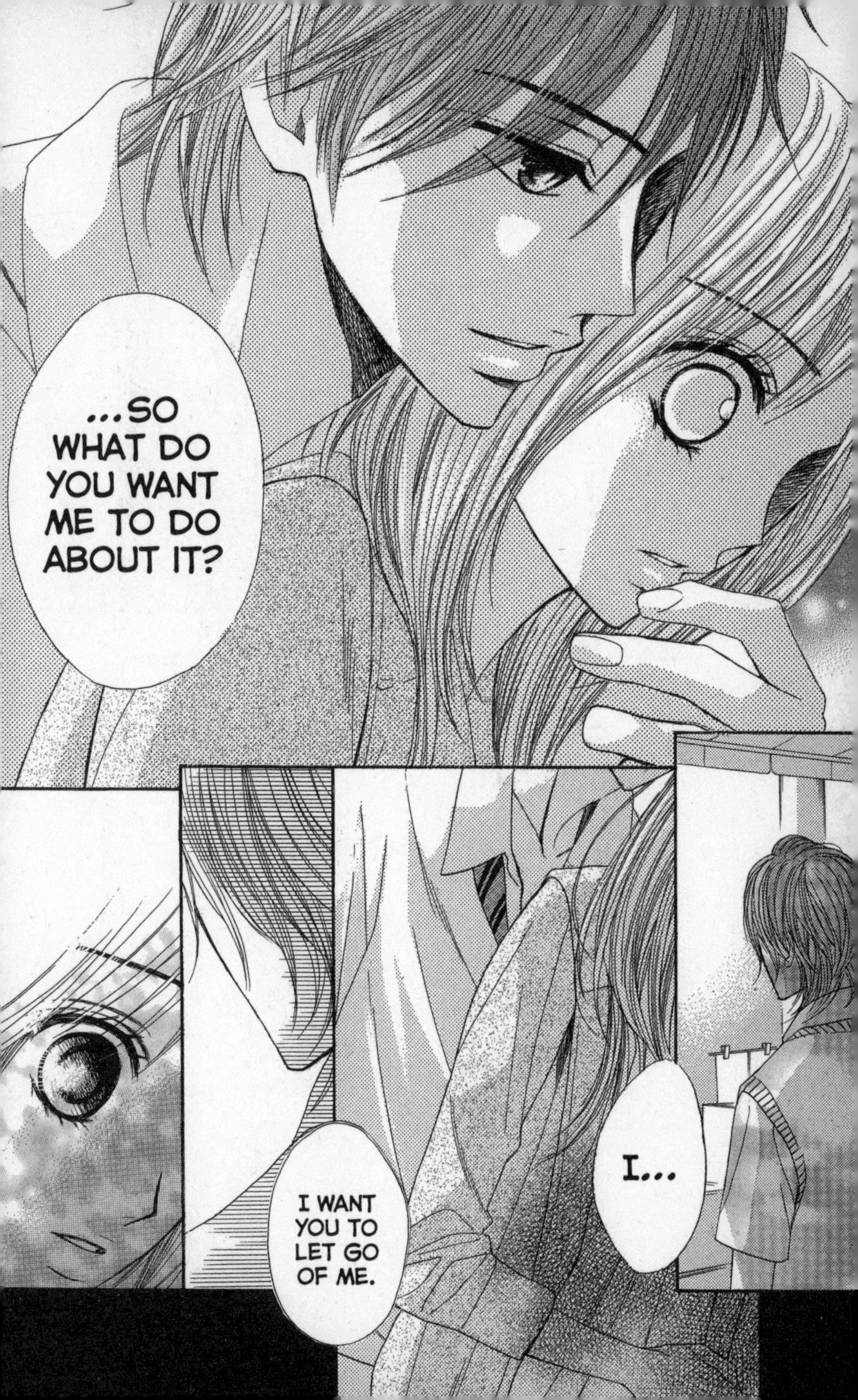
...SO WHAT DO YOU WANT ME TO DO ABOUT IT?
I...
I WANT YOU TO LET GO OF ME.

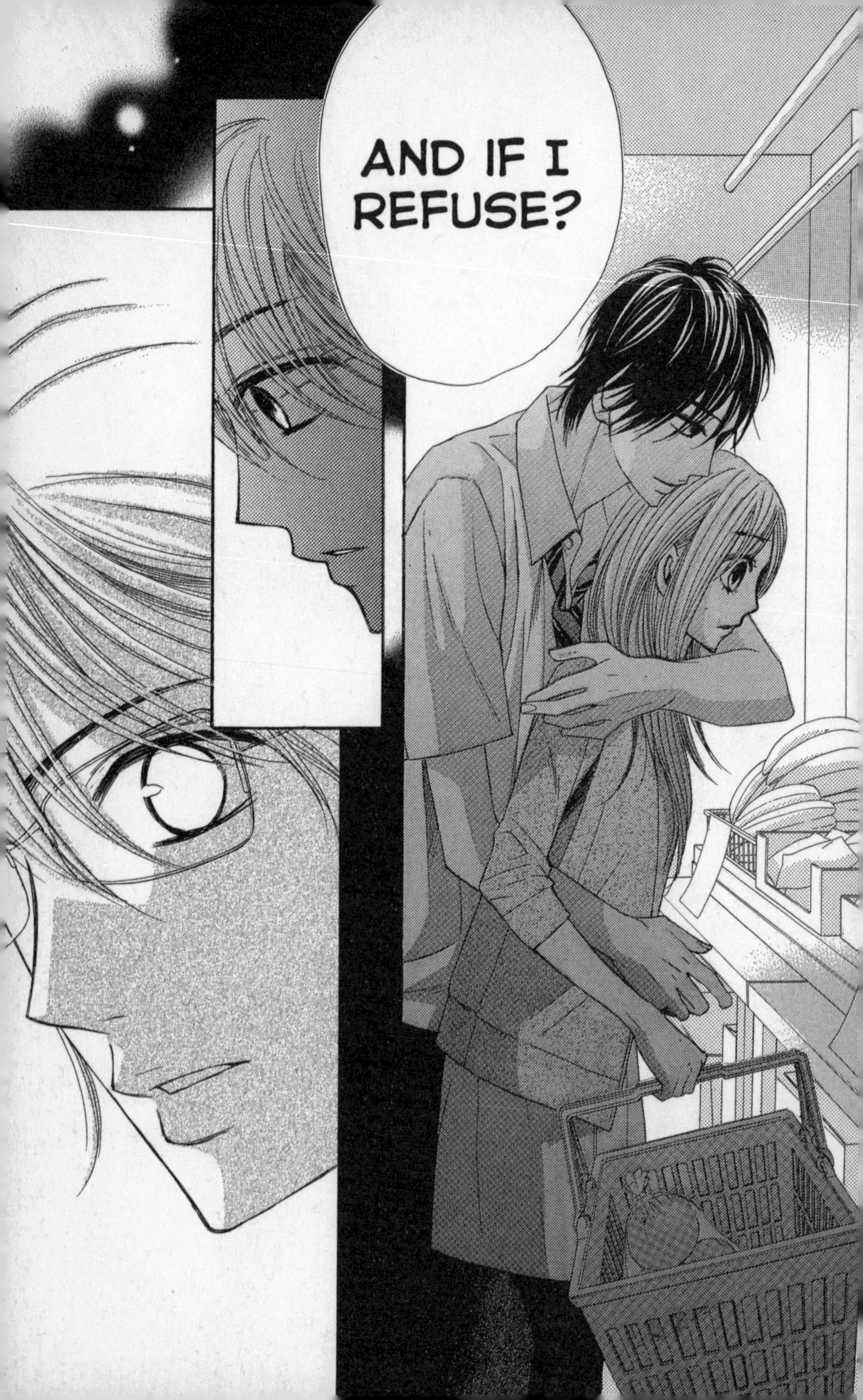
AND IF I REFUSE?

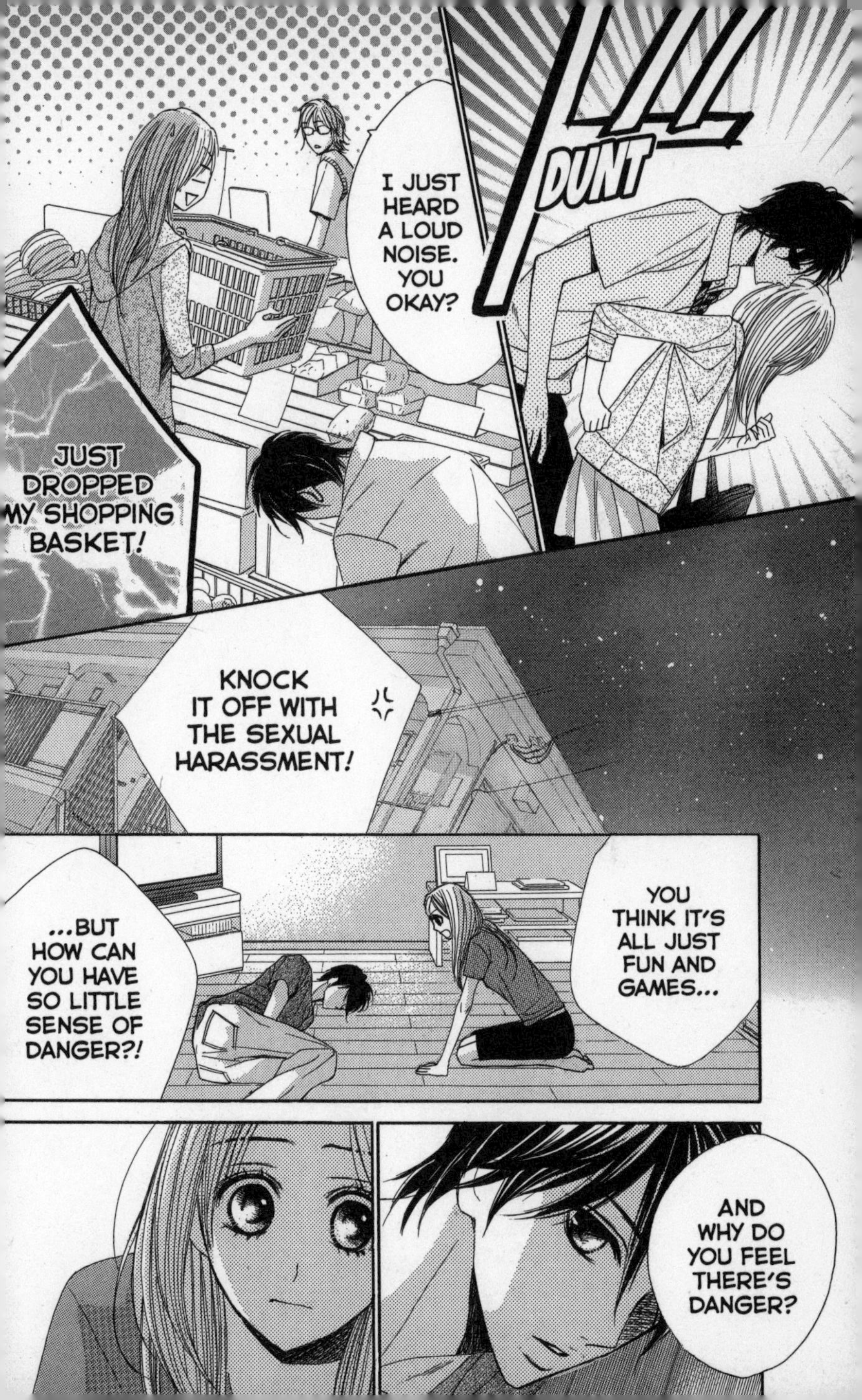
DUNT
I JUST HEARD A LOUD NOISE. YOU OKAY?
JUST DROPPED MY SHOPPING BASKET!
KNOCK IT OFF WITH THE SEXUAL HARASSMENT!
YOU THINK IT'S ALL JUST FUN AND GAMES...
...BUT HOW CAN YOU HAVE SO LITTLE SENSE OF DANGER?!
AND WHY DO YOU FEEL THERE'S DANGER?

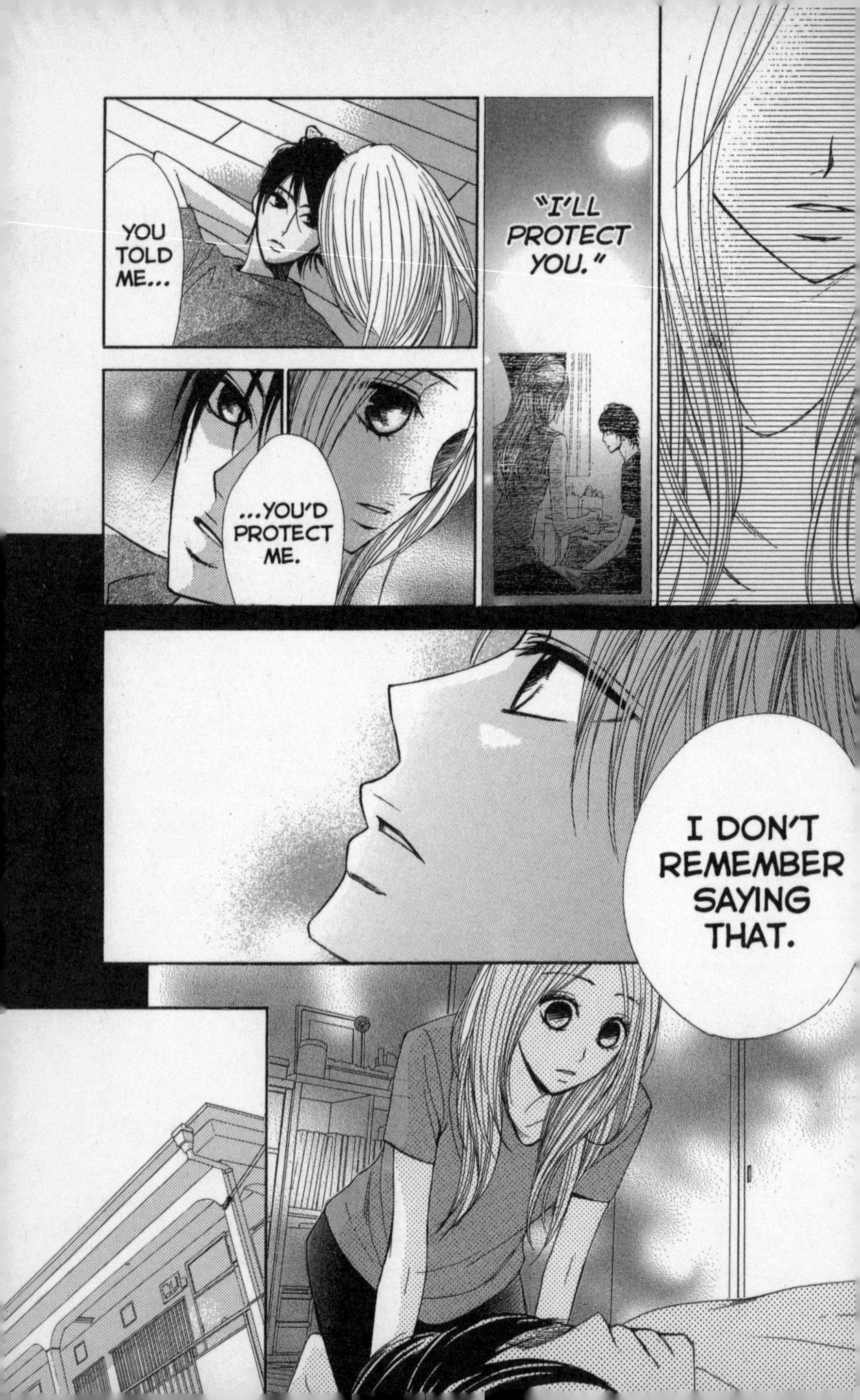
"I'LL PROTECT YOU."
YOU TOLD ME...
...YOU'D PROTECT ME.
I DON'T REMEMBER SAYING THAT.

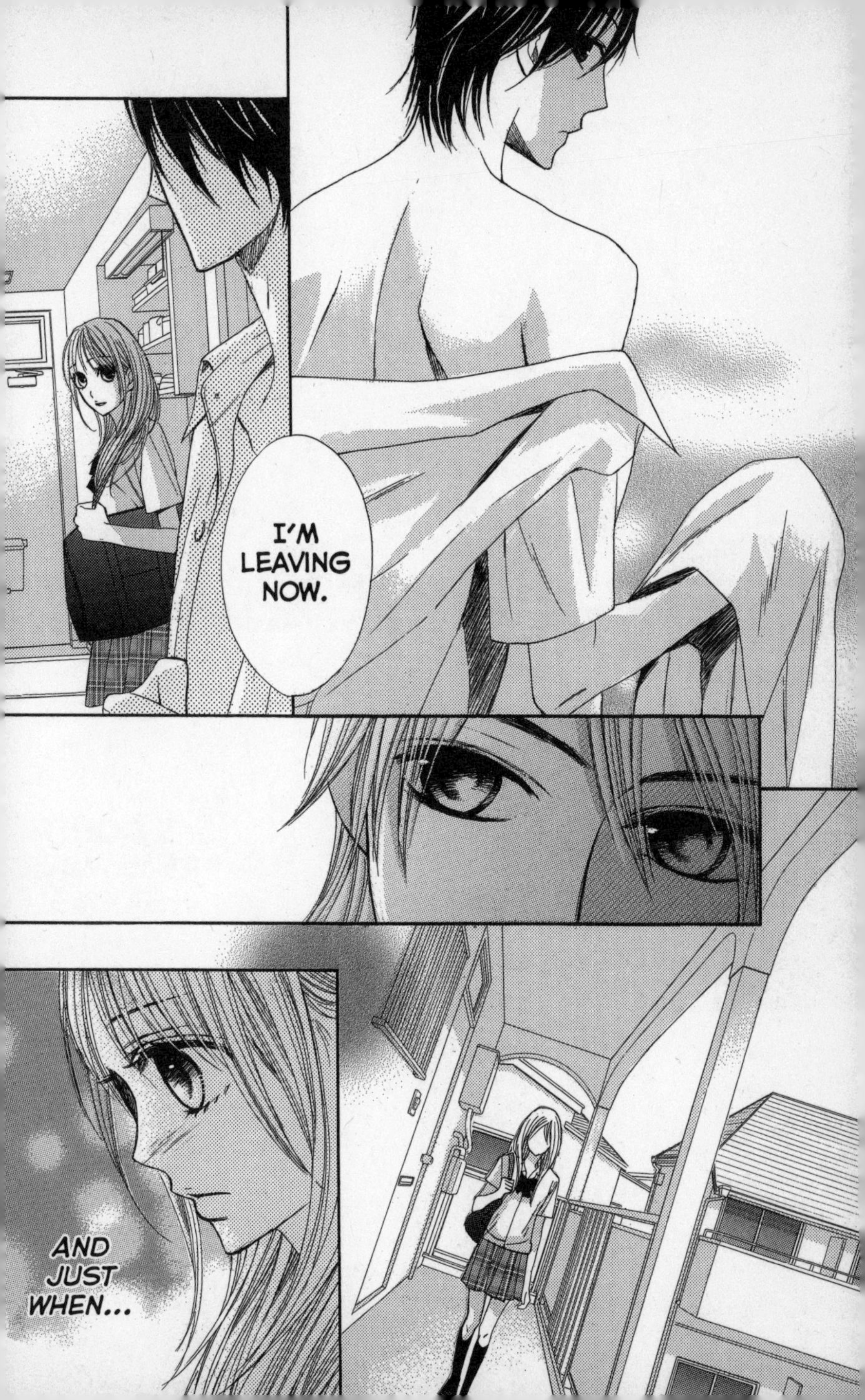
I'M LEAVING NOW.
AND JUST WHEN...

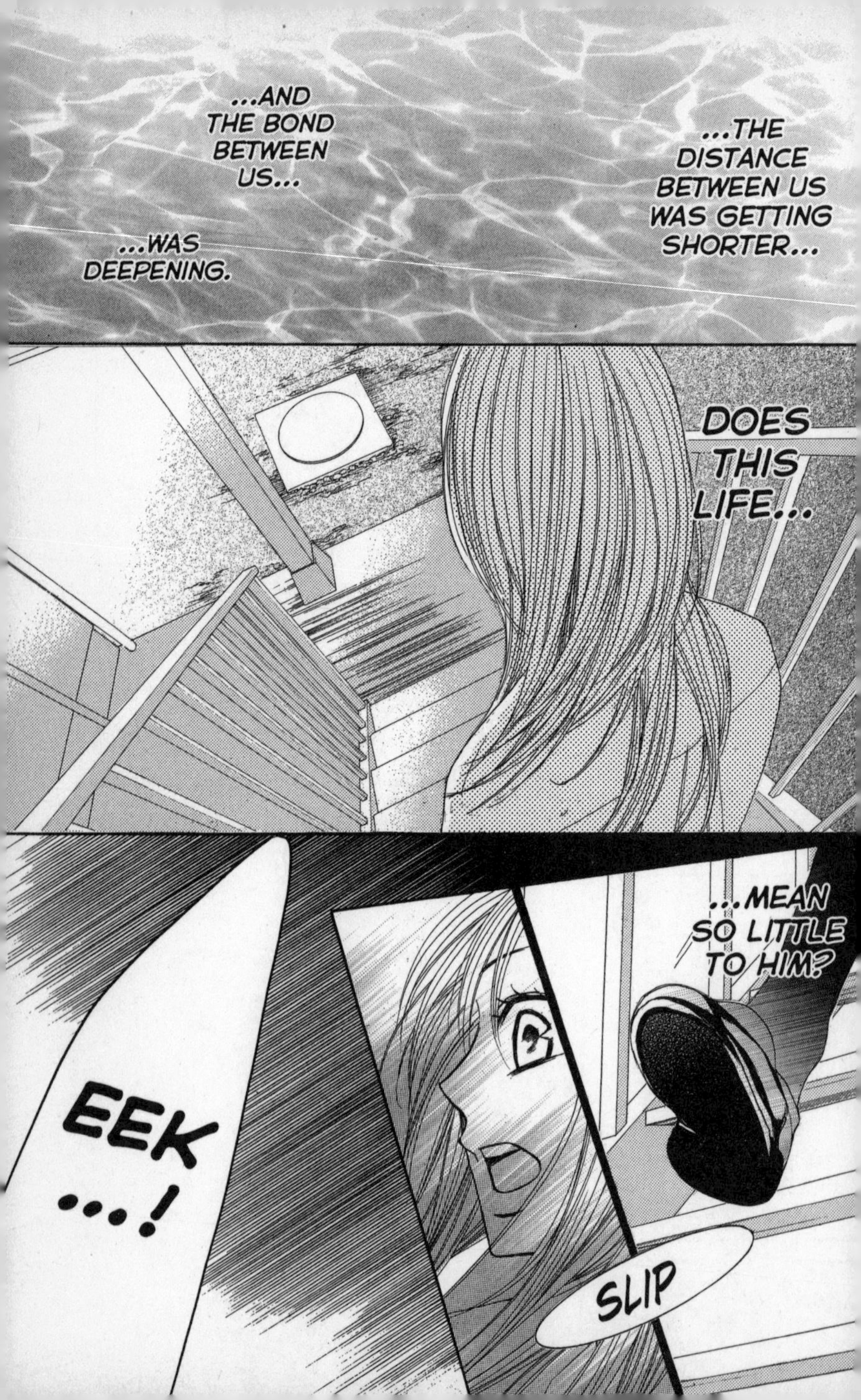
...THE DISTANCE BETWEEN US WAS GETTING SHORTER...
...AND THE BOND BETWEEN US...
...WAS DEEPENING.
DOES THIS LIFE...
...MEAN SO LITTLE TO HIM?
SLIP
EEK ...!

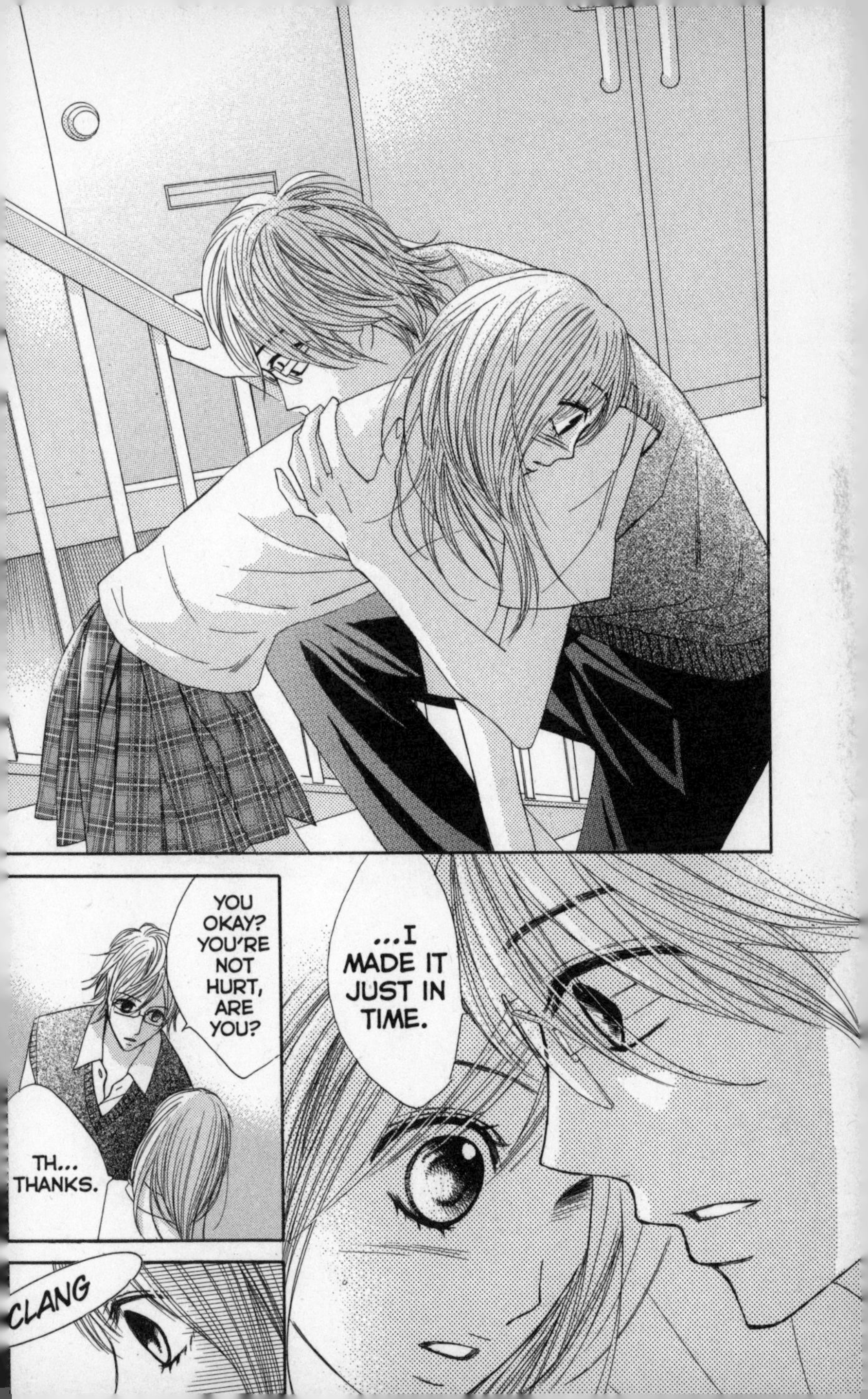
...I MADE IT JUST IN TIME.
YOU OKAY? YOU'RE NOT HURT, ARE YOU?
TH... THANKS.
CLANG

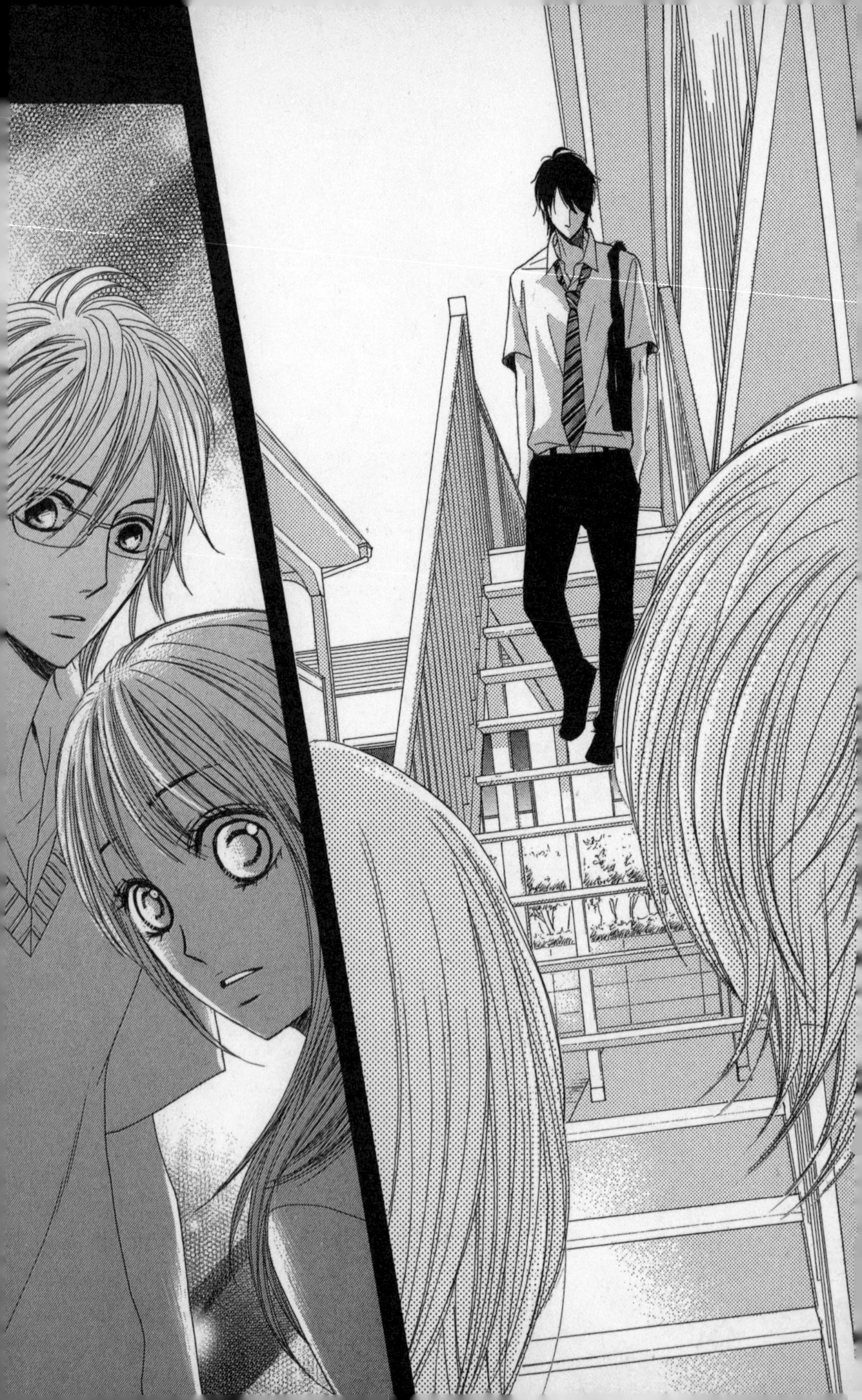

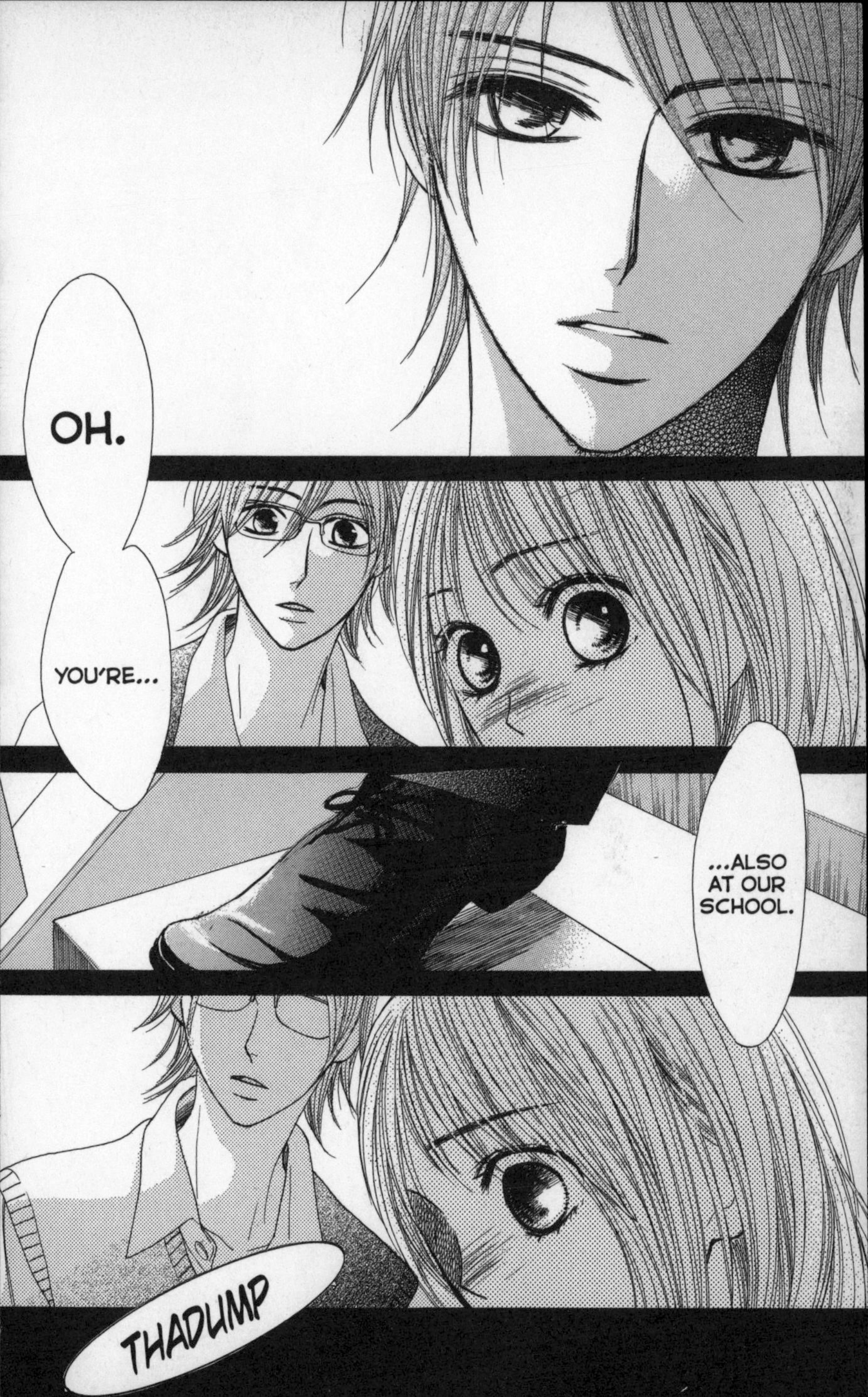
OH.
YOU'RE...
...ALSO AT OUR SCHOOL.
THADUMP

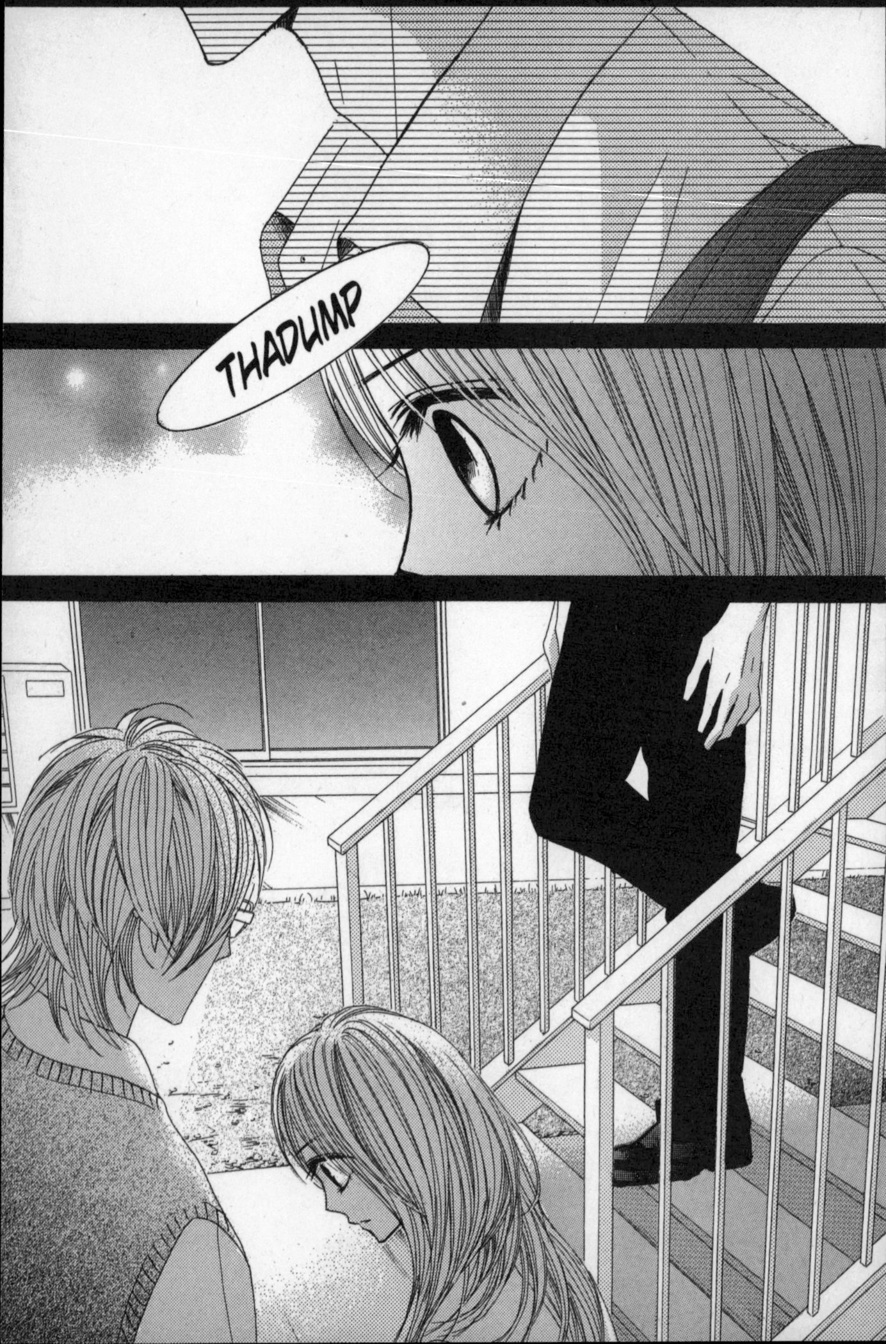
THADUMP

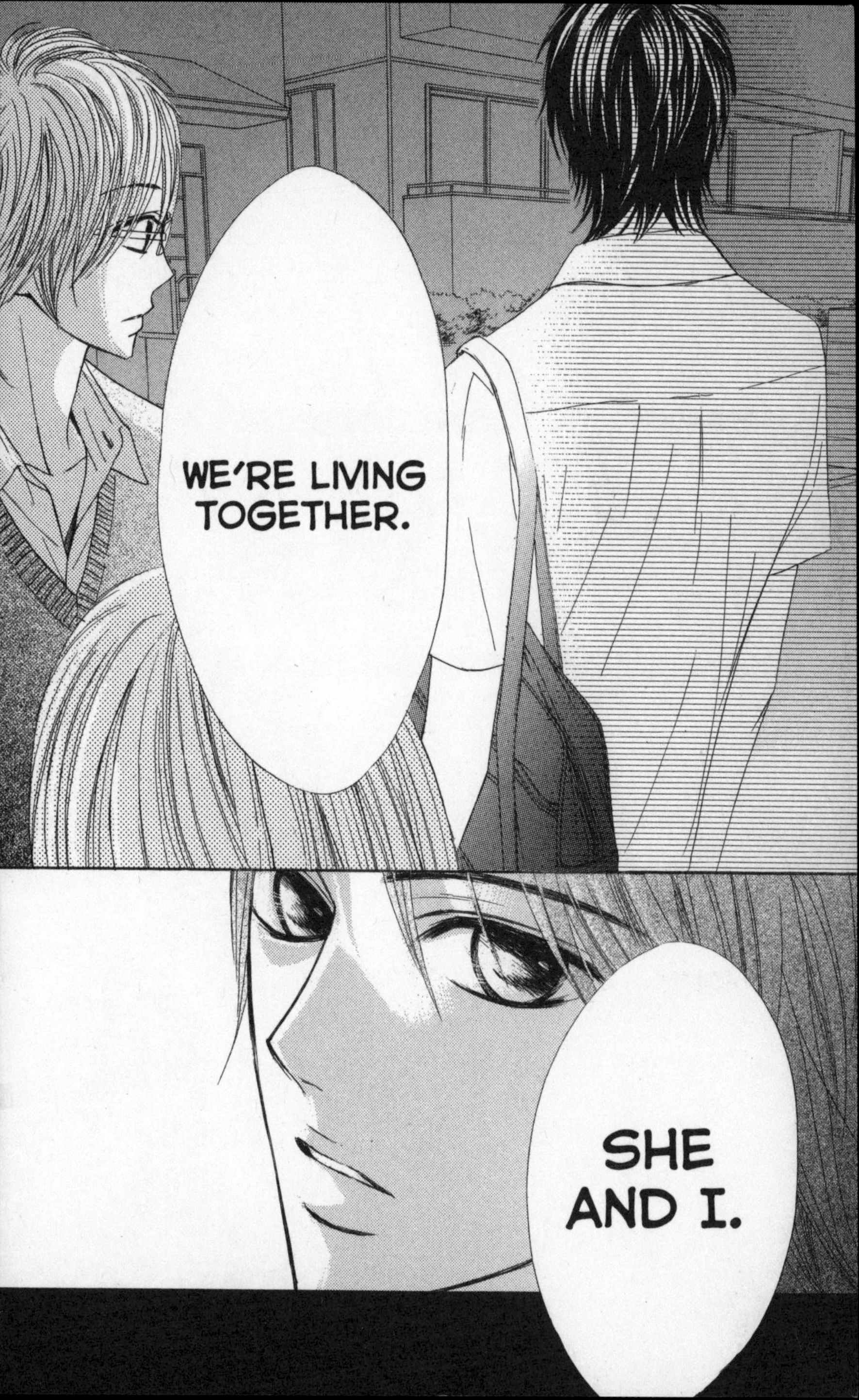
WE'RE LIVING TOGETHER.
SHE AND I.

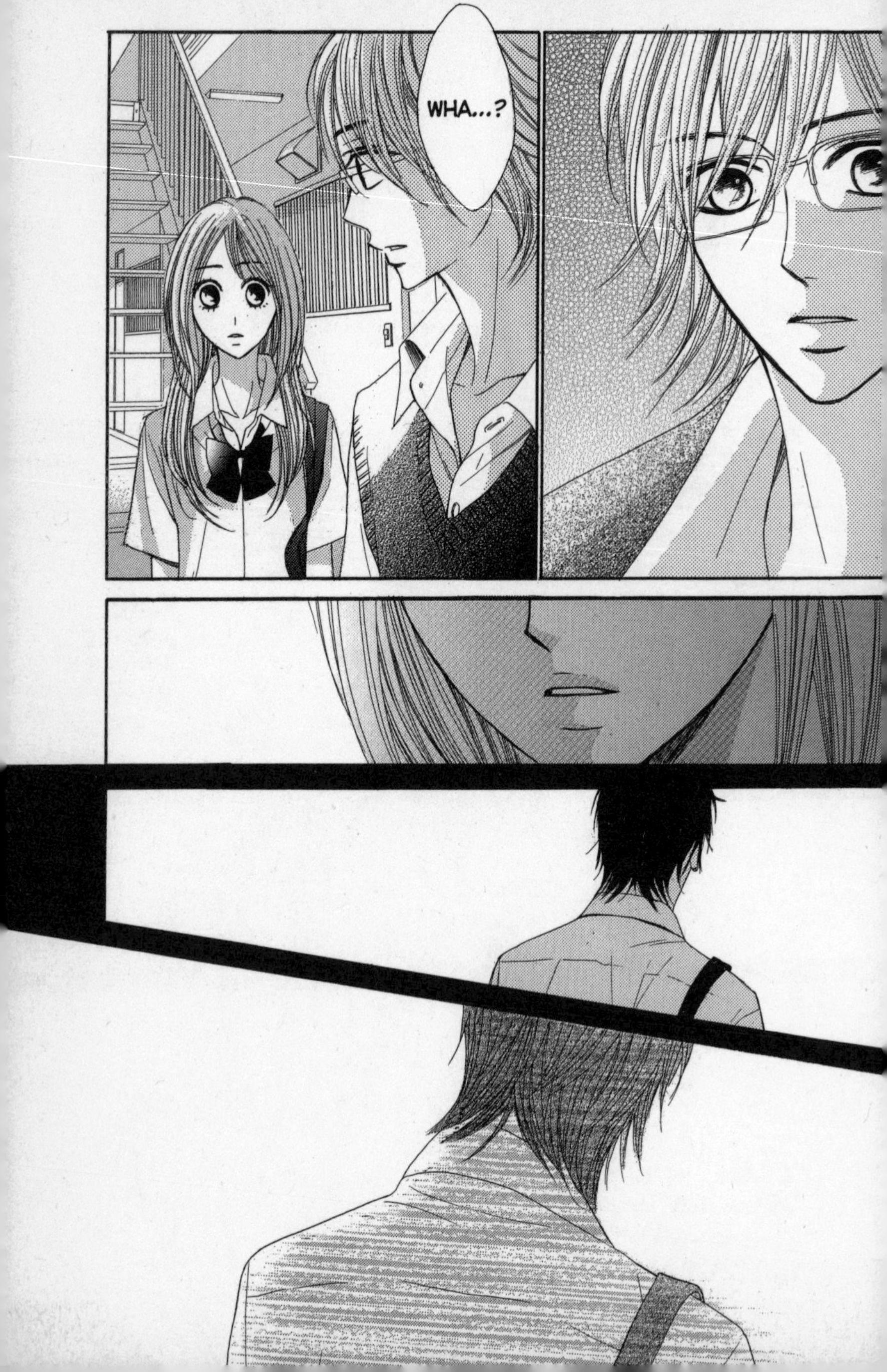
WHA...?

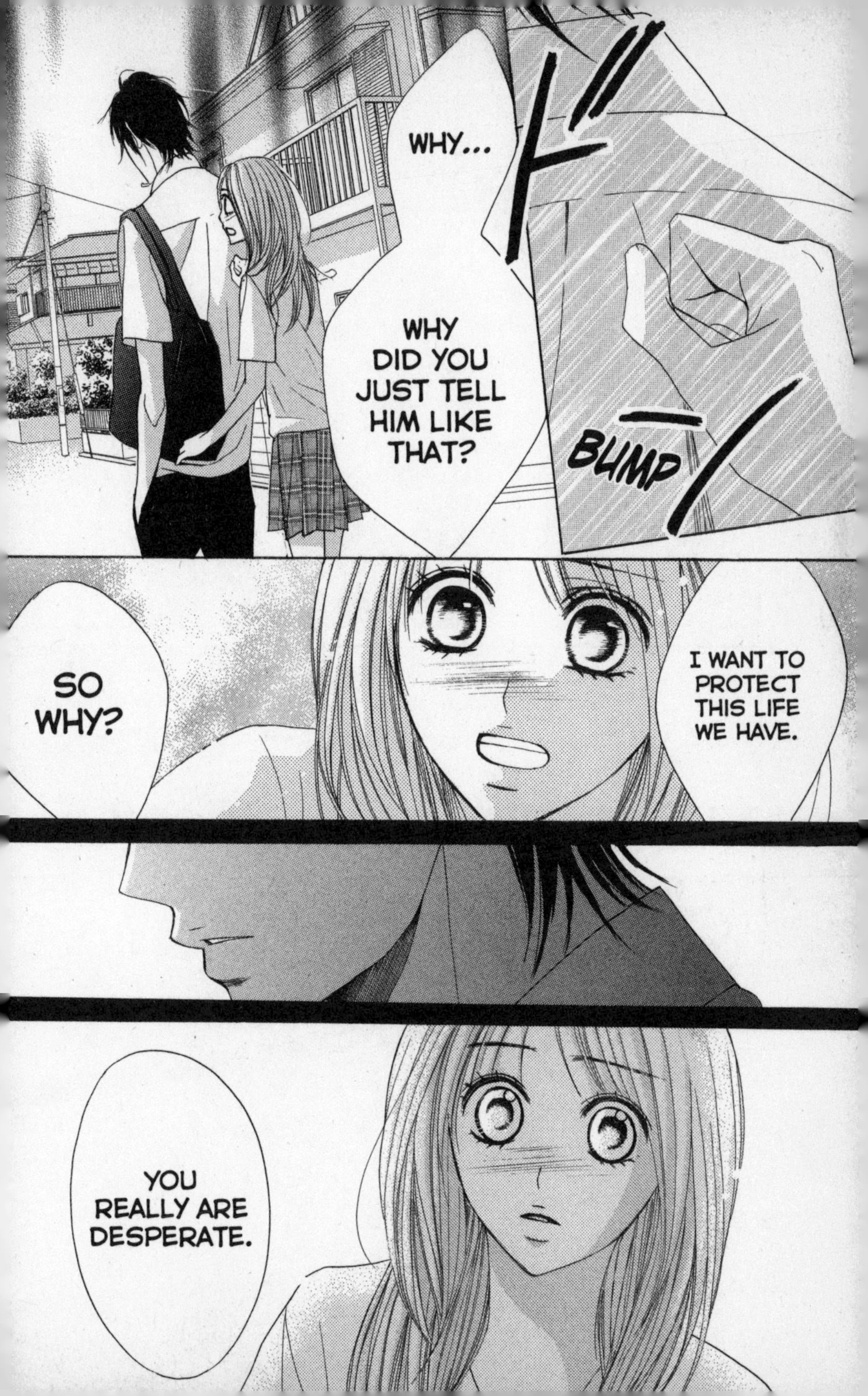
BUMP
WHY...
WHY DID YOU JUST TELL HIM LIKE THAT?
I WANT TO PROTECT THIS LIFE WE HAVE.
SO WHY?
YOU REALLY ARE DESPERATE.

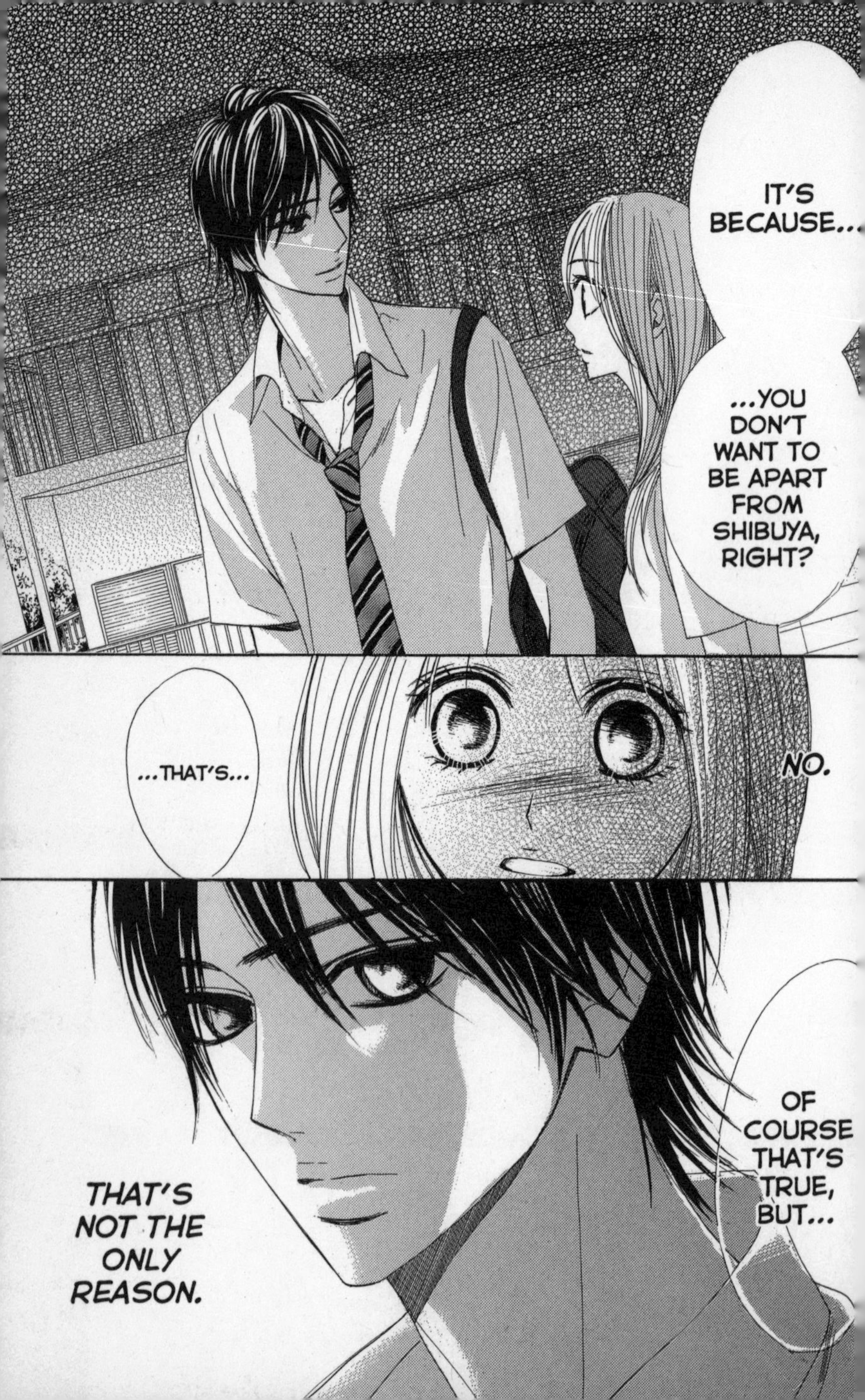
IT'S BECAUSE...
...YOU DON'T WANT TO BE APART FROM SHIBUYA, RIGHT?
NO.
...THAT'S...
OF COURSE THAT'S TRUE, BUT...
THAT'S NOT THE ONLY REASON.

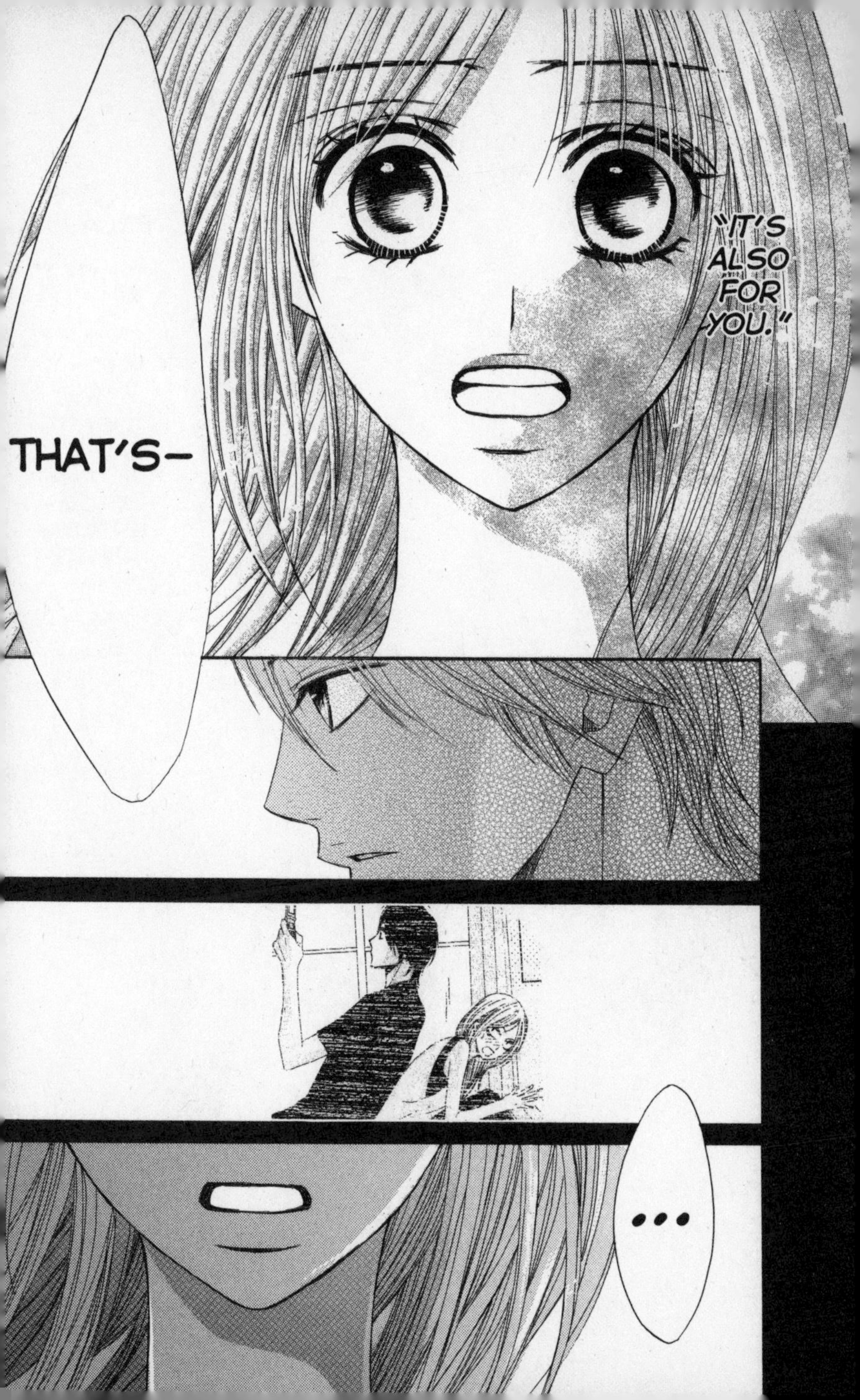
"IT'S ALSO FOR YOU."
THAT'S-
...

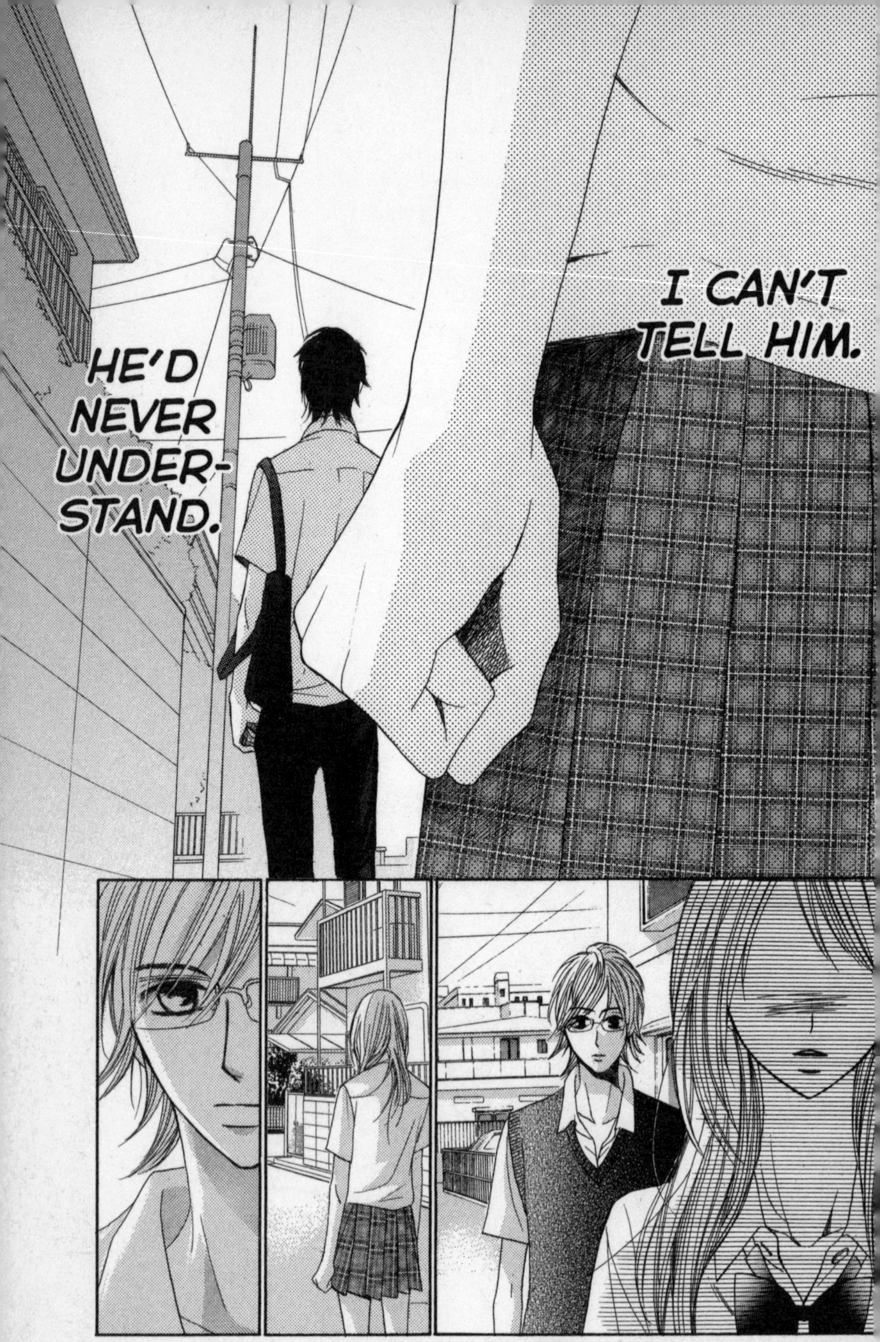
I CAN'T TELL HIM.
HE'D NEVER UNDER-STAND.

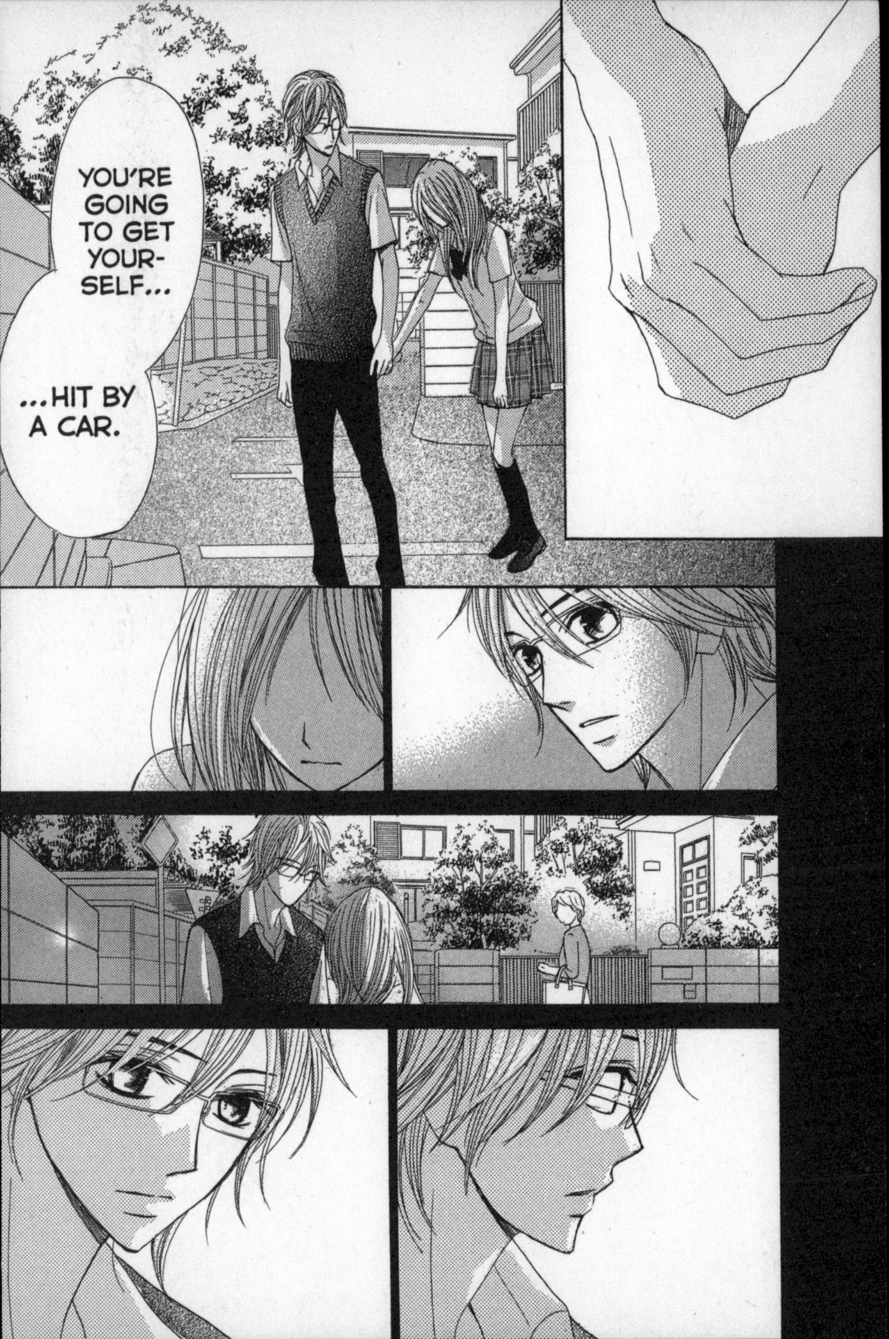
YOU'RE GOING TO GET YOUR-SELF...
...HIT BY A CAR.

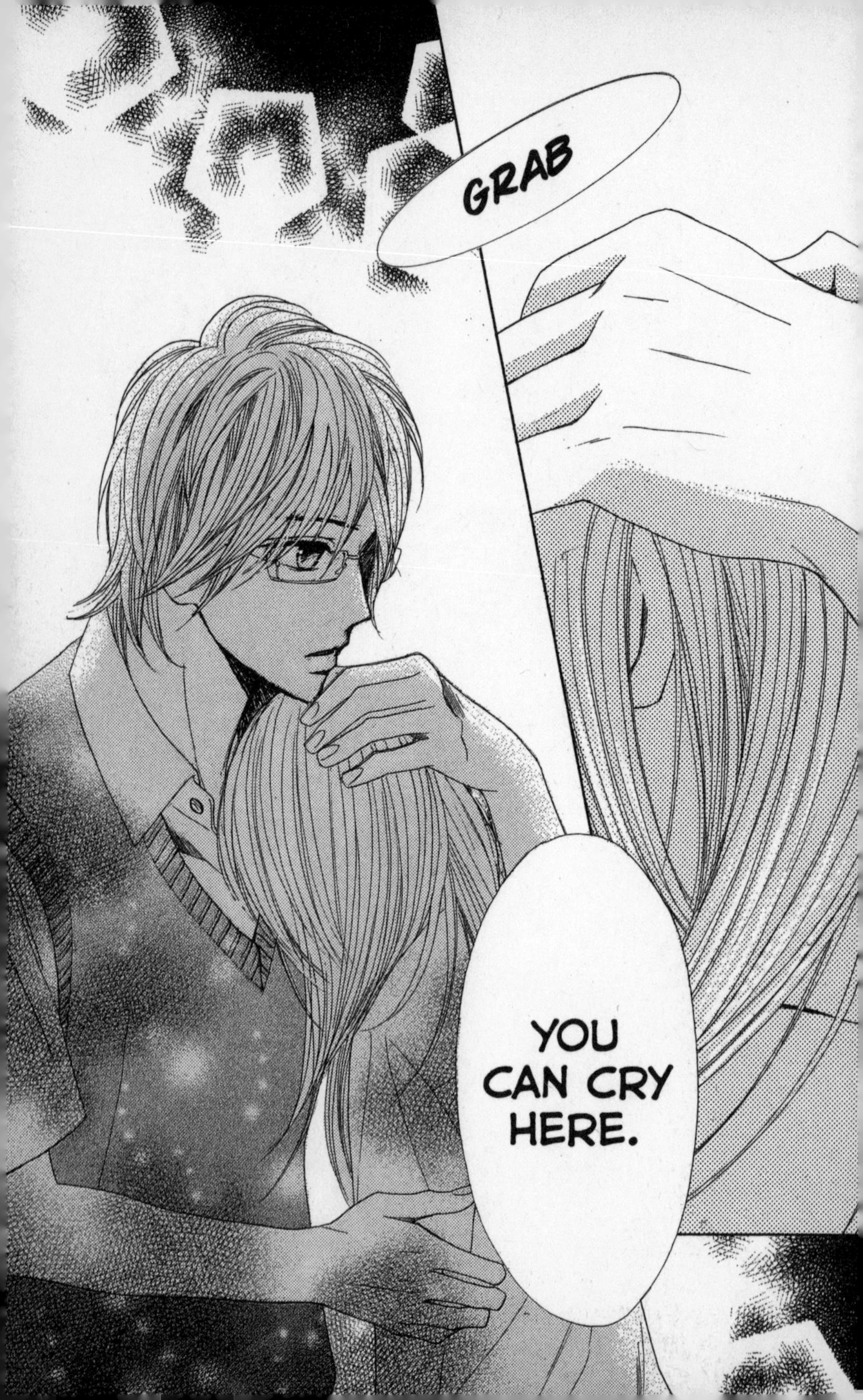
GRAB
YOU CAN CRY HERE.

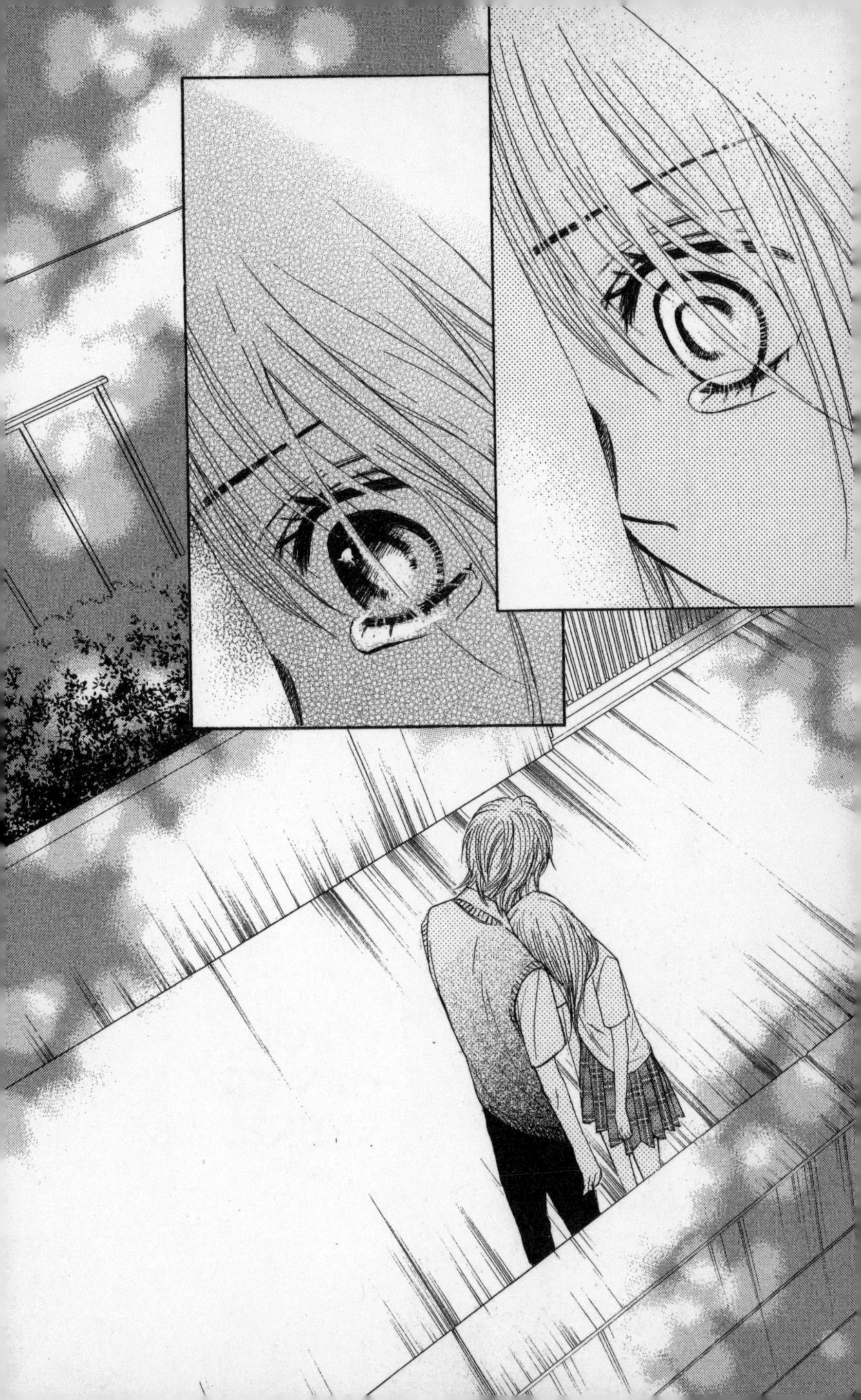

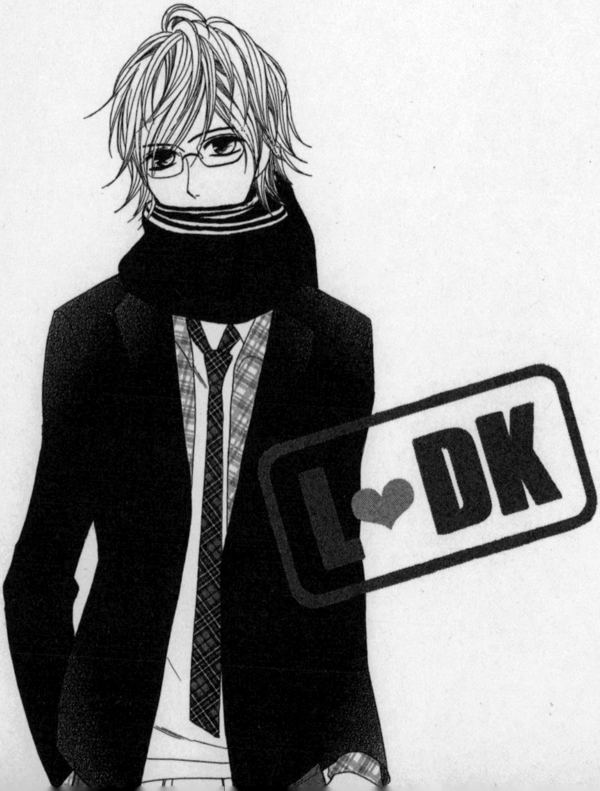
L♥DK

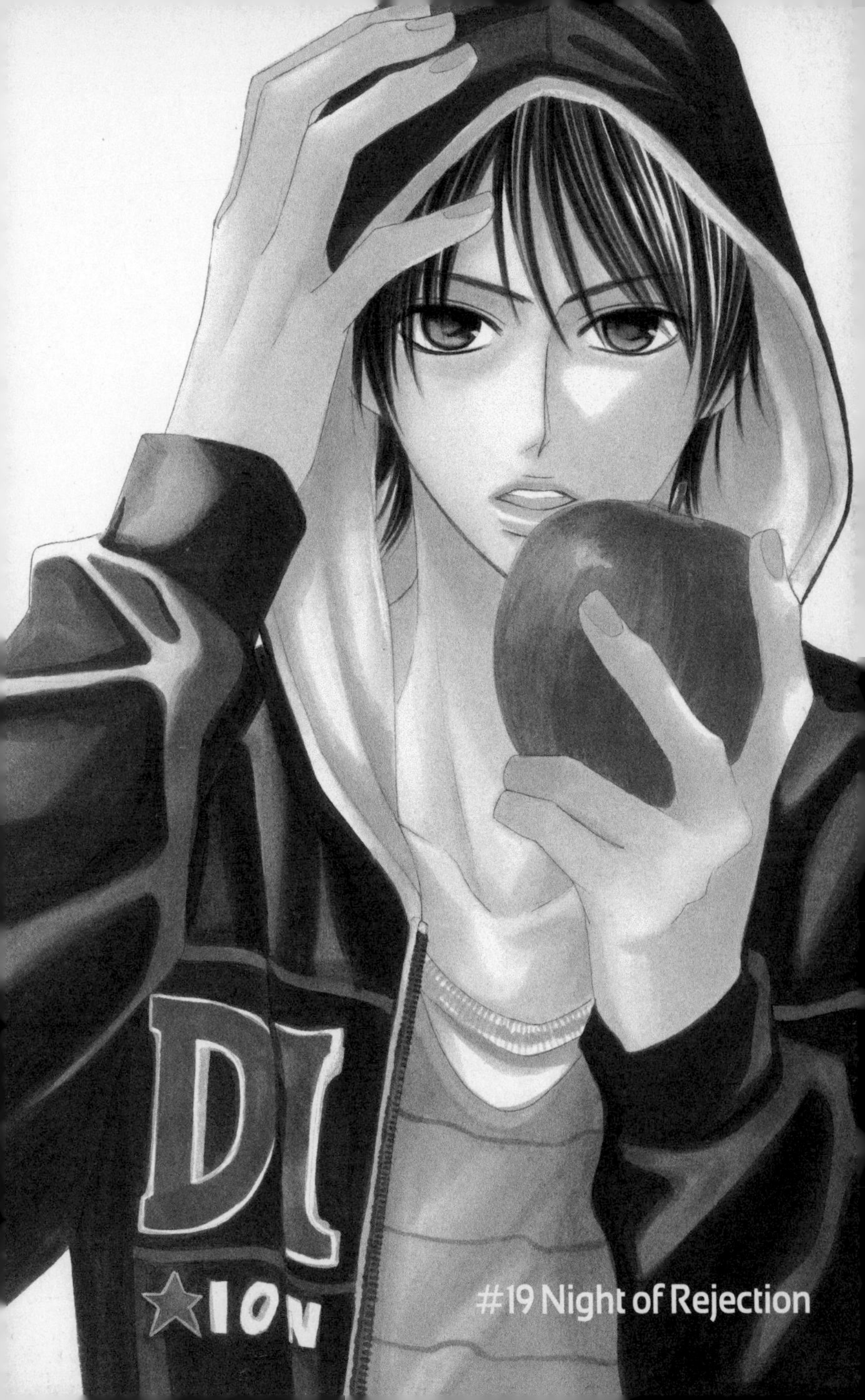
DI
ION

#19 Night of Rejection

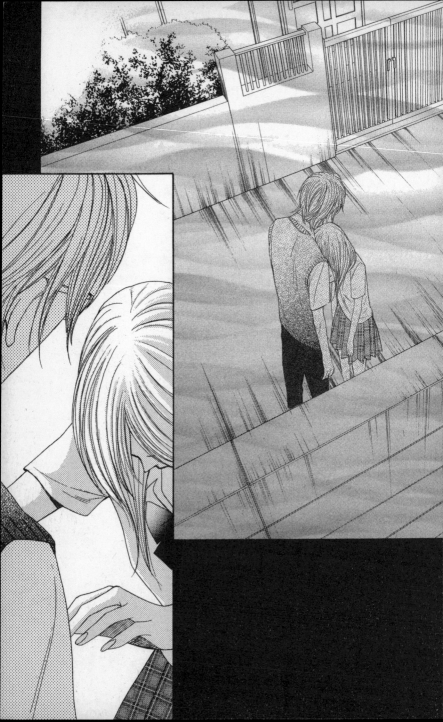

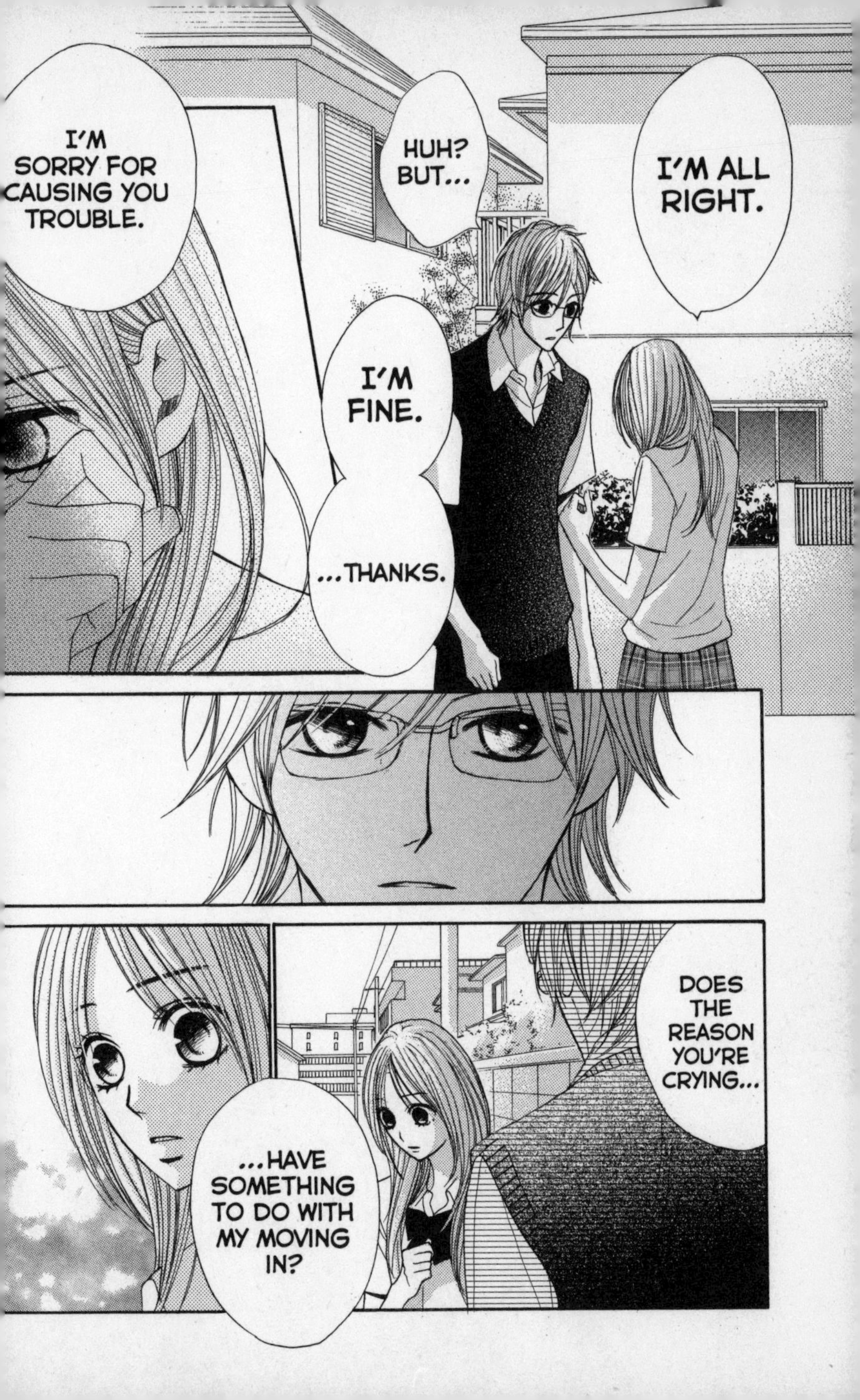
I'M ALL RIGHT.
HUH? BUT...
I'M FINE.
...THANKS.
I'M SORRY FOR CAUSING YOU TROUBLE.
DOES THE REASON YOU'RE CRYING...
...HAVE SOMETHING TO DO WITH MY MOVING IN?

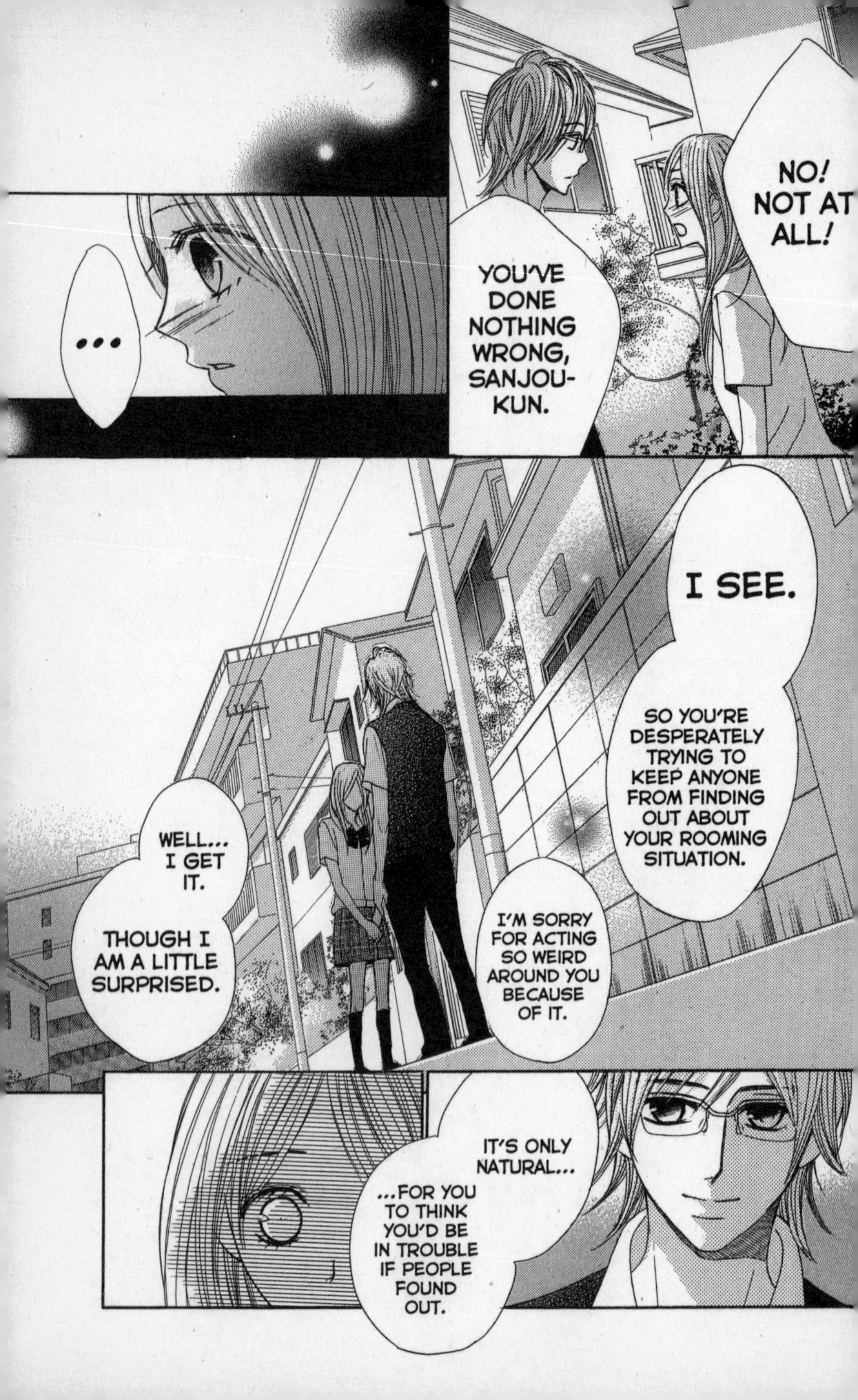
NO! NOT AT ALL!
YOU'VE DONE NOTHING WRONG, SANJOU-KUN.
...
I SEE.
SO YOU'RE DESPERATELY TRYING TO KEEP ANYONE FROM FINDING OUT ABOUT YOUR ROOMING SITUATION.
I'M SORRY FOR ACTING SO WEIRD AROUND YOU BECAUSE OF IT.
WELL... I GET IT.
THOUGH I AM A LITTLE SURPRISED.
IT'S ONLY NATURAL...
...FOR YOU TO THINK YOU'D BE IN TROUBLE IF PEOPLE FOUND OUT.

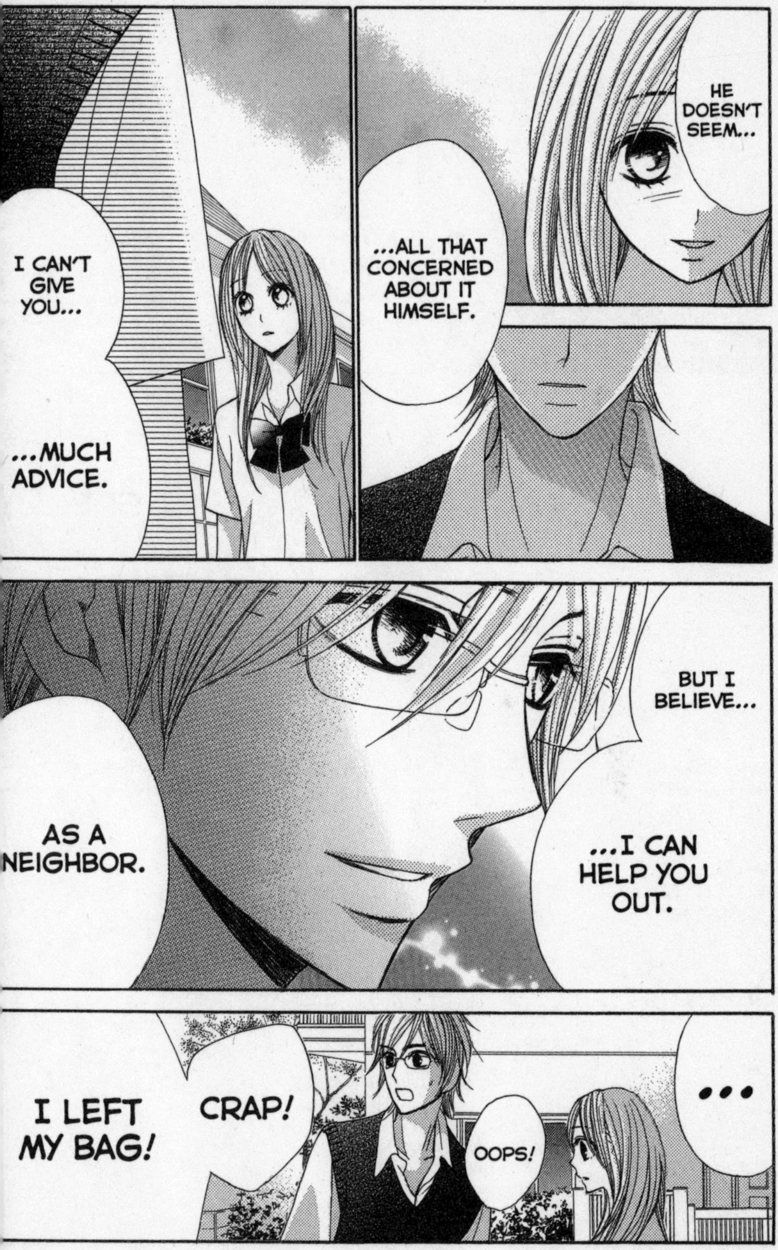
HE DOESN'T SEEM...
...ALL THAT CONCERNED ABOUT IT HIMSELF.
I CAN'T GIVE YOU...
...MUCH ADVICE.
BUT I BELIEVE...
...I CAN HELP YOU OUT.
AS A NEIGHBOR.
...
OOPS!
CRAP!
I LEFT MY BAG!

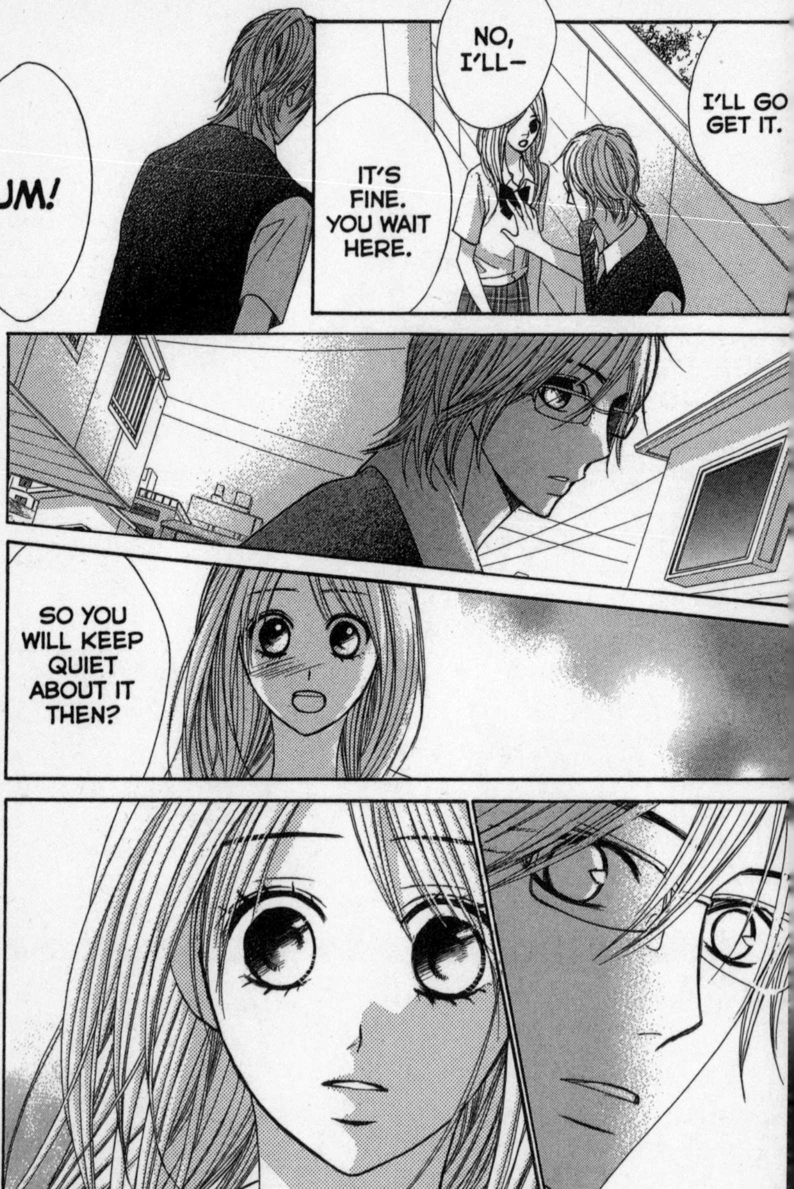
I'LL GO GET IT.
NO, I'LL—
IT'S FINE. YOU WAIT HERE.
UM!
SO YOU WILL KEEP QUIET ABOUT IT THEN?

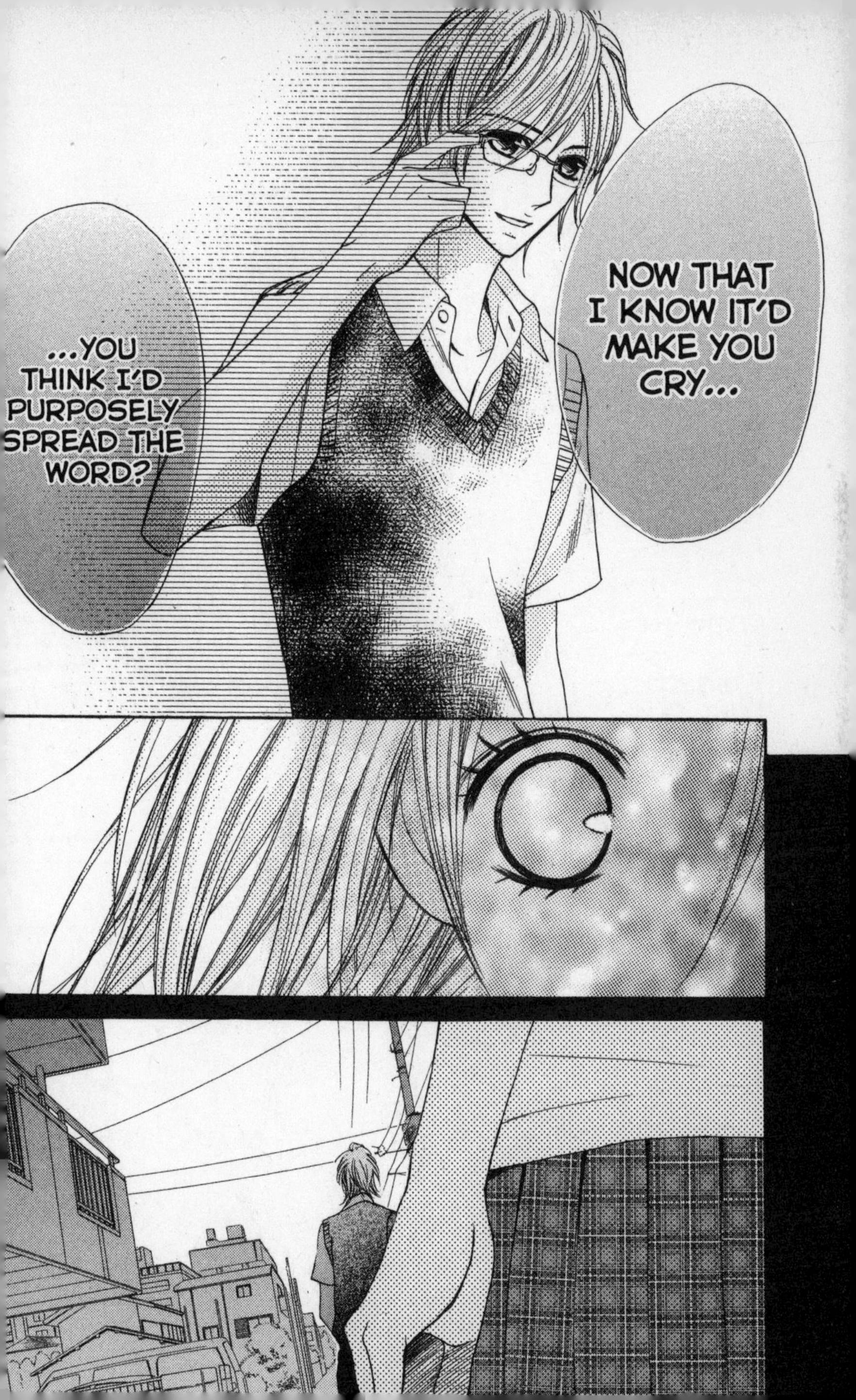
NOW THAT I KNOW IT'D MAKE YOU CRY...
...YOU THINK I'D PURPOSELY SPREAD THE WORD?

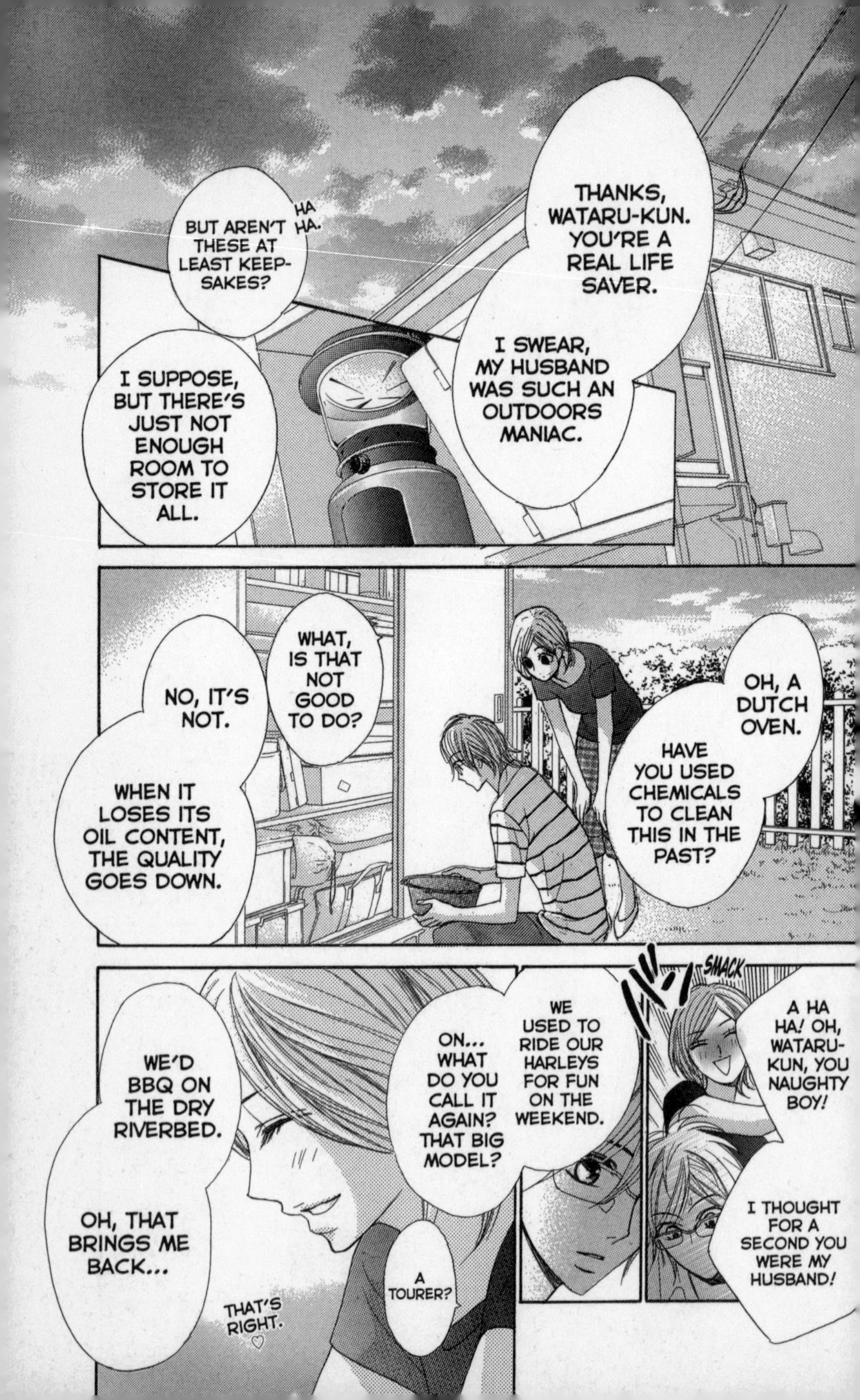
THANKS, WATARU-KUN. YOU'RE A REAL LIFE SAVER.
I SWEAR, MY HUSBAND WAS SUCH AN OUTDOORS MANIAC.
HA HA.
BUT AREN'T THESE AT LEAST KEEP-SAKES?
I SUPPOSE, BUT THERE'S JUST NOT ENOUGH ROOM TO STORE IT ALL.
OH, A DUTCH OVEN.
HAVE YOU USED CHEMICALS TO CLEAN THIS IN THE PAST?
WHAT, IS THAT NOT GOOD TO DO?
NO, IT'S NOT.
WHEN IT LOSES ITS OIL CONTENT, THE QUALITY GOES DOWN.
SMACK
A HA HA! OH, WATARU-KUN, YOU NAUGHTY BOY!
I THOUGHT FOR A SECOND YOU WERE MY HUSBAND!
WE USED TO RIDE OUR HARLEYS FOR FUN ON THE WEEKEND.
ON... WHAT DO YOU CALL IT AGAIN? THAT BIG MODEL?
A TOURER?
THAT'S RIGHT. ♡
WE'D BBQ ON THE DRY RIVERBED.
OH, THAT BRINGS ME BACK...

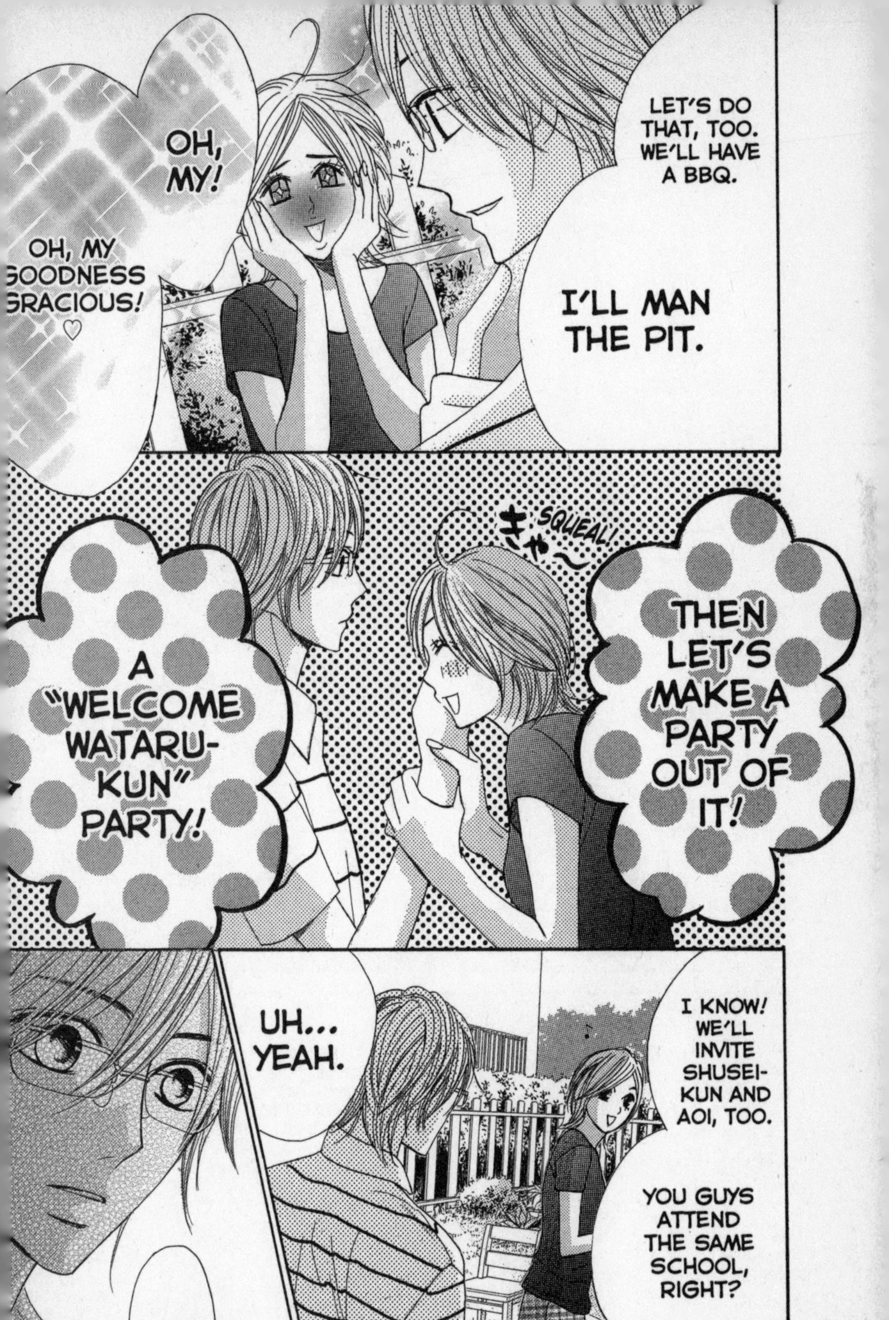
LET'S DO THAT, TOO. WE'LL HAVE A BBQ.
I'LL MAN THE PIT.
OH, MY!
OH, MY GOODNESS GRACIOUS! ♡
きゃ〜 SQUEAL!
THEN LET'S MAKE A PARTY OUT OF IT!
A "WELCOME WATARU-KUN" PARTY!
I KNOW! WE'LL INVITE SHUSEI-KUN AND AOI, TOO.
YOU GUYS ATTEND THE SAME SCHOOL, RIGHT?
UH... YEAH.
...

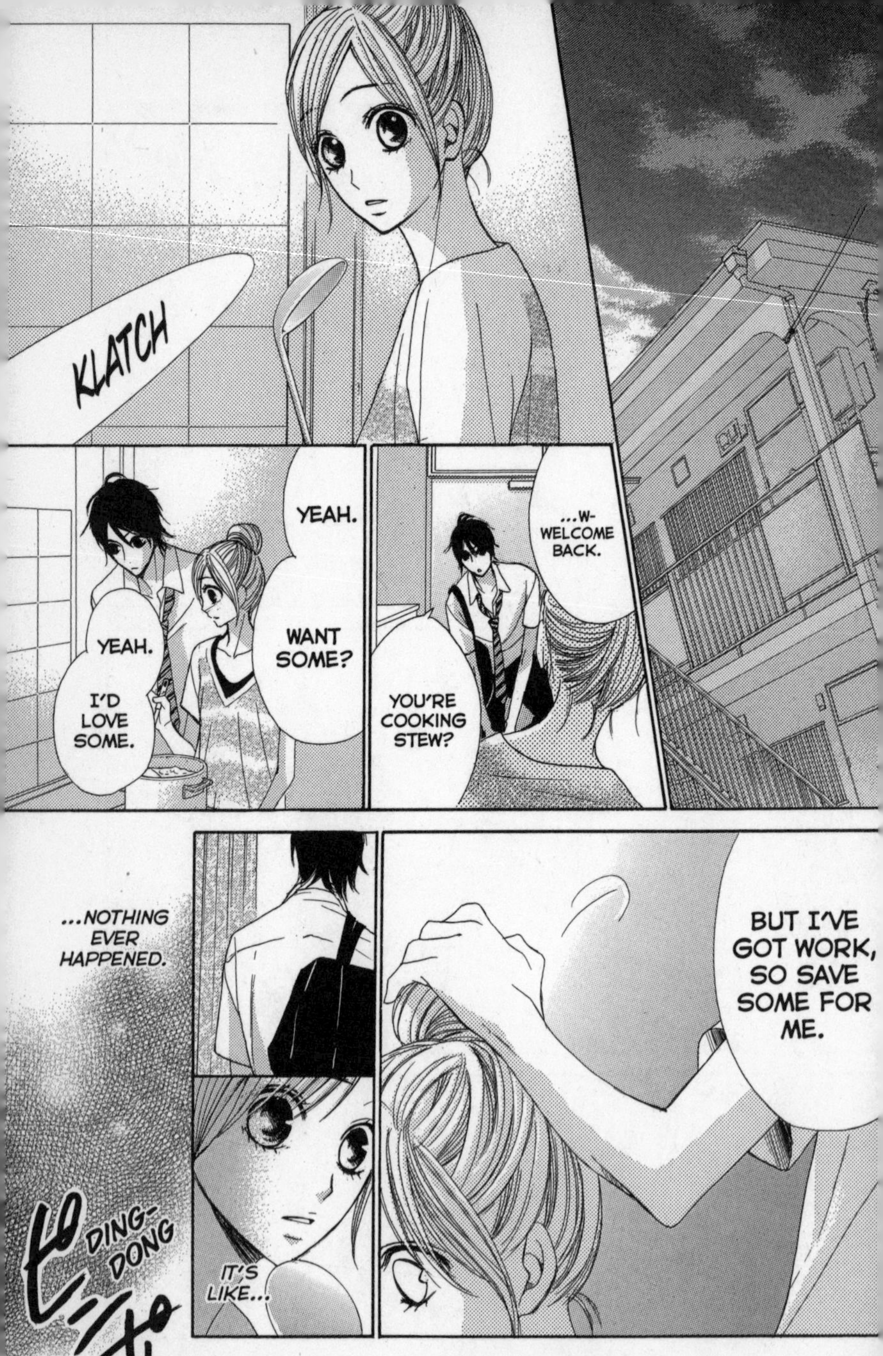
KLATCH
...W-WELCOME BACK.
YOU'RE COOKING STEW?
YEAH.
WANT SOME?
YEAH.
I'D LOVE SOME.
BUT I'VE GOT WORK, SO SAVE SOME FOR ME.
ピンポーン
DING-DONG
IT'S LIKE...
...NOTHING EVER HAPPENED.

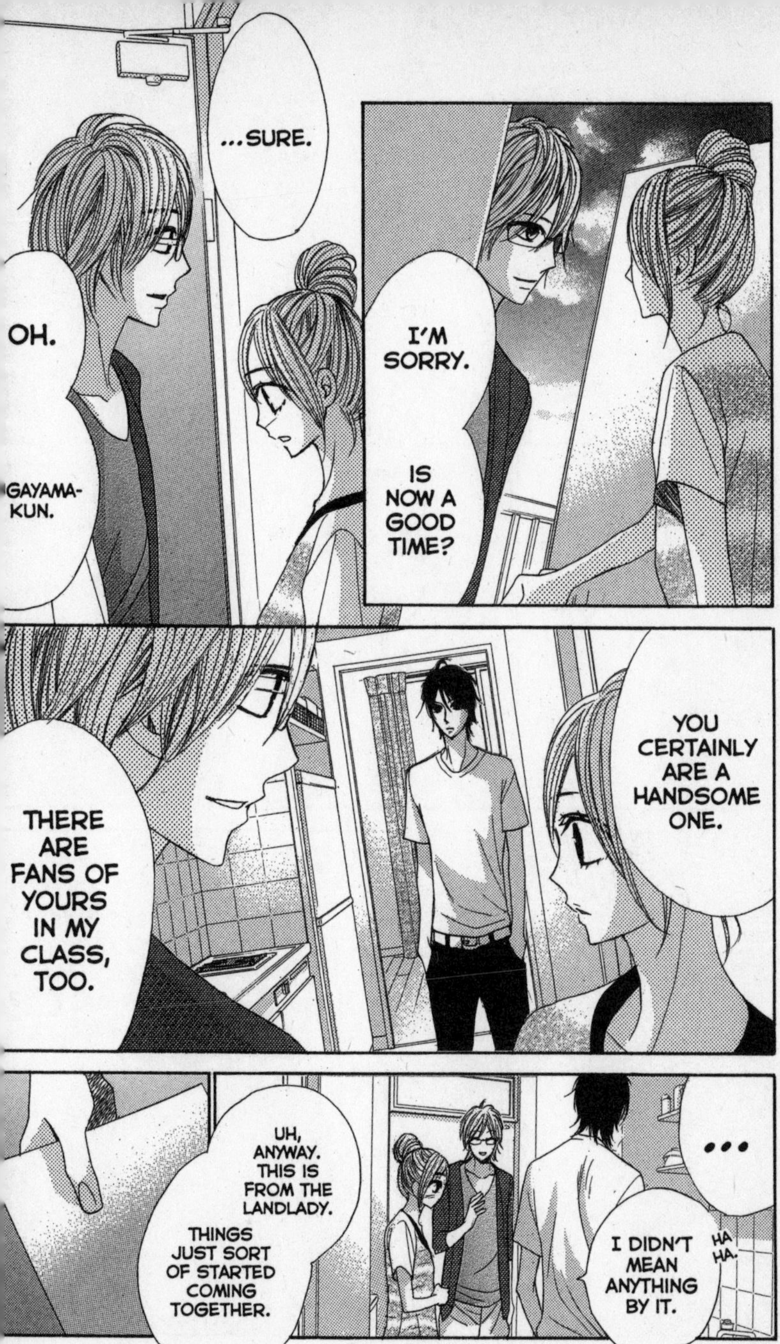
I'M SORRY.
IS NOW A GOOD TIME?
...SURE.
OH.
GAYAMA-KUN.
YOU CERTAINLY ARE A HANDSOME ONE.
THERE ARE FANS OF YOURS IN MY CLASS, TOO.
...
HA HA.
I DIDN'T MEAN ANYTHING BY IT.
UH, ANYWAY. THIS IS FROM THE LANDLADY.
THINGS JUST SORT OF STARTED COMING TOGETHER.

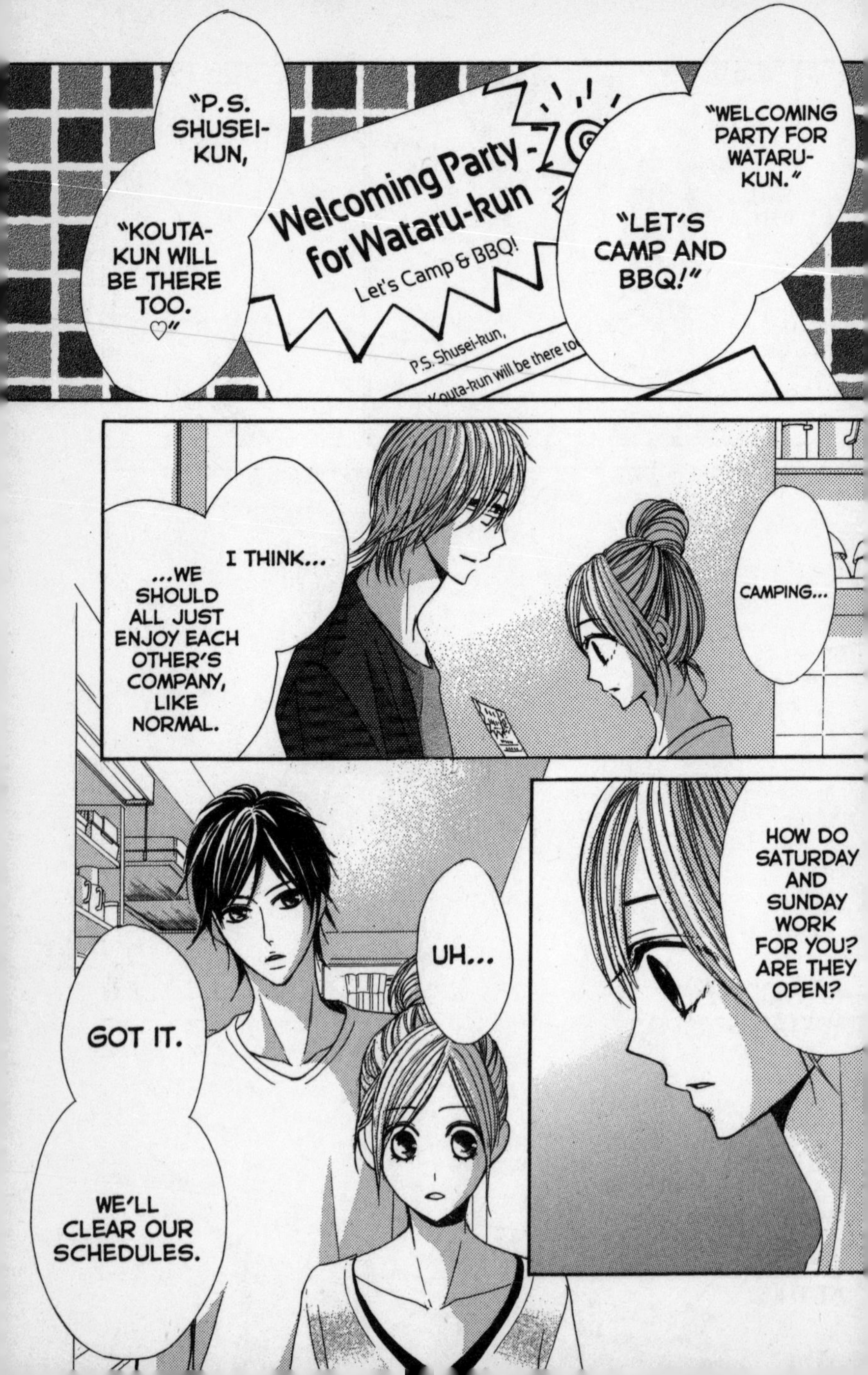
"WELCOMING PARTY FOR WATARU-KUN."
"LET'S CAMP AND BBQ!"
Welcoming Party for Wataru-kun
Let's Camp & BBQ!
P.S. Shusei-kun,
"P.S. SHUSEI-KUN,
"KOUTA-KUN WILL BE THERE TOO. ♡"
CAMPING...
I THINK...
...WE SHOULD ALL JUST ENJOY EACH OTHER'S COMPANY, LIKE NORMAL.
HOW DO SATURDAY AND SUNDAY WORK FOR YOU? ARE THEY OPEN?
UH...
GOT IT.
WE'LL CLEAR OUR SCHEDULES.

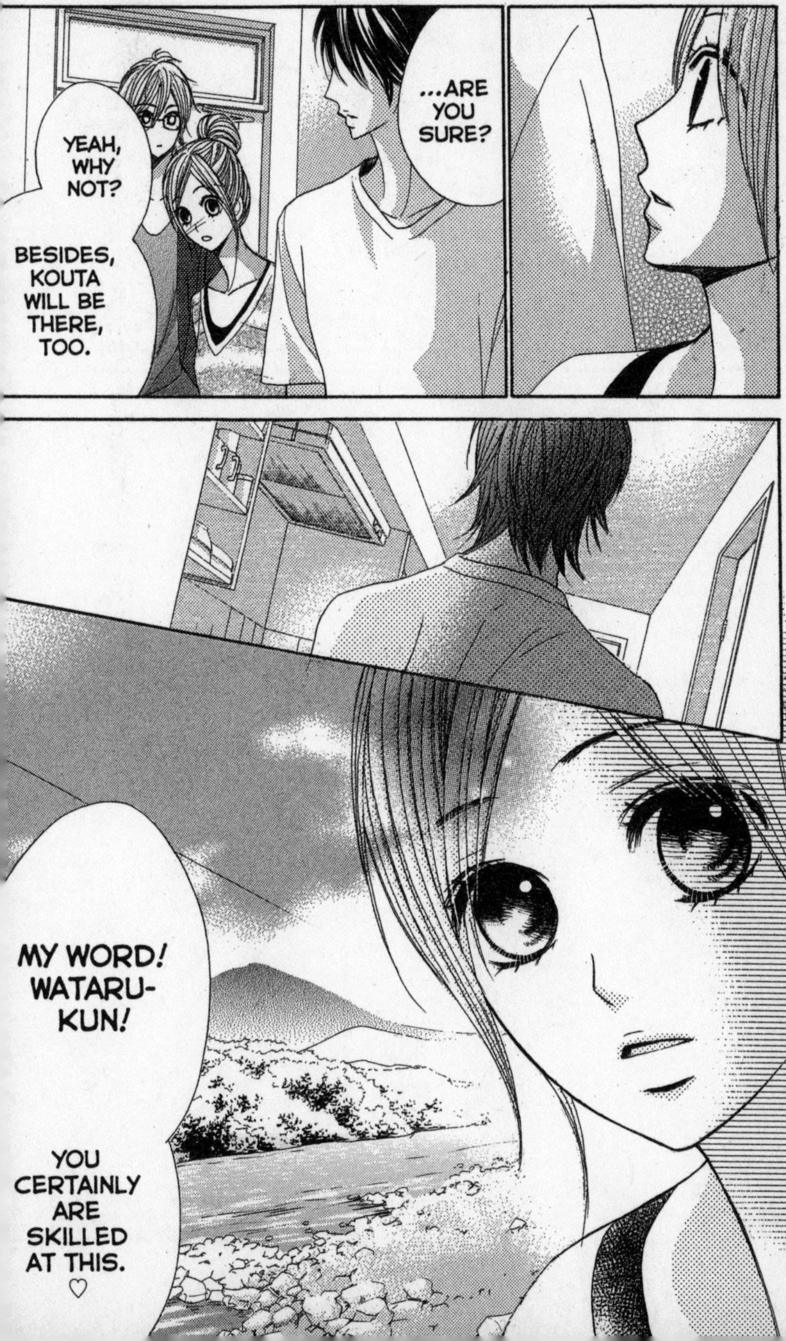
...ARE YOU SURE?
YEAH, WHY NOT?
BESIDES, KOUTA WILL BE THERE, TOO.
MY WORD! WATARU-KUN!
YOU CERTAINLY ARE SKILLED AT THIS. ♡

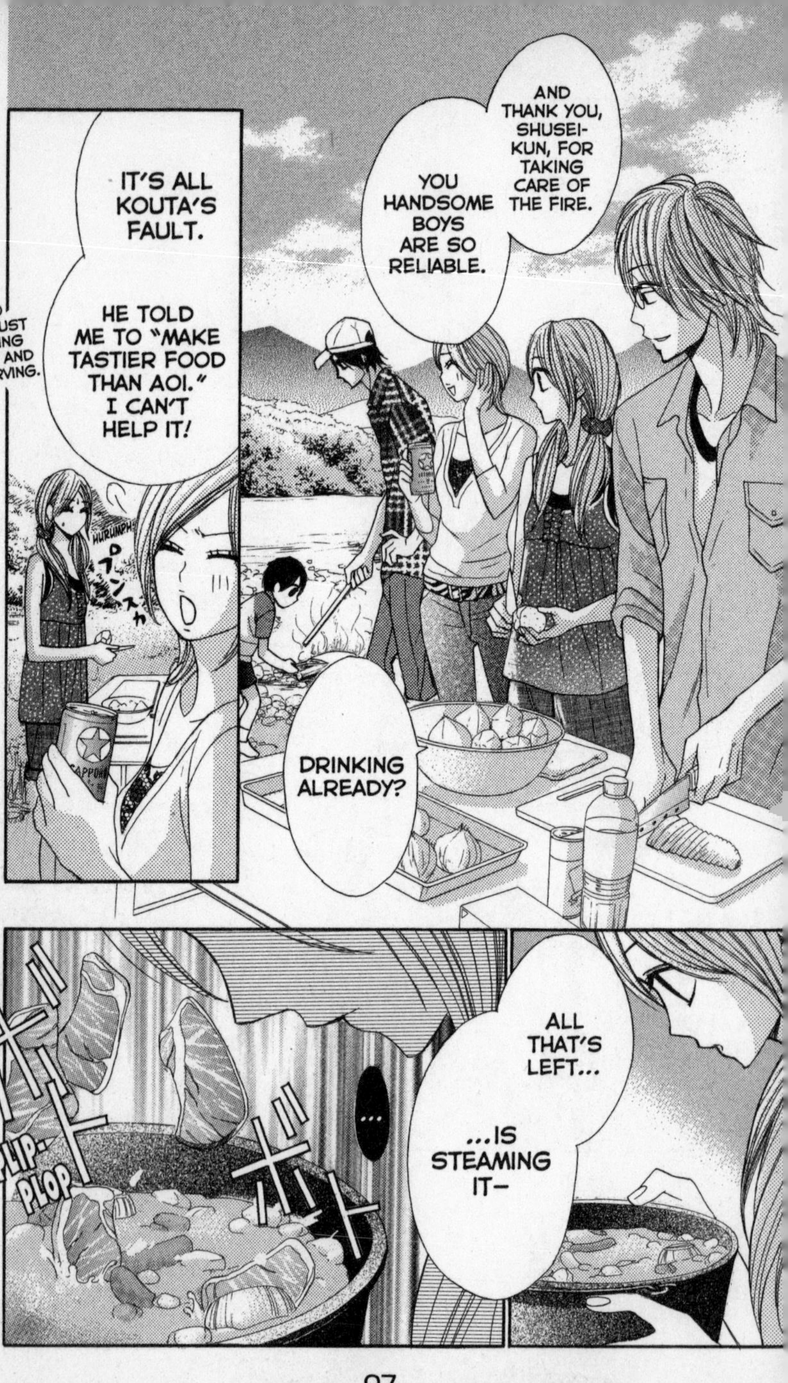
AND THANK YOU, SHUSEI-KUN, FOR TAKING CARE OF THE FIRE.
YOU HANDSOME BOYS ARE SO RELIABLE.
DRINKING ALREADY?
IT'S ALL KOUTA'S FAULT.
HE TOLD ME TO "MAKE TASTIER FOOD THAN AOI." I CAN'T HELP IT!
HURUMPH
SO I'M JUST SITTING BACK AND OBSERVING.
ALL THAT'S LEFT...
...IS STEAMING IT—
...
PLIP-PLOP

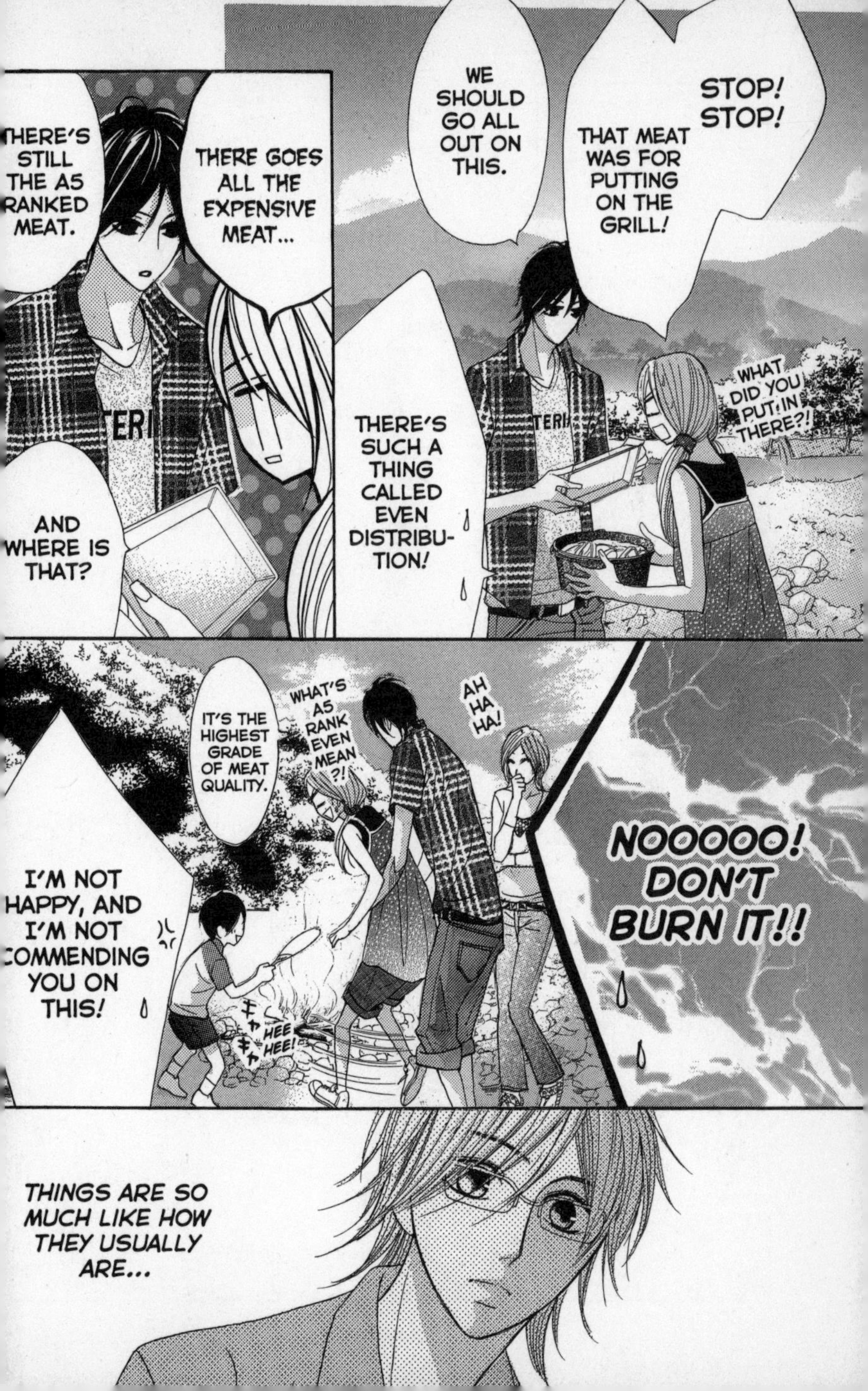
STOP! STOP! THAT MEAT WAS FOR PUTTING ON THE GRILL!
WE SHOULD GO ALL OUT ON THIS.
WHAT DID YOU PUT IN THERE?!
THERE'S SUCH A THING CALLED EVEN DISTRIBUTION!
THERE GOES ALL THE EXPENSIVE MEAT...
THERE'S STILL THE A5 RANKED MEAT.
AND WHERE IS THAT?
NOOOOO! DON'T BURN IT!!
AH HA HA!
WHAT'S A5 RANK EVEN MEAN?!
IT'S THE HIGHEST GRADE OF MEAT QUALITY.
I'M NOT HAPPY, AND I'M NOT COMMENDING YOU ON THIS!
HEE HEE!
THINGS ARE SO MUCH LIKE HOW THEY USUALLY ARE...

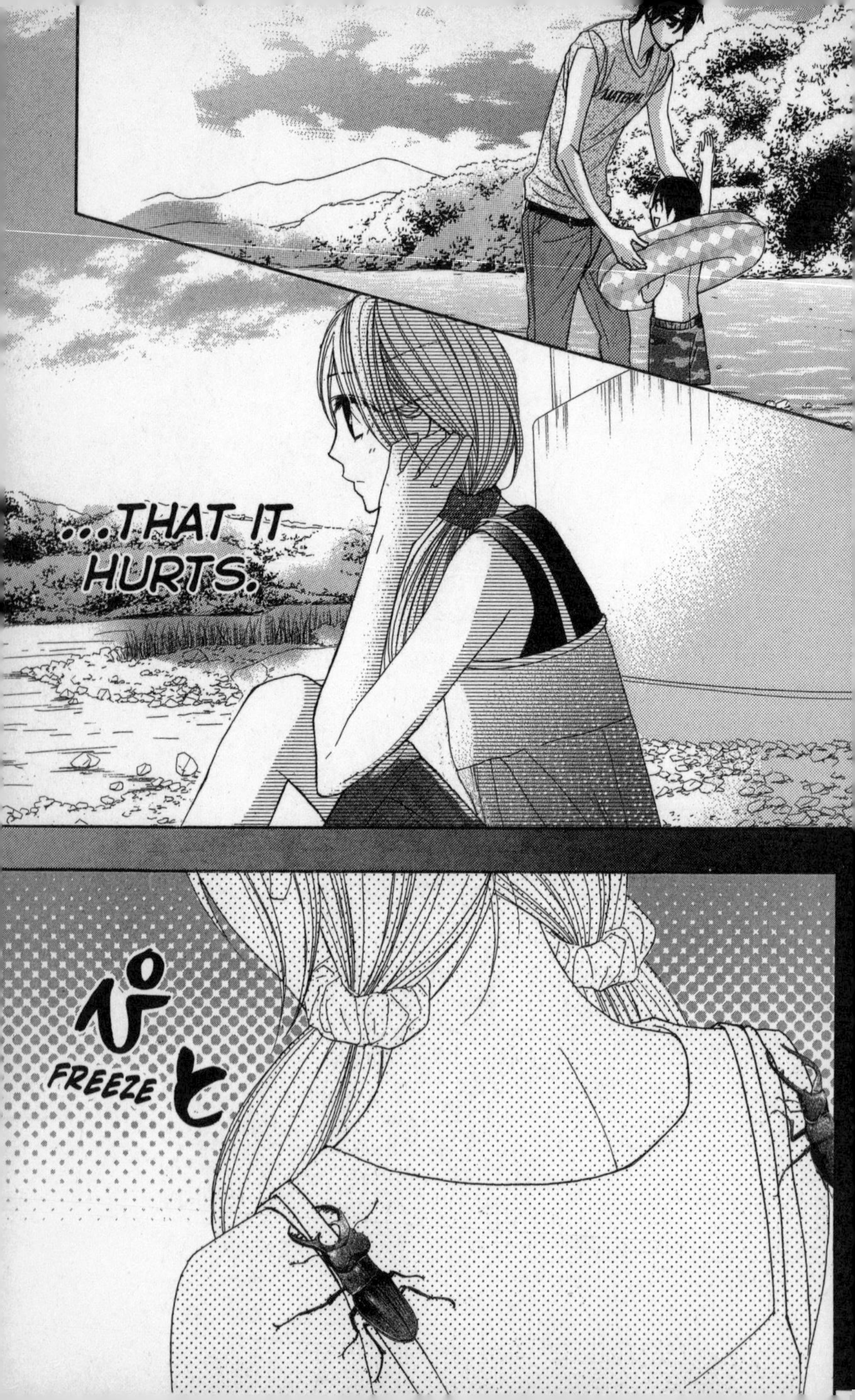
...THAT IT HURTS.
ぴと
FREEZE

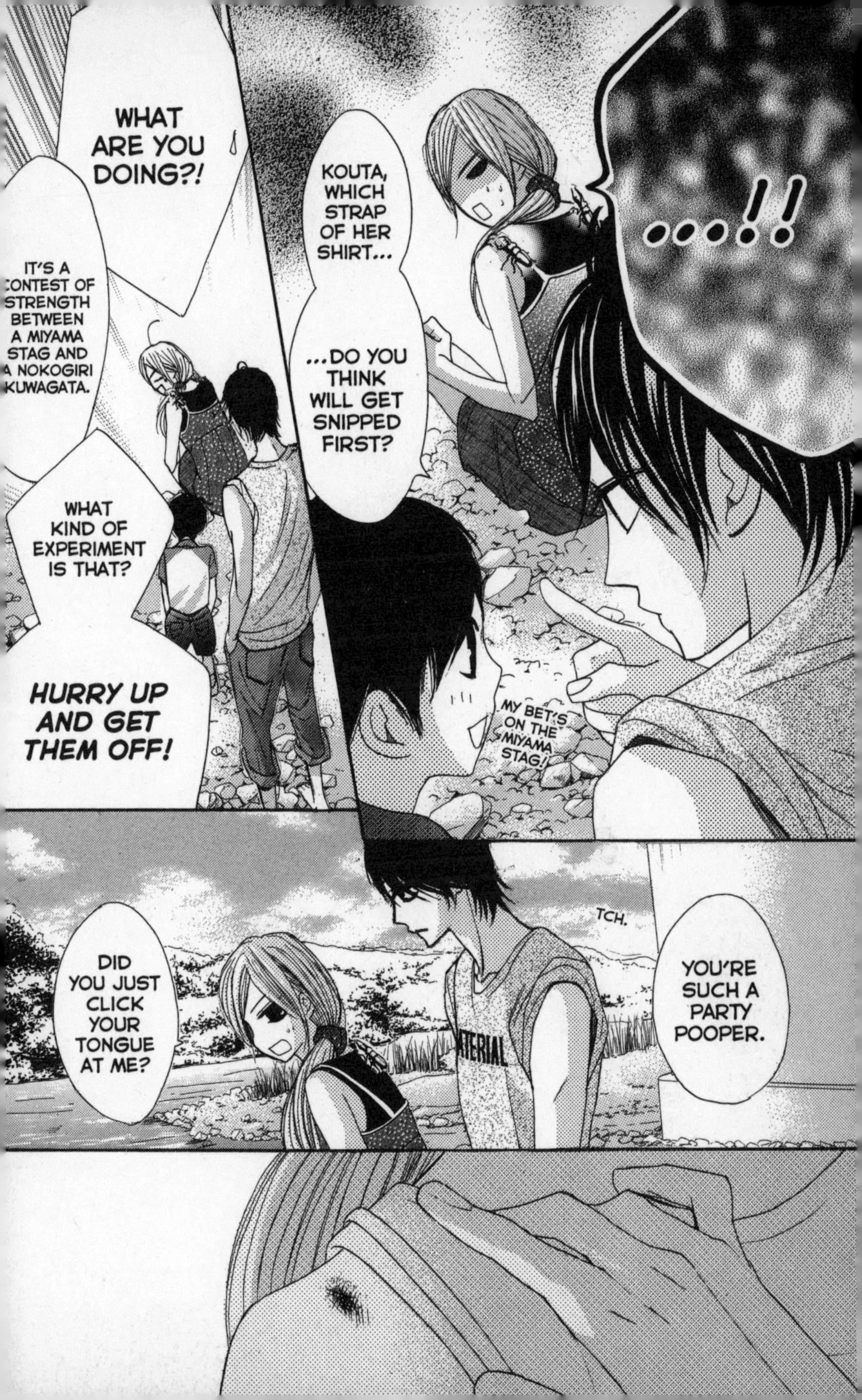
...!!
KOUTA, WHICH STRAP OF HER SHIRT...
...DO YOU THINK WILL GET SNIPPED FIRST?
MY BET'S ON THE MIYAMA STAG!
WHAT ARE YOU DOING?!
IT'S A CONTEST OF STRENGTH BETWEEN A MIYAMA STAG AND A NOKOGIRI KUWAGATA.
WHAT KIND OF EXPERIMENT IS THAT?
HURRY UP AND GET THEM OFF!
YOU'RE SUCH A PARTY POOPER.
TCH.
DID YOU JUST CLICK YOUR TONGUE AT ME?

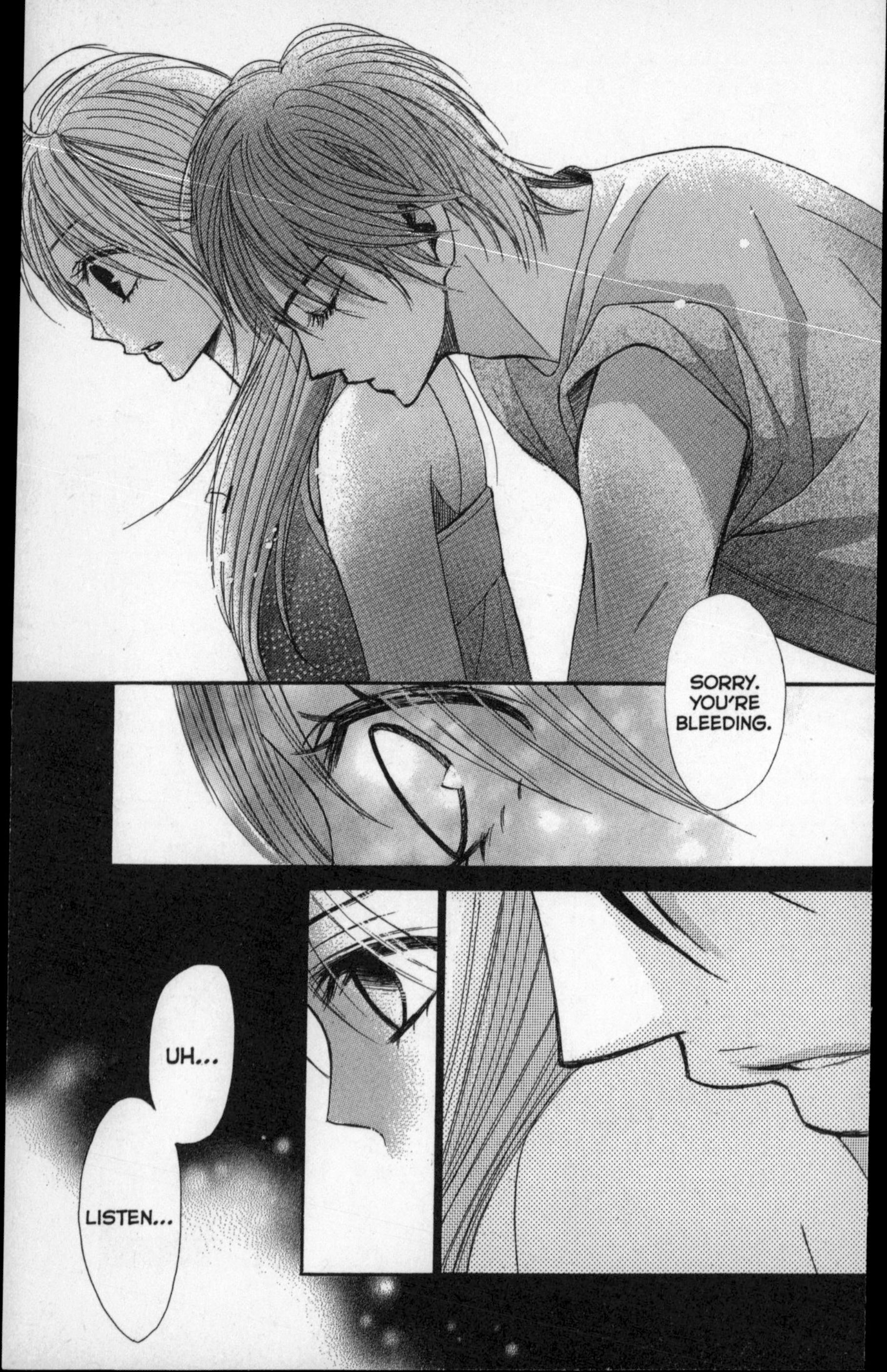
SORRY. YOU'RE BLEEDING.
UH...
LISTEN...

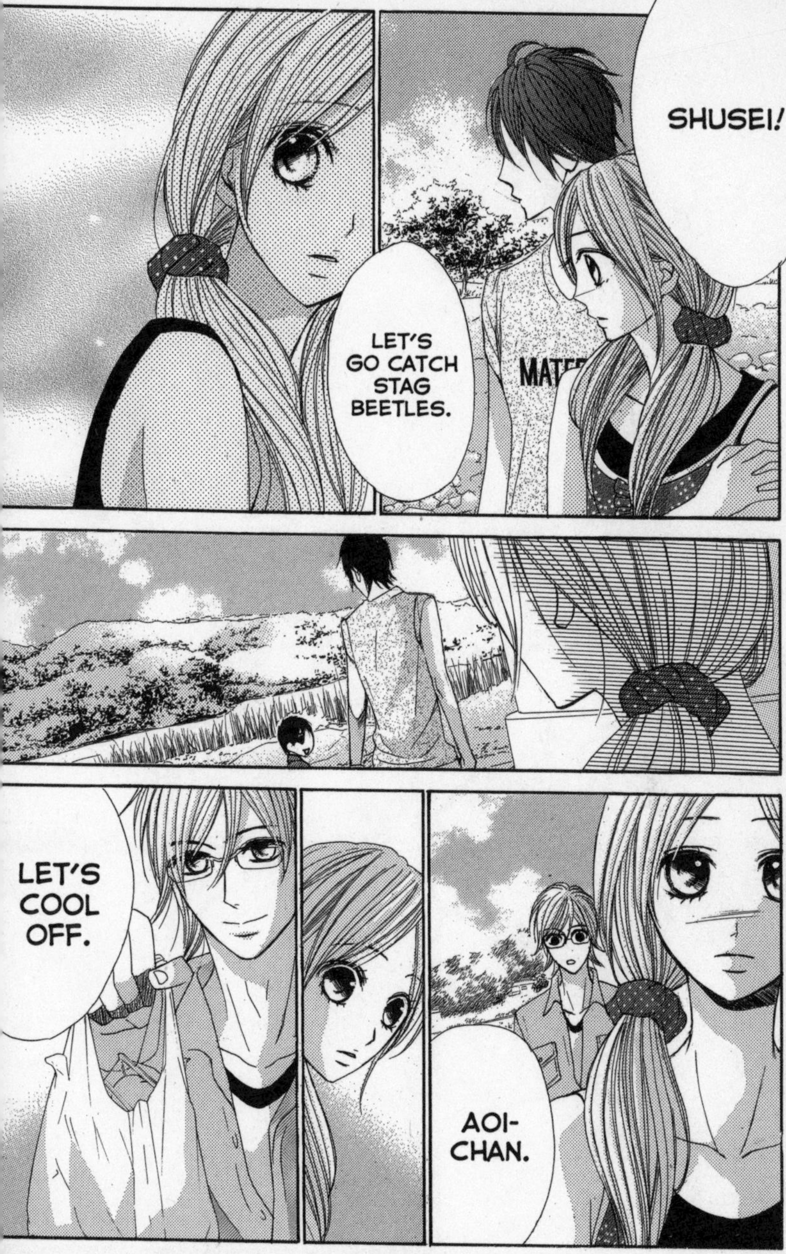
SHUSEI!
LET'S GO CATCH STAG BEETLES.
AOI-CHAN.
LET'S COOL OFF.

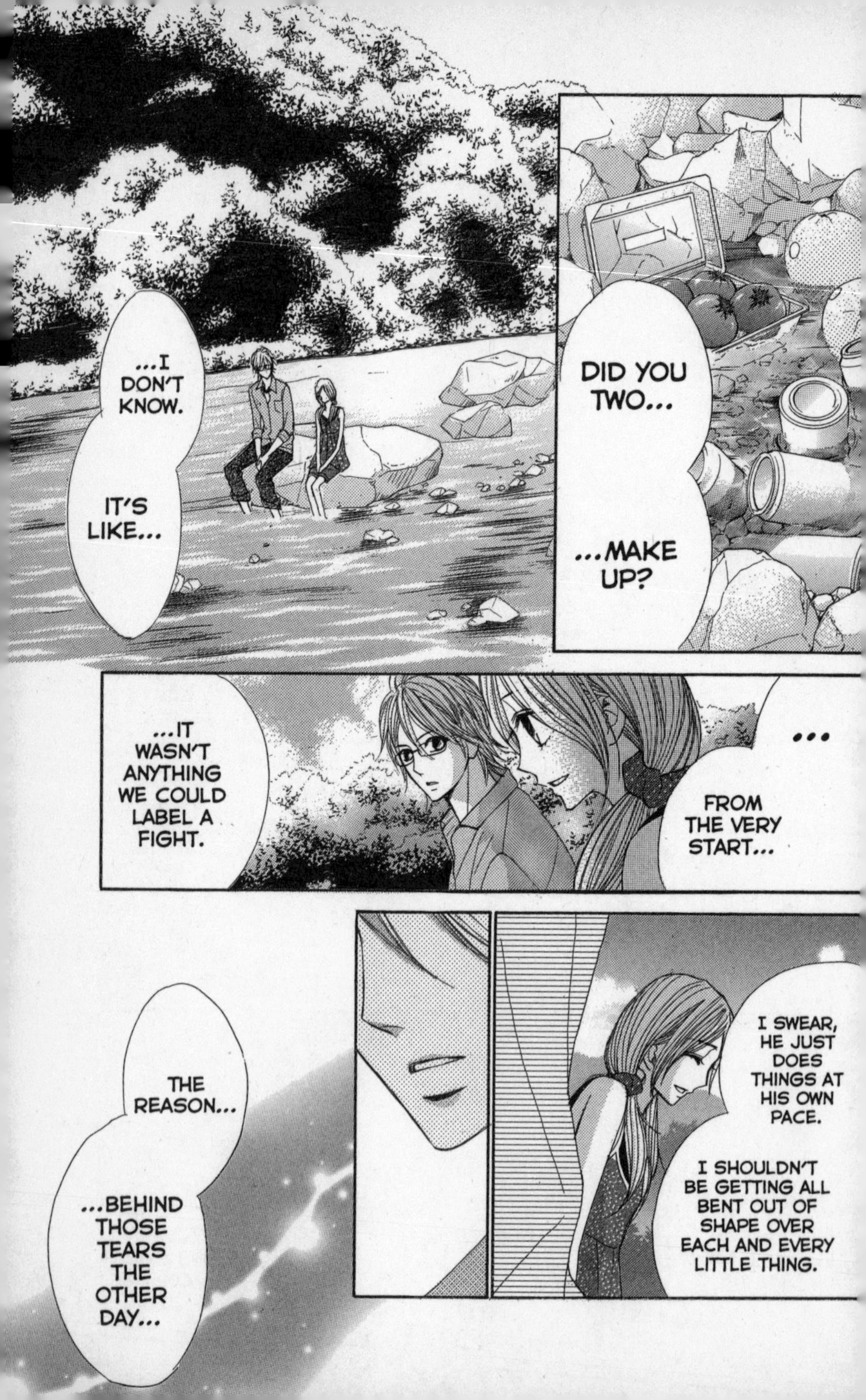
DID YOU TWO...
...MAKE UP?
...I DON'T KNOW.
IT'S LIKE...
...
FROM THE VERY START...
...IT WASN'T ANYTHING WE COULD LABEL A FIGHT.
I SWEAR, HE JUST DOES THINGS AT HIS OWN PACE.
I SHOULDN'T BE GETTING ALL BENT OUT OF SHAPE OVER EACH AND EVERY LITTLE THING.
THE REASON...
...BEHIND THOSE TEARS THE OTHER DAY...

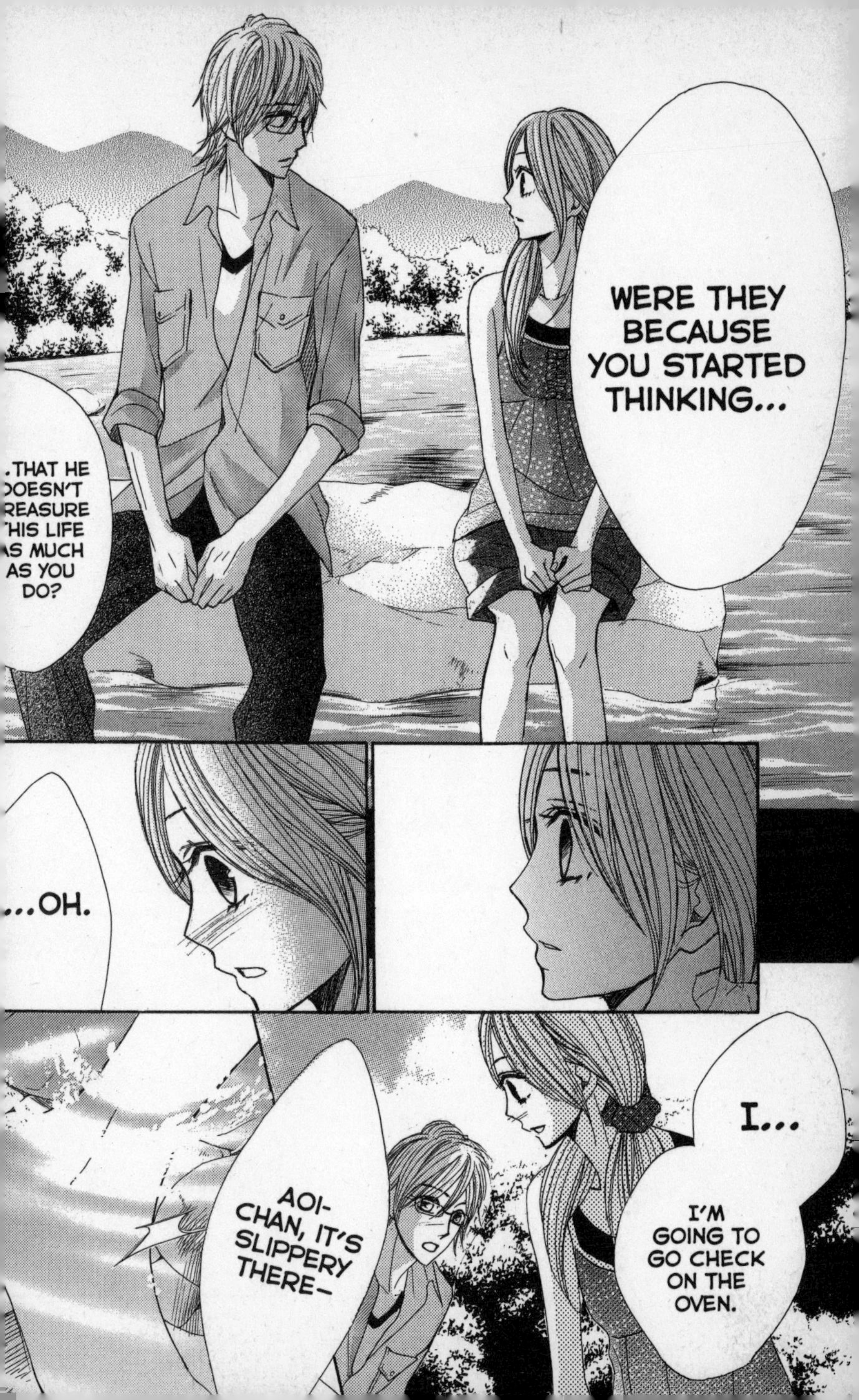
WERE THEY BECAUSE YOU STARTED THINKING...
.THAT HE DOESN'T TREASURE THIS LIFE AS MUCH AS YOU DO?
...OH.
I...
I'M GOING TO GO CHECK ON THE OVEN.
AOI-CHAN, IT'S SLIPPERY THERE–

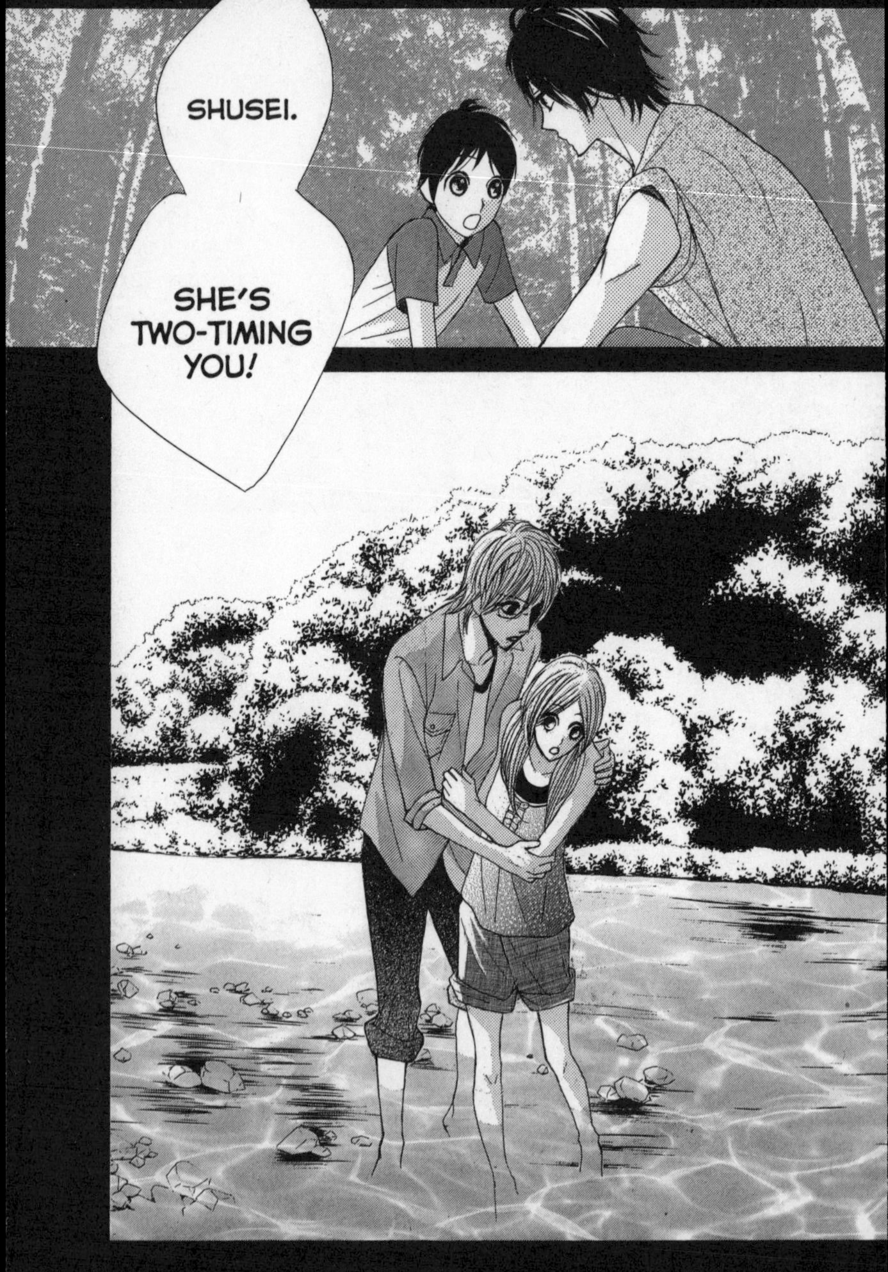
SHUSEI.
SHE'S TWO-TIMING YOU!

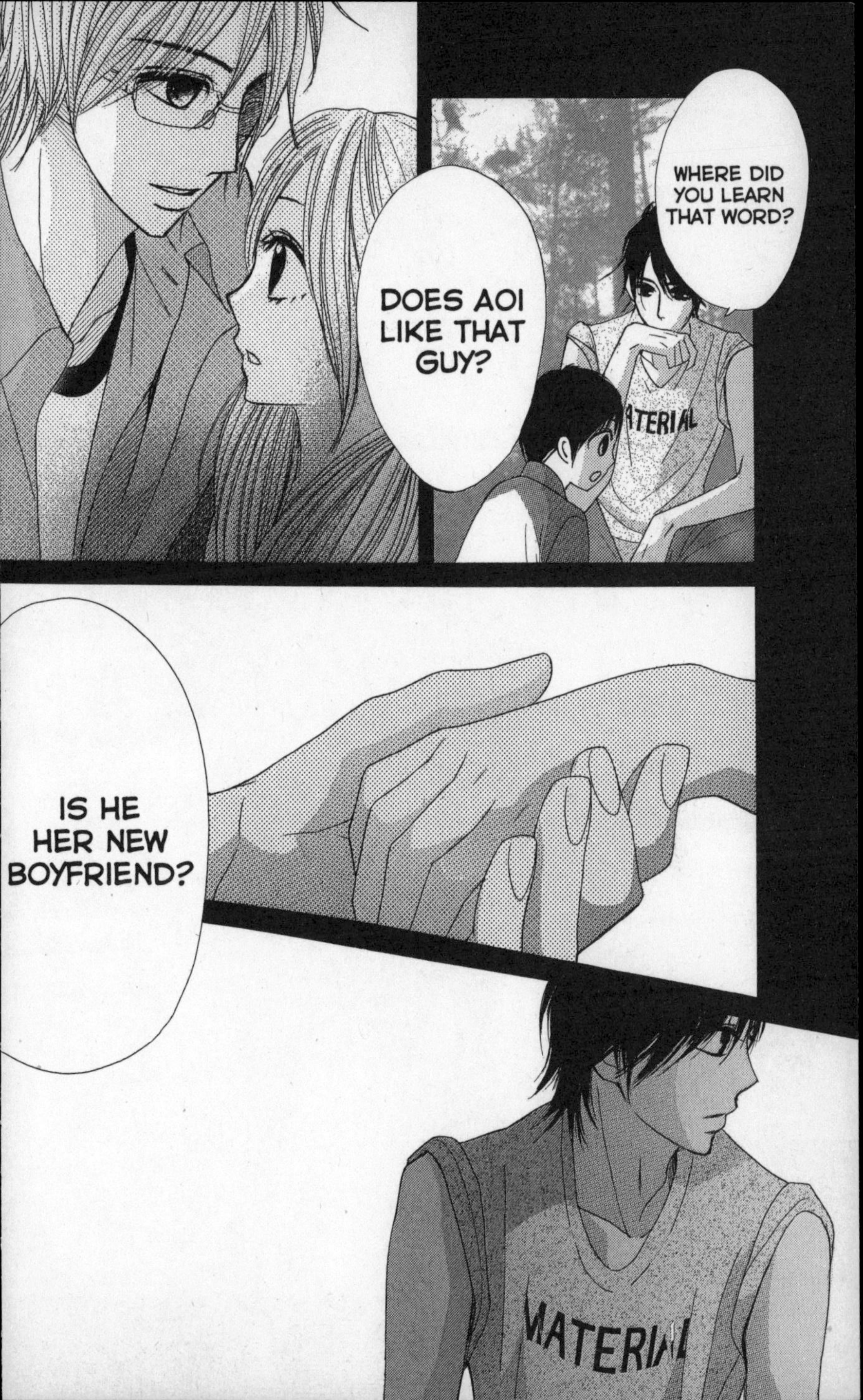
WHERE DID YOU LEARN THAT WORD?
DOES AOI LIKE THAT GUY?
IS HE HER NEW BOYFRIEND?

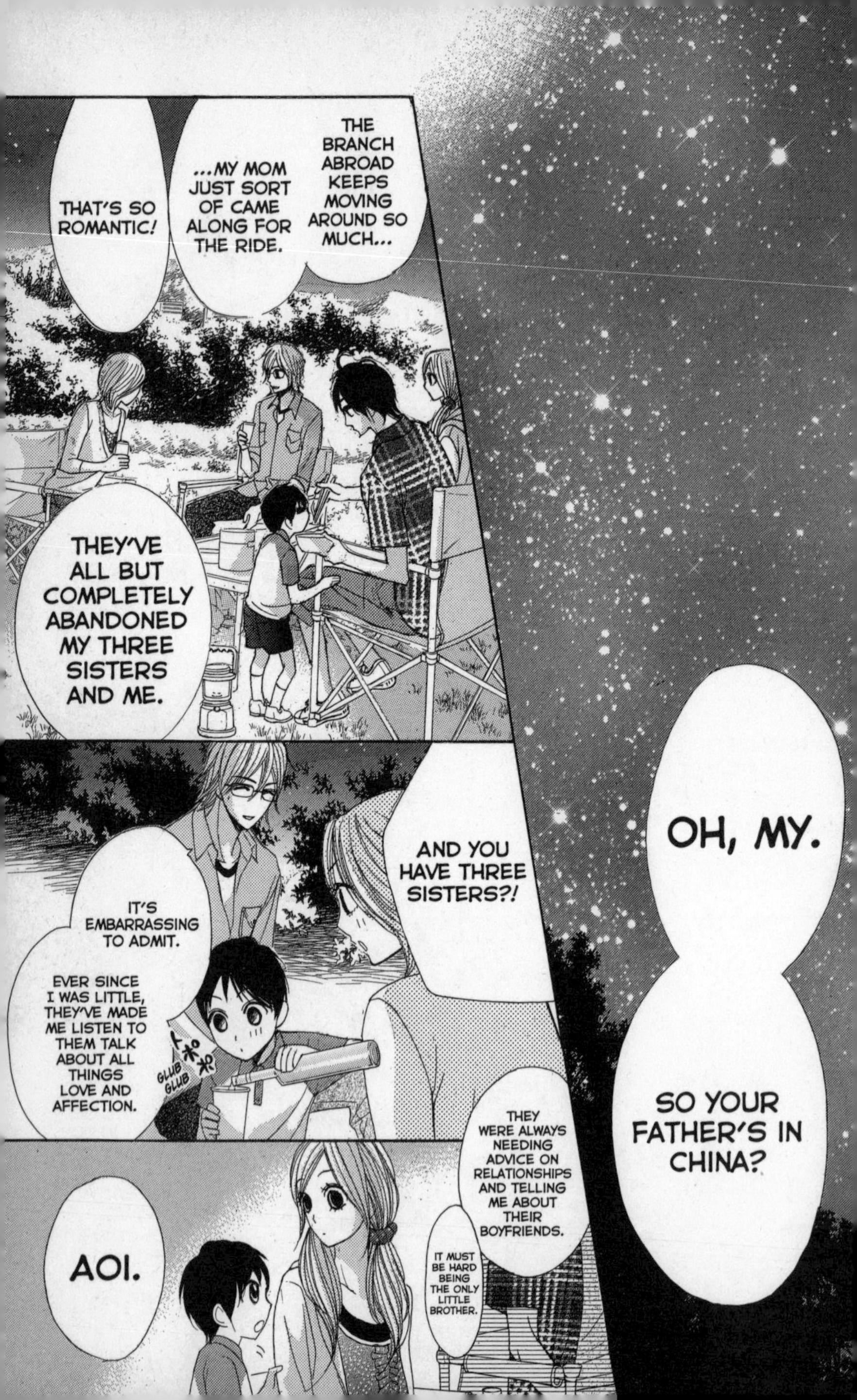
OH, MY.
SO YOUR FATHER'S IN CHINA?
THE BRANCH ABROAD KEEPS MOVING AROUND SO MUCH...
...MY MOM JUST SORT OF CAME ALONG FOR THE RIDE.
THAT'S SO ROMANTIC!
THEY'VE ALL BUT COMPLETELY ABANDONED MY THREE SISTERS AND ME.
AND YOU HAVE THREE SISTERS?!
IT'S EMBARRASSING TO ADMIT.
EVER SINCE I WAS LITTLE, THEY'VE MADE ME LISTEN TO THEM TALK ABOUT ALL THINGS LOVE AND AFFECTION.
トポポ
GLUB GLUB
THEY WERE ALWAYS NEEDING ADVICE ON RELATIONSHIPS AND TELLING ME ABOUT THEIR BOYFRIENDS.
IT MUST BE HARD BEING THE ONLY LITTLE BROTHER.
AOI.

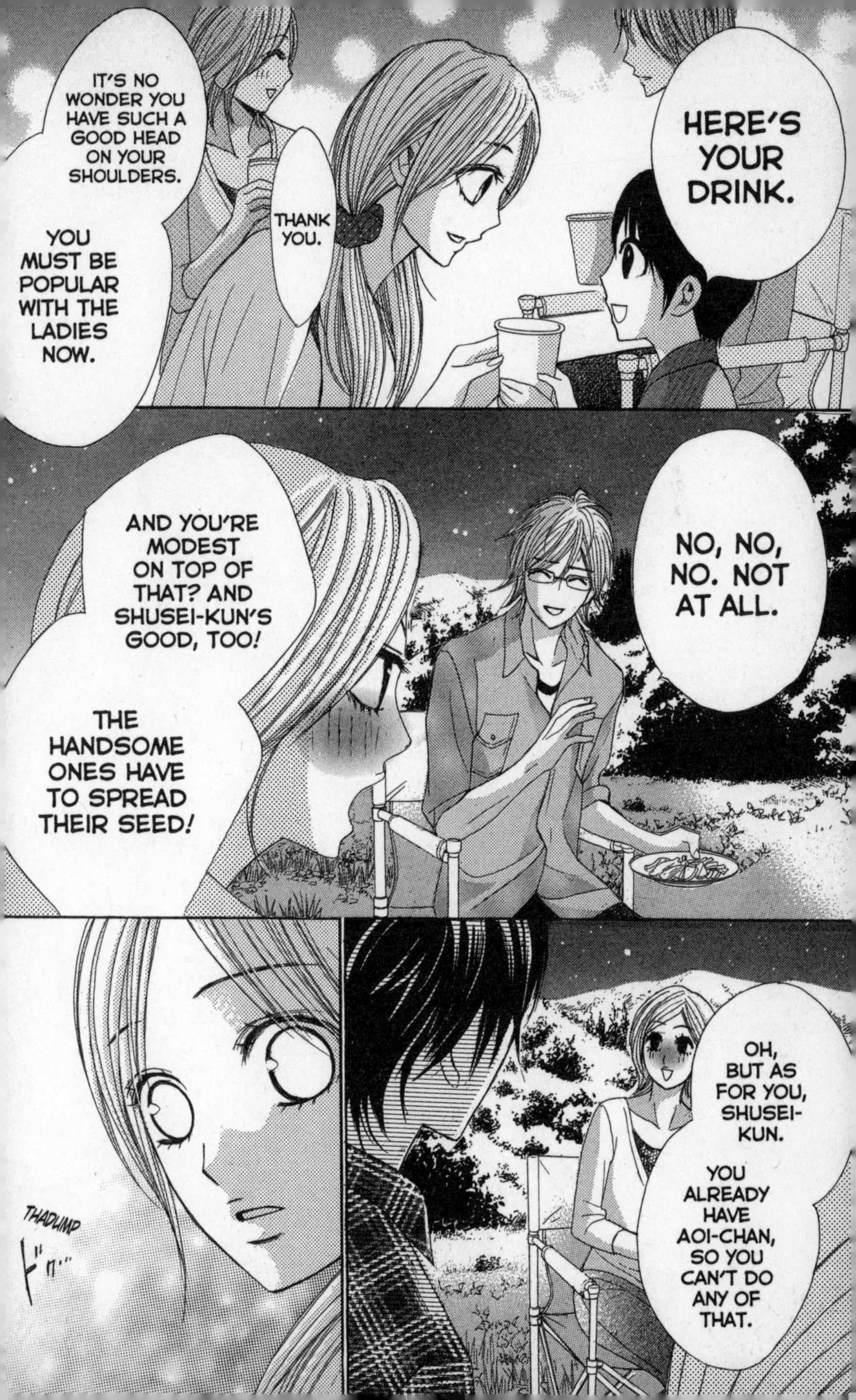
HERE'S YOUR DRINK.
THANK YOU.
IT'S NO WONDER YOU HAVE SUCH A GOOD HEAD ON YOUR SHOULDERS.
YOU MUST BE POPULAR WITH THE LADIES NOW.
NO, NO, NO. NOT AT ALL.
AND YOU'RE MODEST ON TOP OF THAT? AND SHUSEI-KUN'S GOOD, TOO!
THE HANDSOME ONES HAVE TO SPREAD THEIR SEED!
OH, BUT AS FOR YOU, SHUSEI-KUN.
YOU ALREADY HAVE AOI-CHAN, SO YOU CAN'T DO ANY OF THAT.
THADUMP

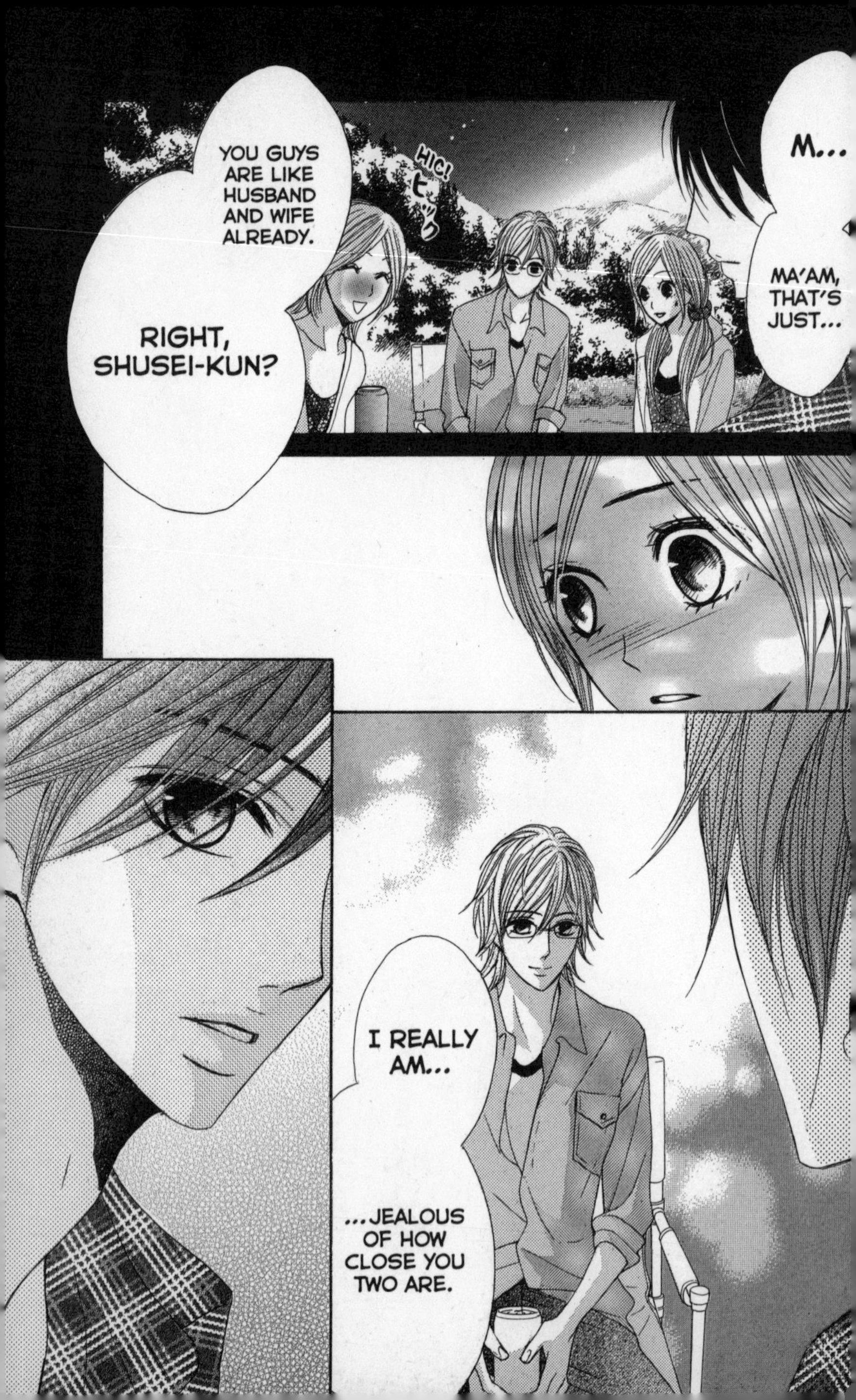
M...
MA'AM, THAT'S JUST...
YOU GUYS ARE LIKE HUSBAND AND WIFE ALREADY.
HIC!
RIGHT, SHUSEI-KUN?
I REALLY AM...
...JEALOUS OF HOW CLOSE YOU TWO ARE.

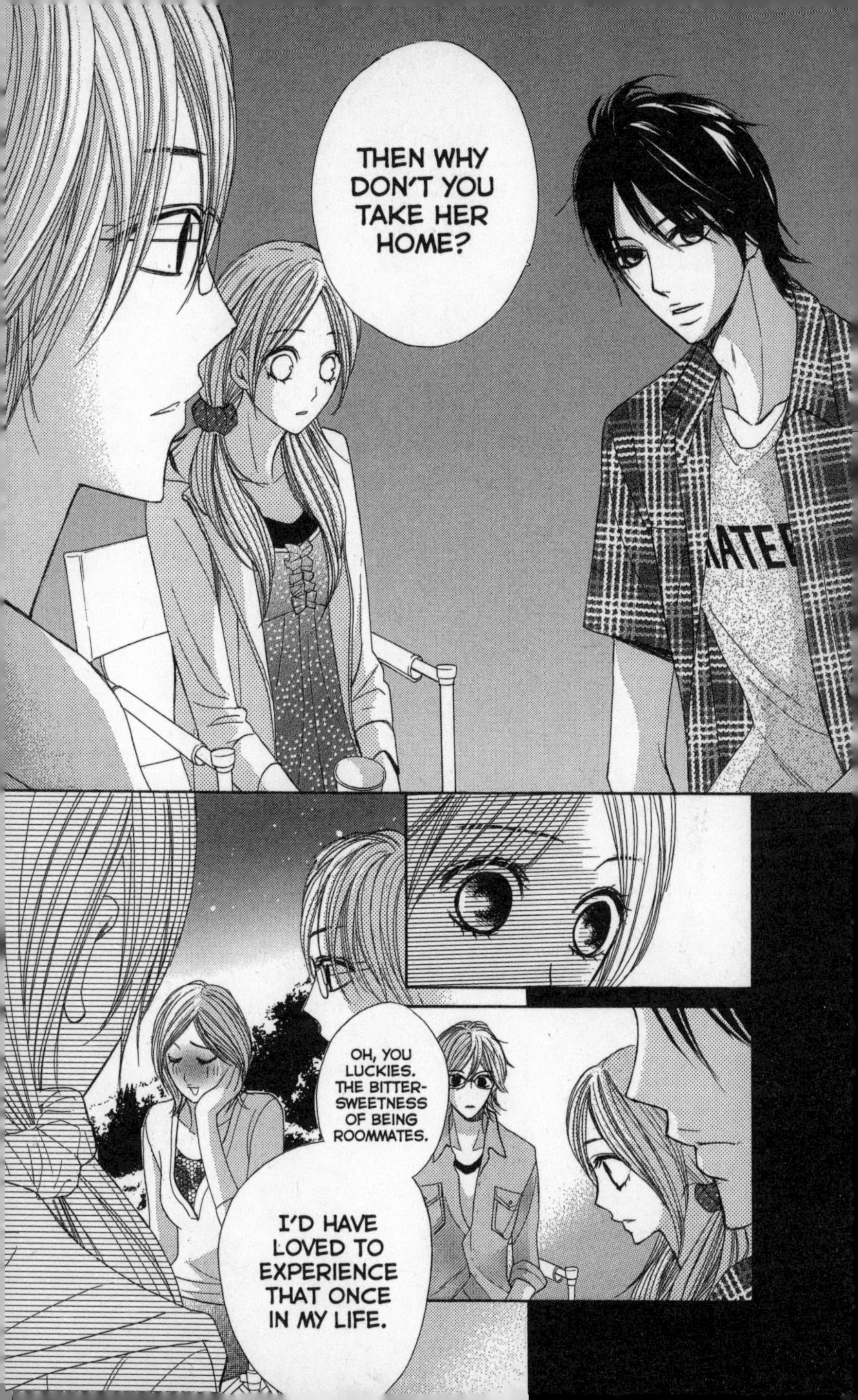
THEN WHY DON'T YOU TAKE HER HOME?
OH, YOU LUCKIES. THE BITTER-SWEETNESS OF BEING ROOMMATES.
I'D HAVE LOVED TO EXPERIENCE THAT ONCE IN MY LIFE.

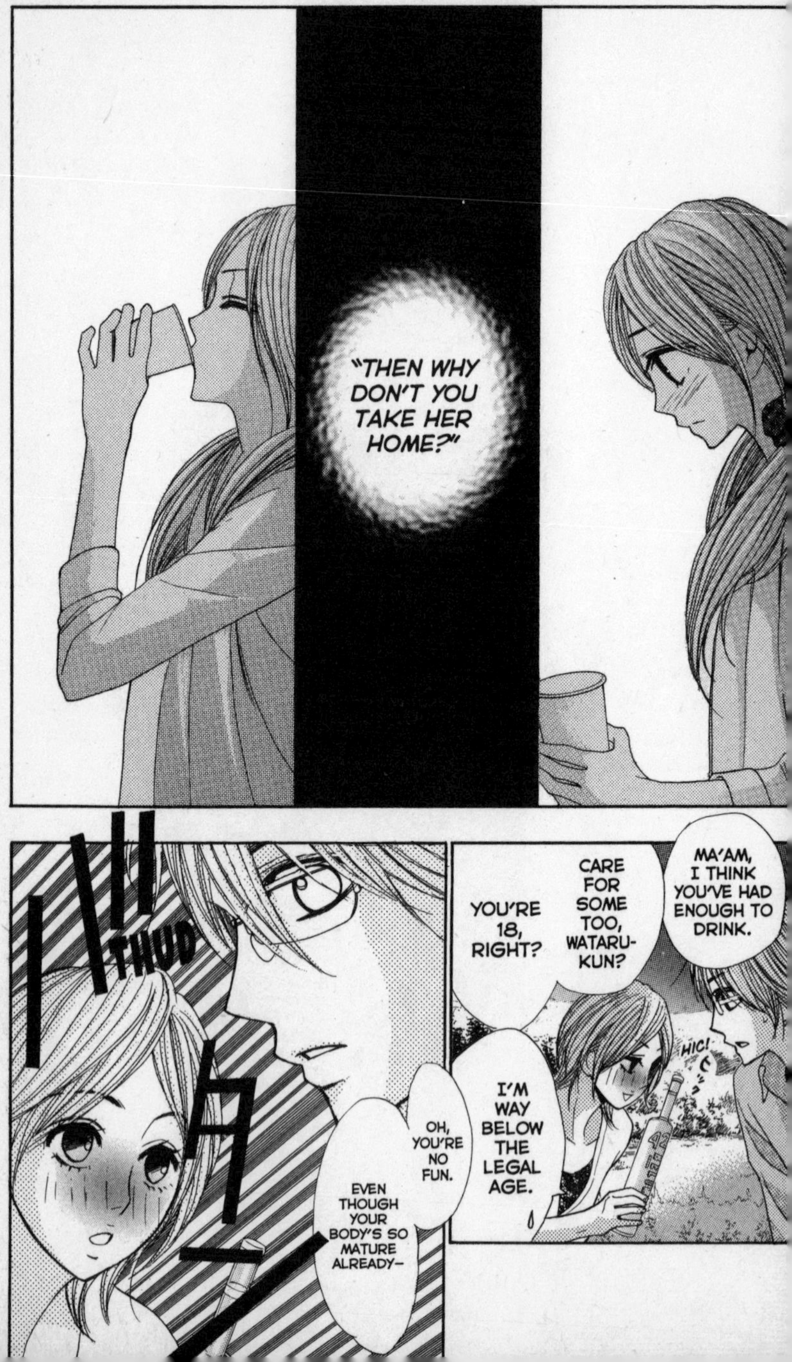
"THEN WHY DON'T YOU TAKE HER HOME?"
MA'AM, I THINK YOU'VE HAD ENOUGH TO DRINK.
CARE FOR SOME TOO, WATARU-KUN?
YOU'RE 18, RIGHT?
HIC!
I'M WAY BELOW THE LEGAL AGE.
THUD
OH, YOU'RE NO FUN.
EVEN THOUGH YOUR BODY'S SO MATURE ALREADY—

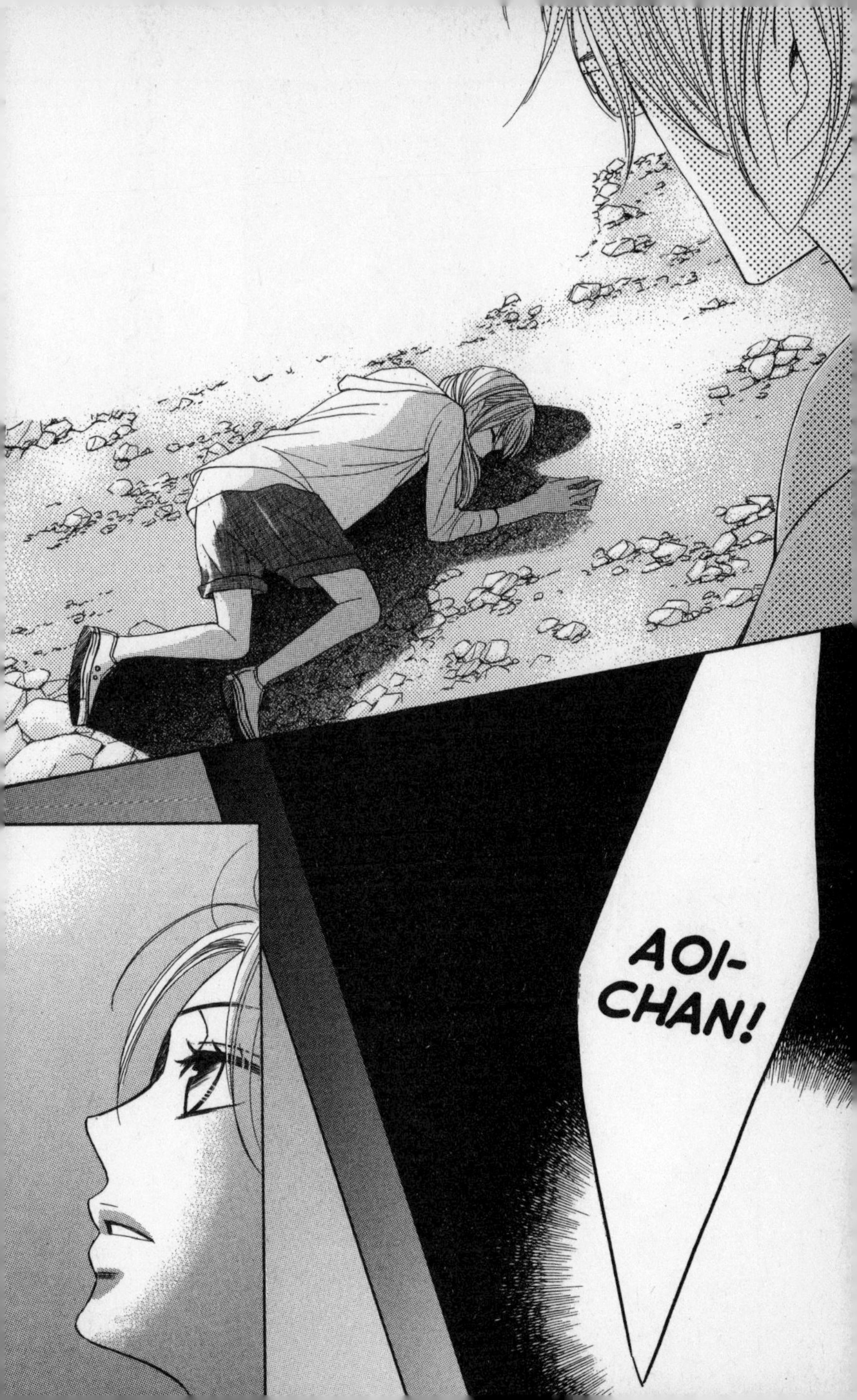
AOI-CHAN!

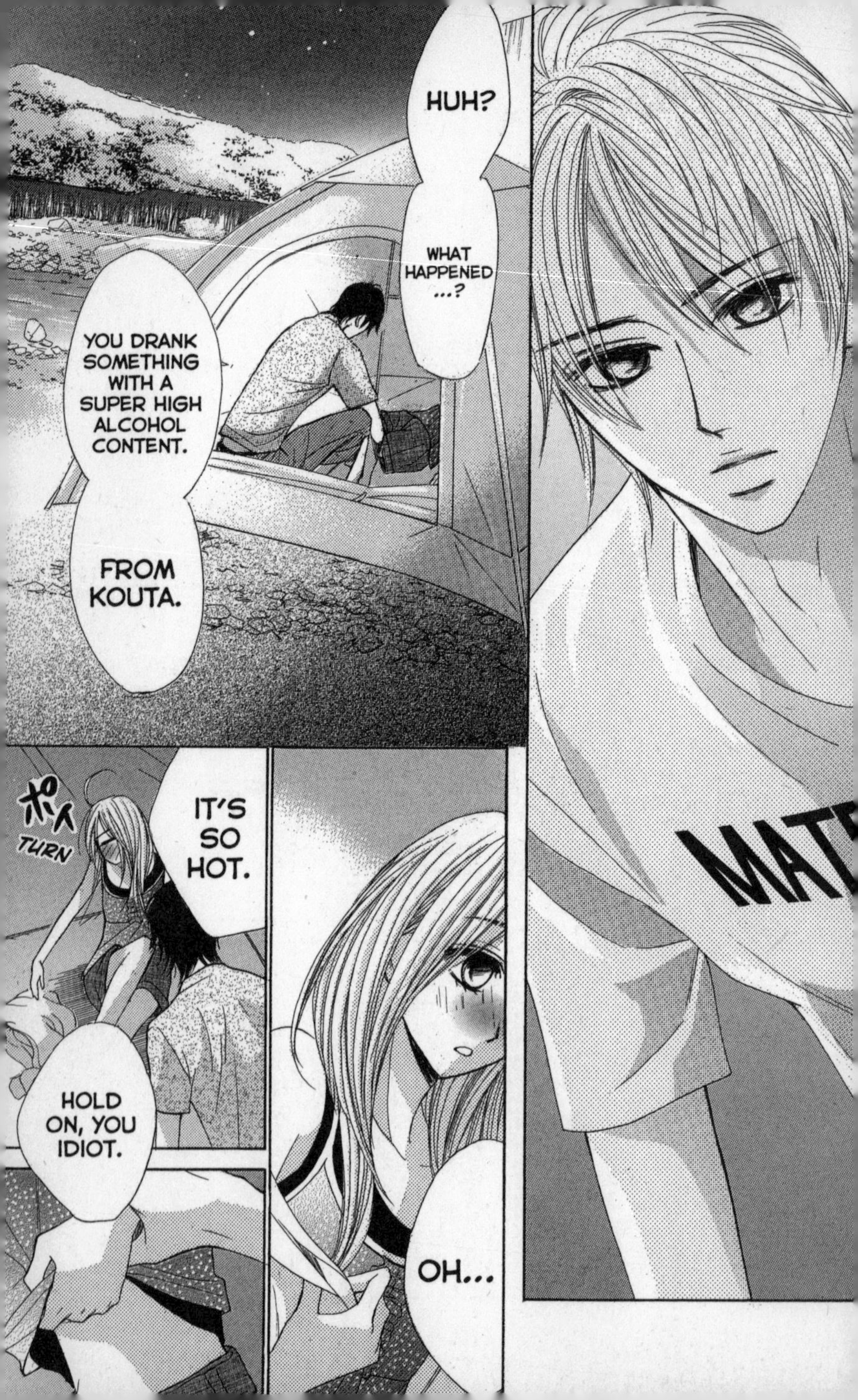
MATE
HUH?
WHAT HAPPENED ...?
YOU DRANK SOMETHING WITH A SUPER HIGH ALCOHOL CONTENT.
FROM KOUTA.
OH...
IT'S SO HOT.
ポイ
TURN
HOLD ON, YOU IDIOT.

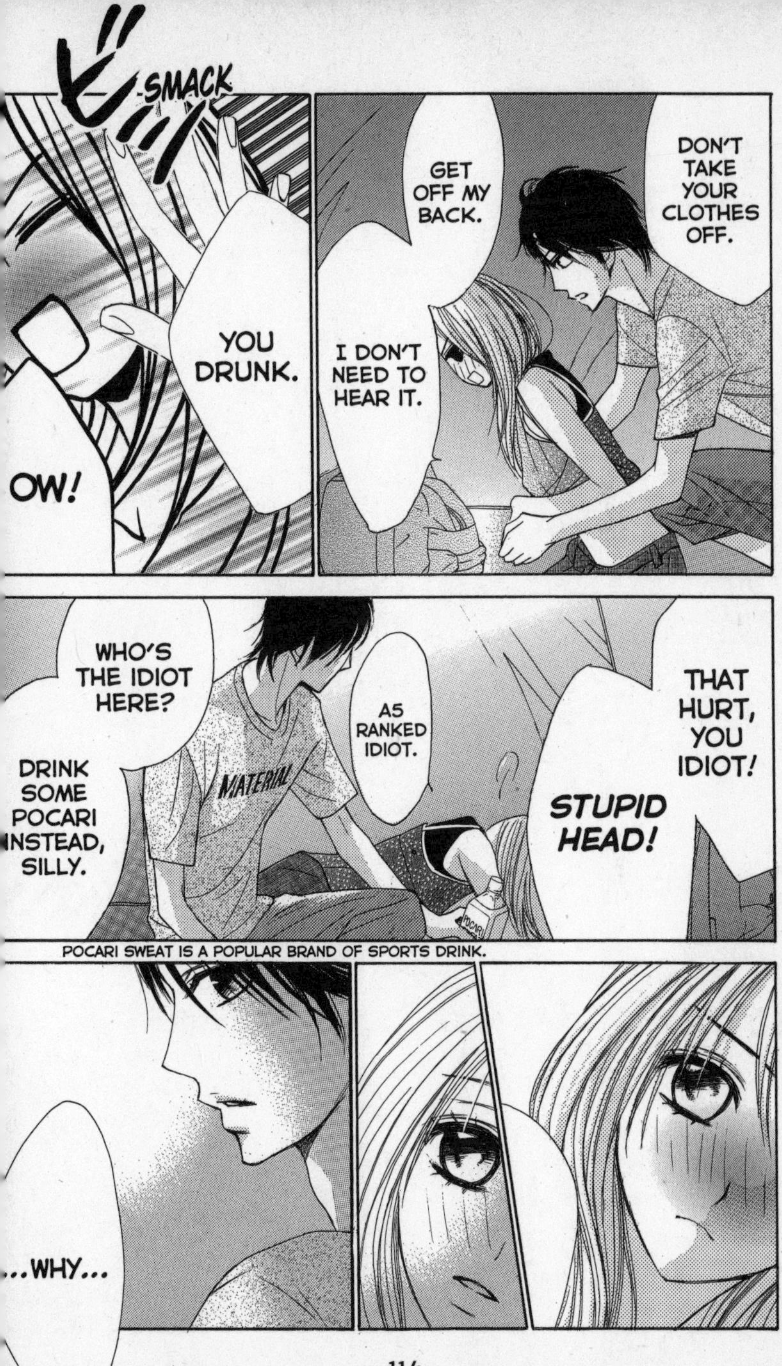
DON'T TAKE YOUR CLOTHES OFF.
GET OFF MY BACK.
I DON'T NEED TO HEAR IT.
SMACK
YOU DRUNK.
OW!
THAT HURT, YOU IDIOT!
STUPID HEAD!
AS RANKED IDIOT.
WHO'S THE IDIOT HERE?
DRINK SOME POCARI INSTEAD, SILLY.
...WHY...
POCARI SWEAT IS A POPULAR BRAND OF SPORTS DRINK.

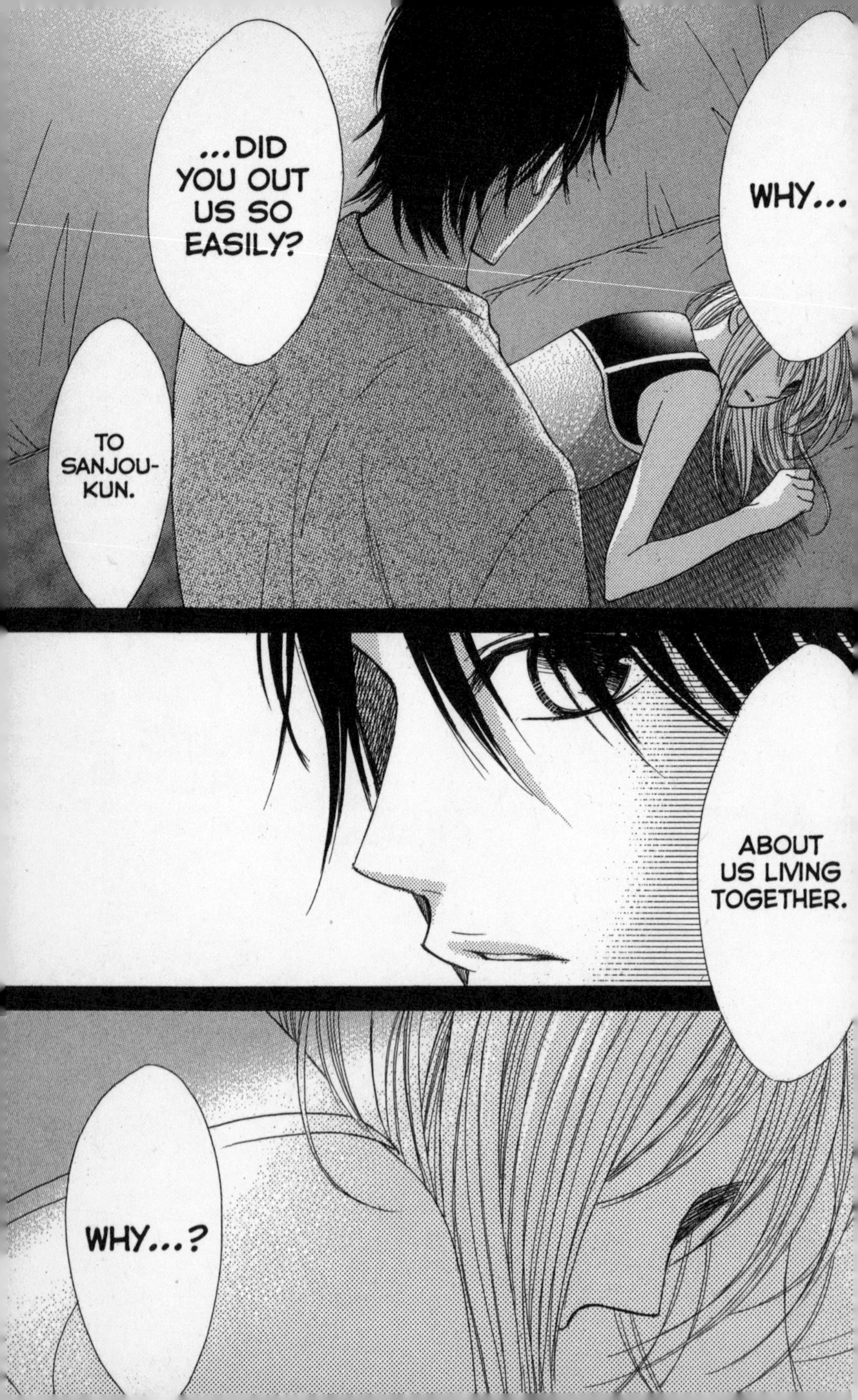
WHY...
...DID YOU OUT US SO EASILY?
TO SANJOU-KUN.
ABOUT US LIVING TOGETHER.
WHY...?

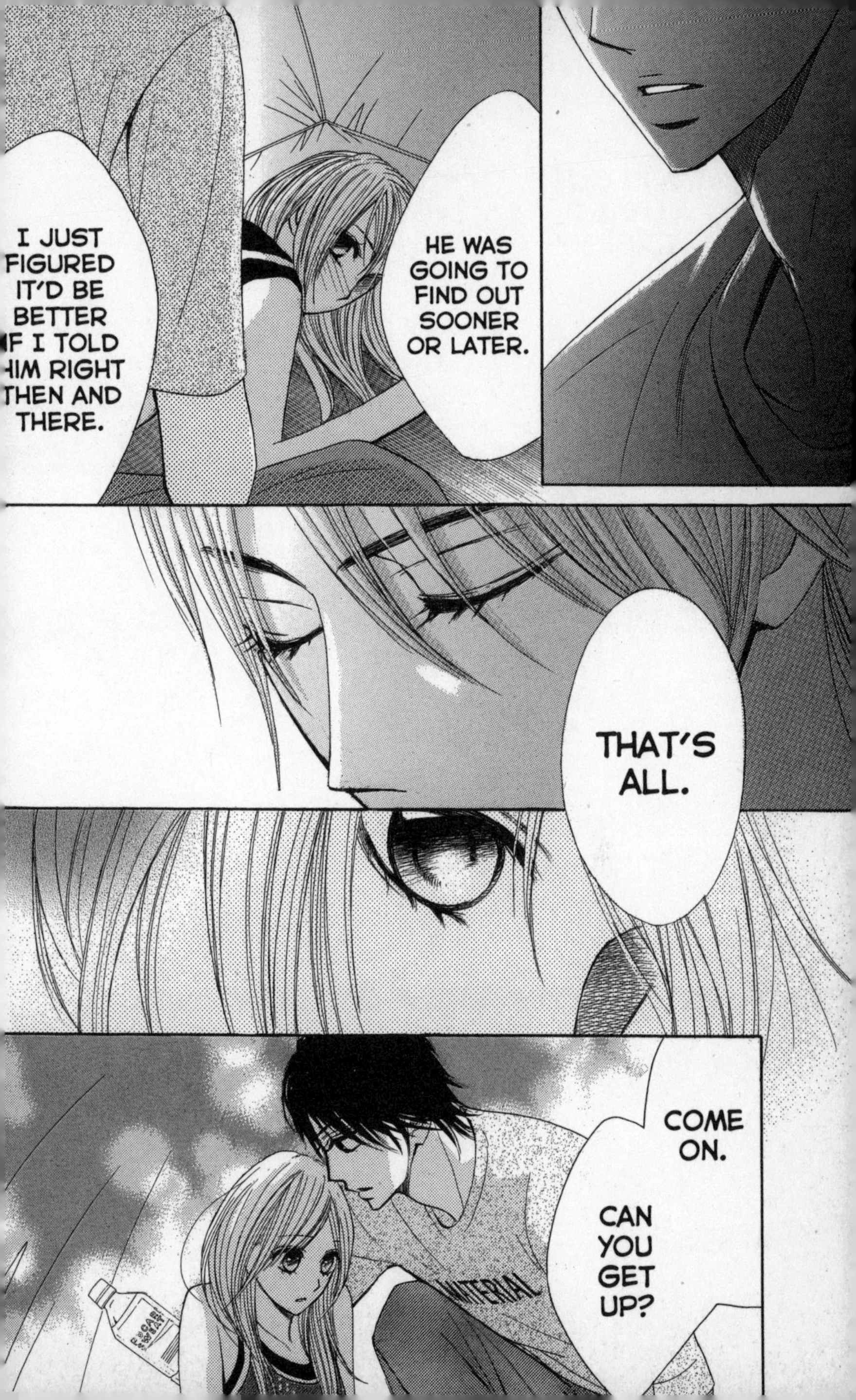
HE WAS GOING TO FIND OUT SOONER OR LATER.
I JUST FIGURED IT'D BE BETTER IF I TOLD HIM RIGHT THEN AND THERE.
THAT'S ALL.
COME ON.
CAN YOU GET UP?

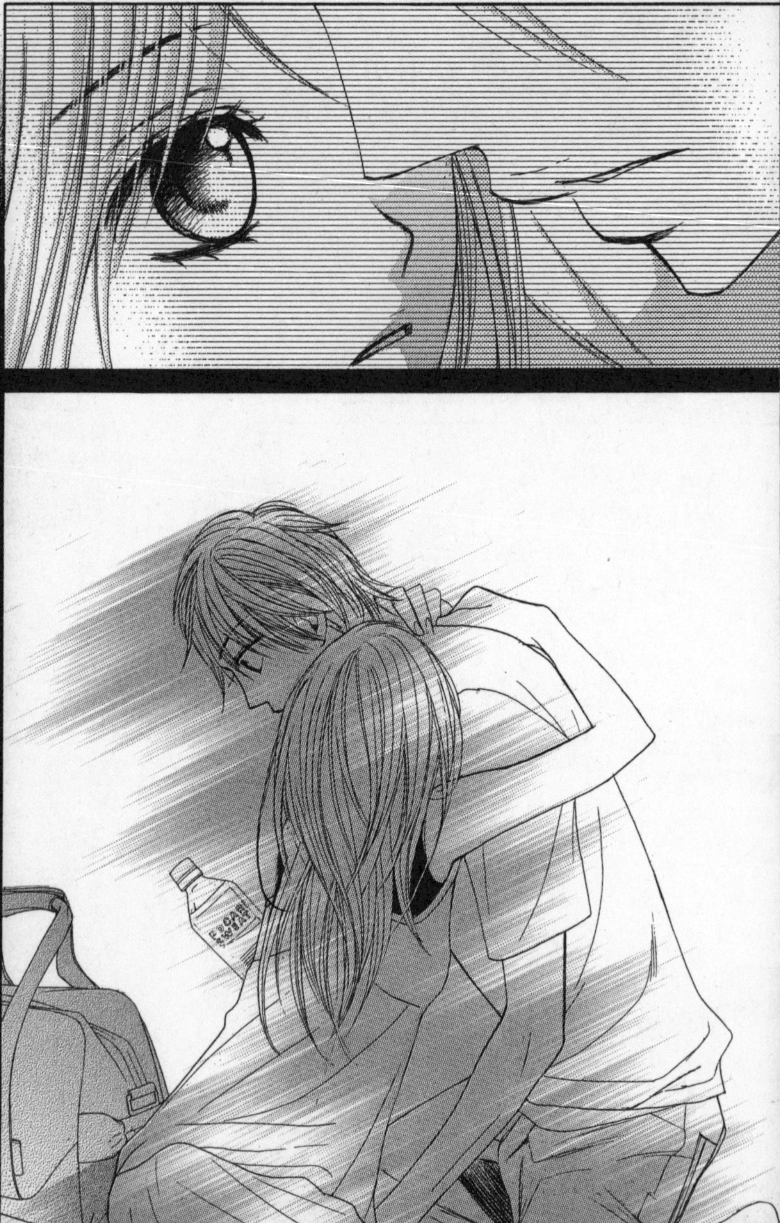

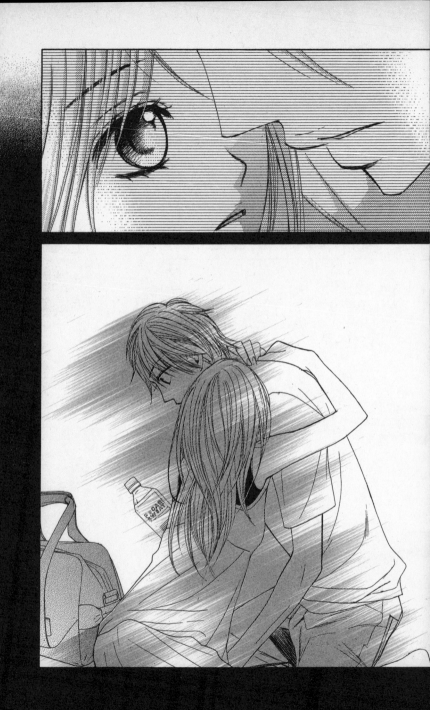

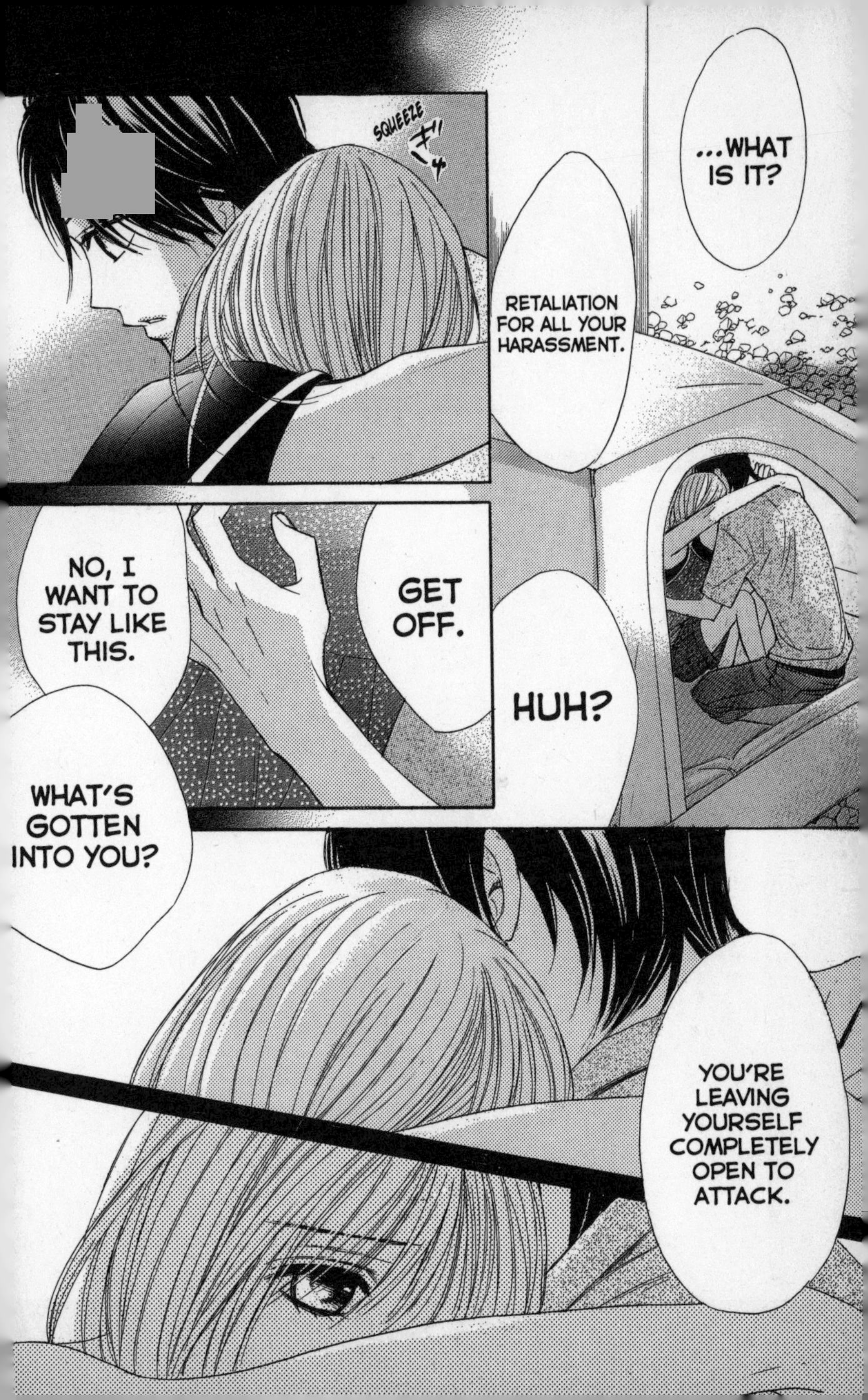
...WHAT IS IT?
RETALIATION FOR ALL YOUR HARASSMENT.
HUH?
SQUEEZE
GET OFF.
NO, I WANT TO STAY LIKE THIS.
WHAT'S GOTTEN INTO YOU?
YOU'RE LEAVING YOURSELF COMPLETELY OPEN TO ATTACK.

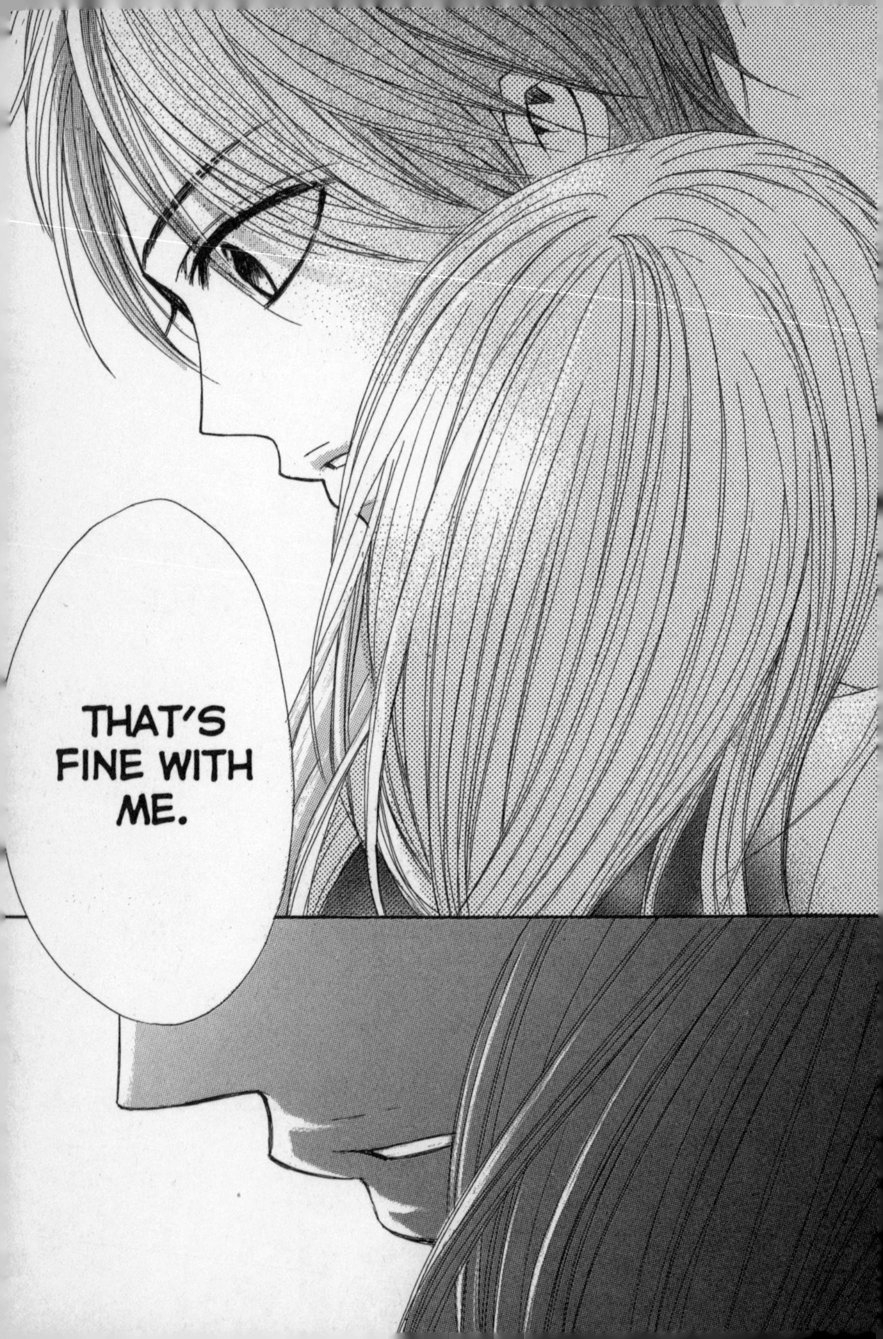
THAT'S FINE WITH ME.

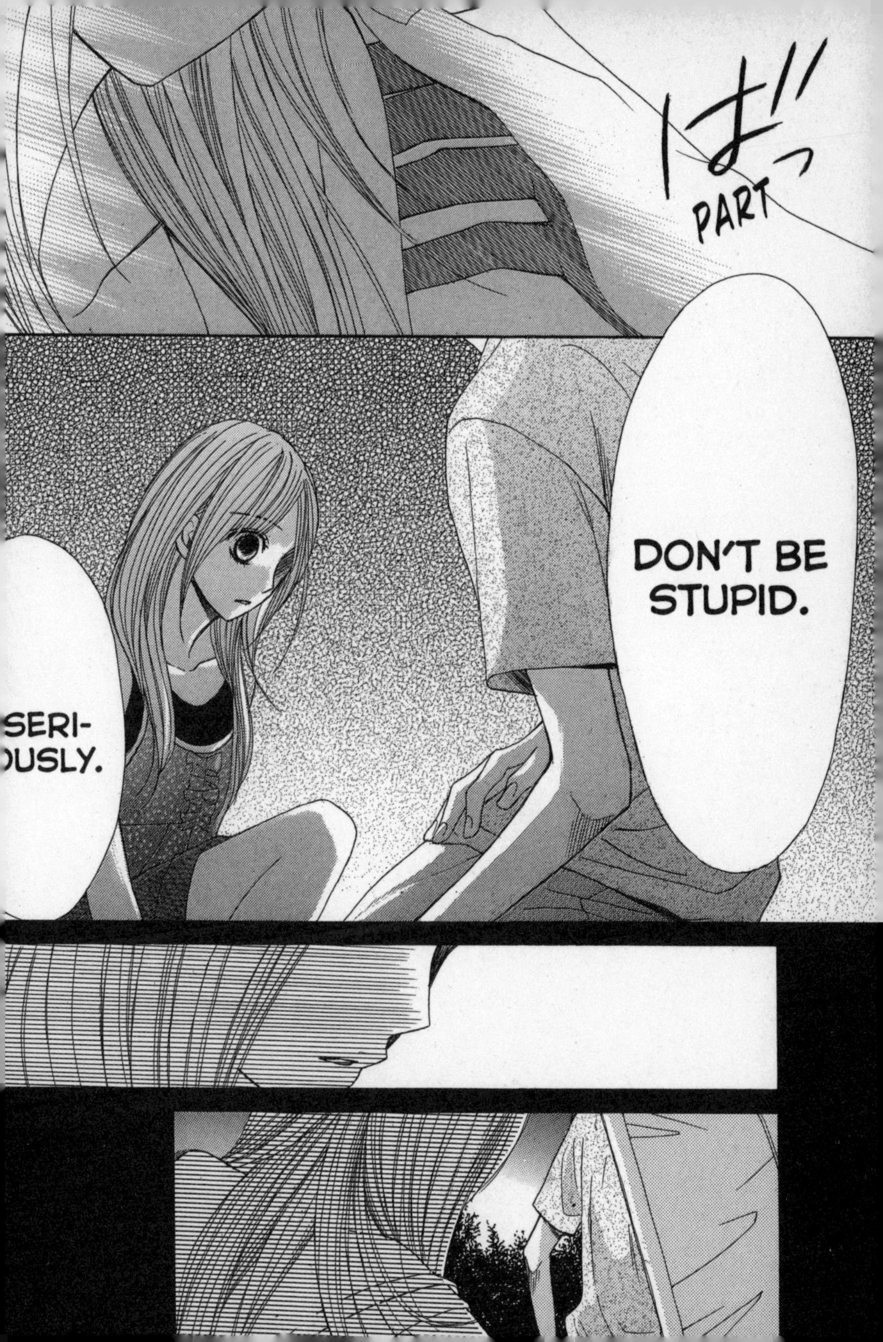

ばっ
PART
DON'T BE STUPID.
SERI- USLY.

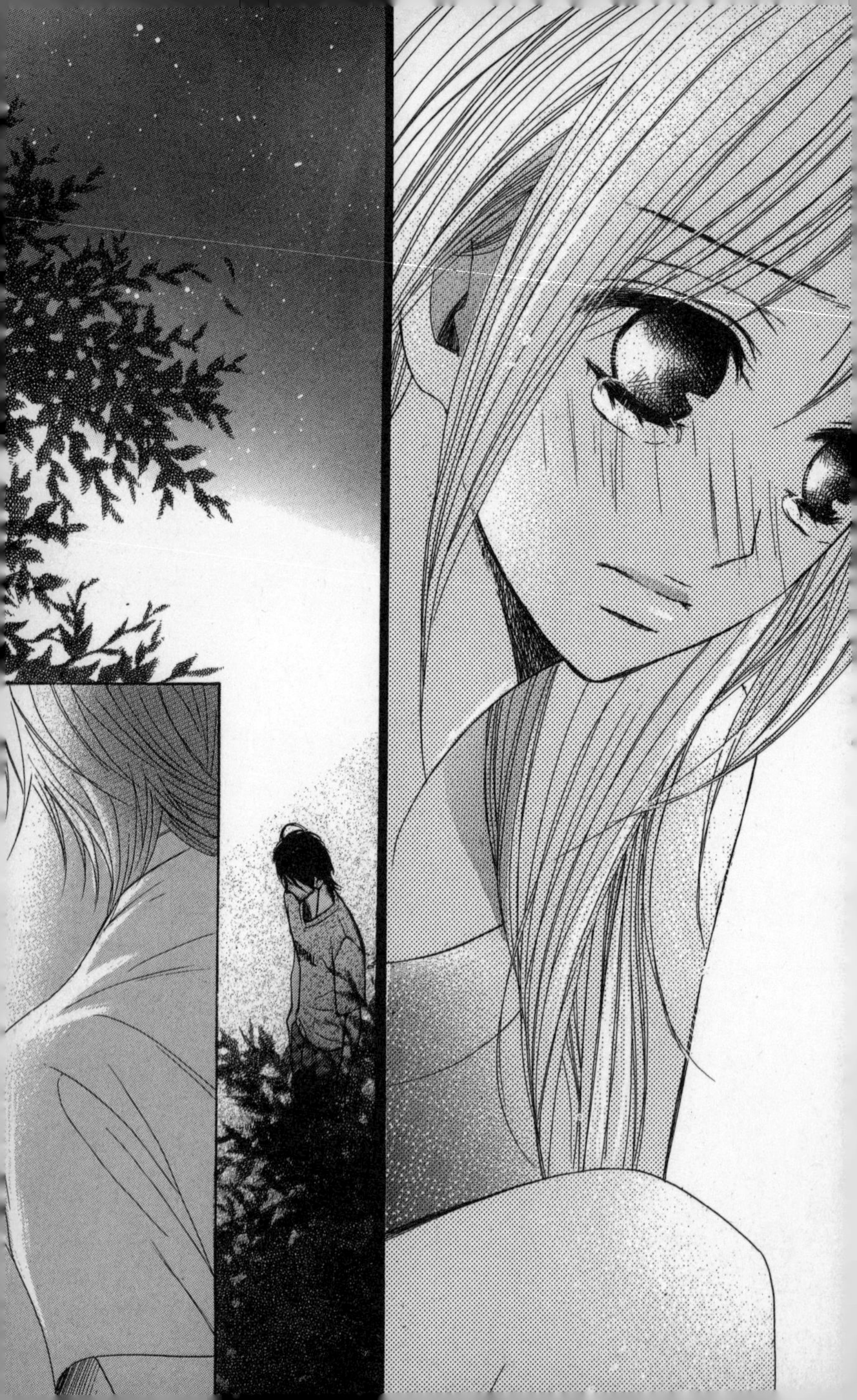

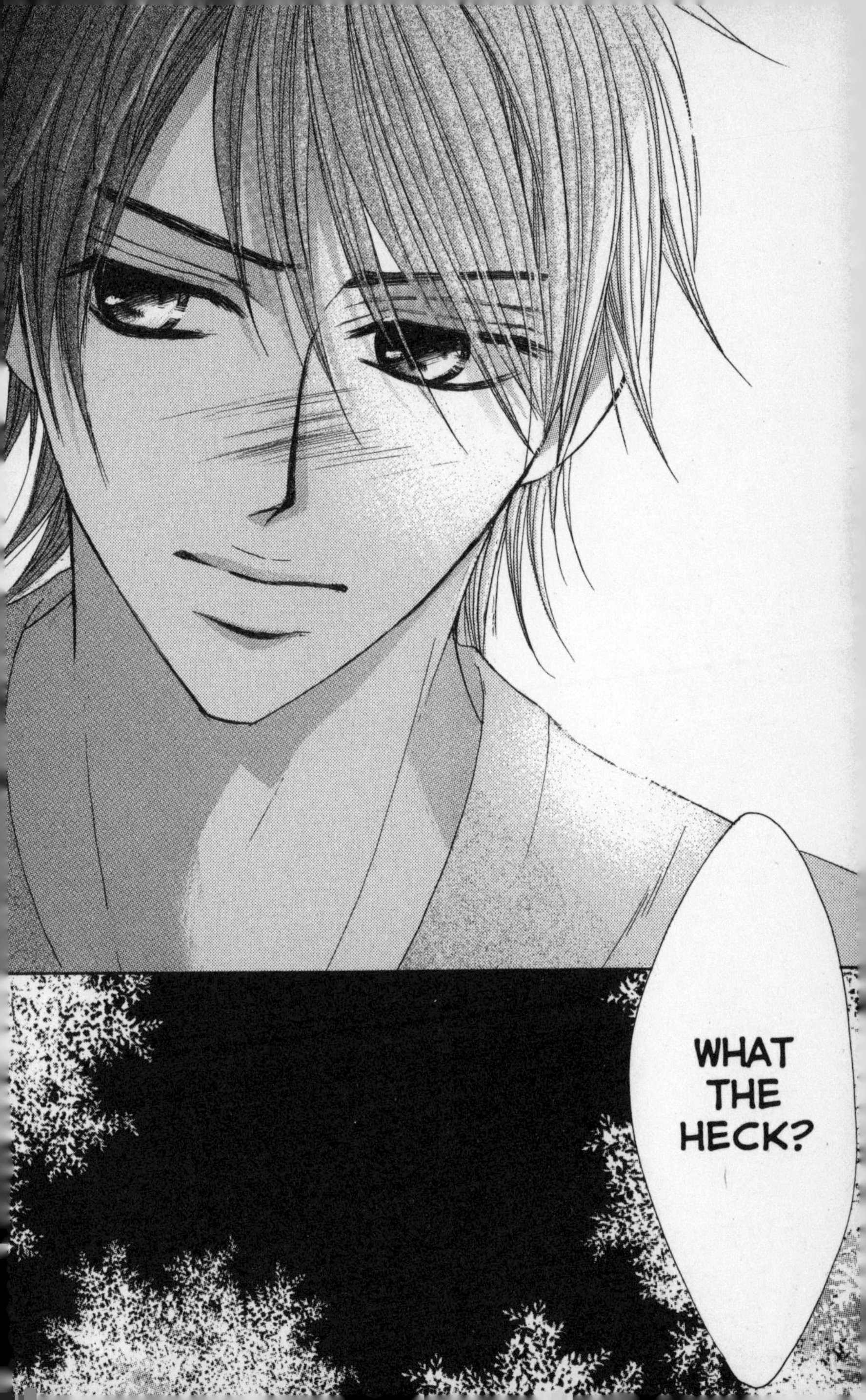
WHAT THE HECK?

L♥DK

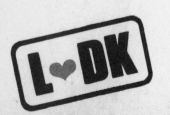

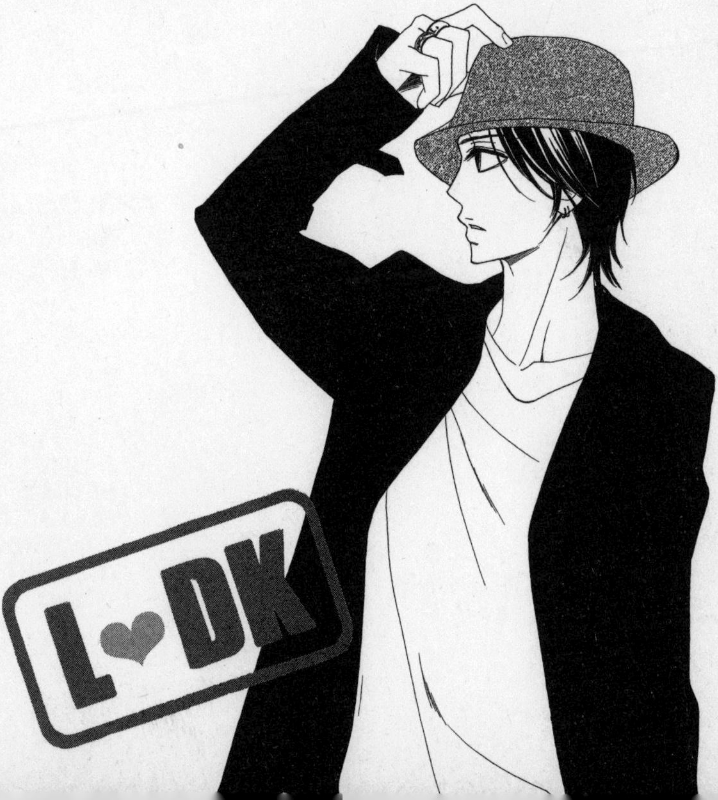
L♥DK

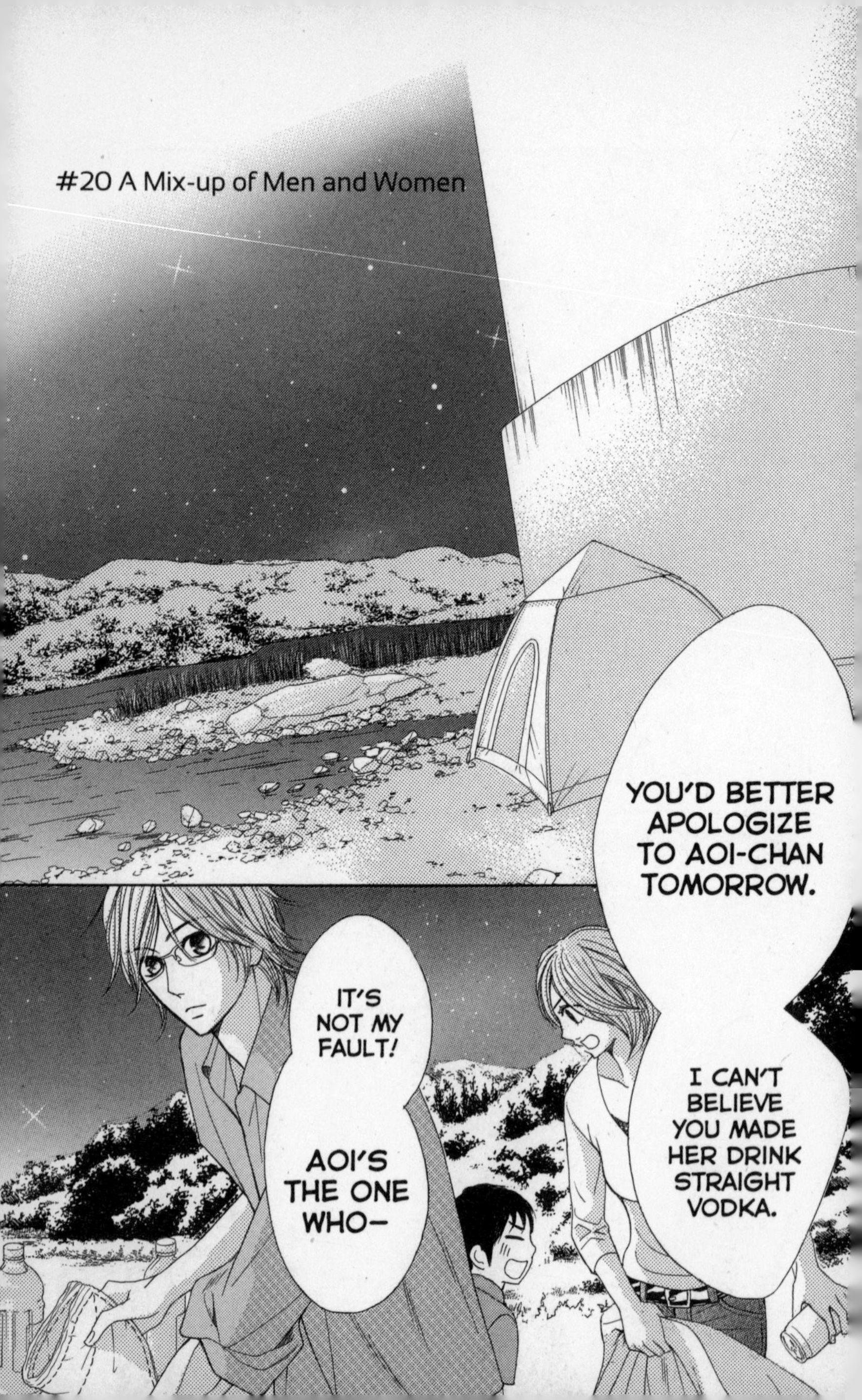
#20 A Mix-up of Men and Women
YOU'D BETTER APOLOGIZE TO AOI-CHAN TOMORROW.
I CAN'T BELIEVE YOU MADE HER DRINK STRAIGHT VODKA.
IT'S NOT MY FAULT!
AOI'S THE ONE WHO–

DON'T SPOUT THAT CRAP!
Former street thug
A CHILD WHO DOESN'T KNOW WHEN TO ADMIT HE'S WRONG AND APOLOGIZE IS NO CHILD OF MINE!
OOPS! OH, DEAR.
SORRY YOU HAD TO SEE THAT, WATARU-KUN. ♡
HEH HEH!
N...NO PROBLEM.

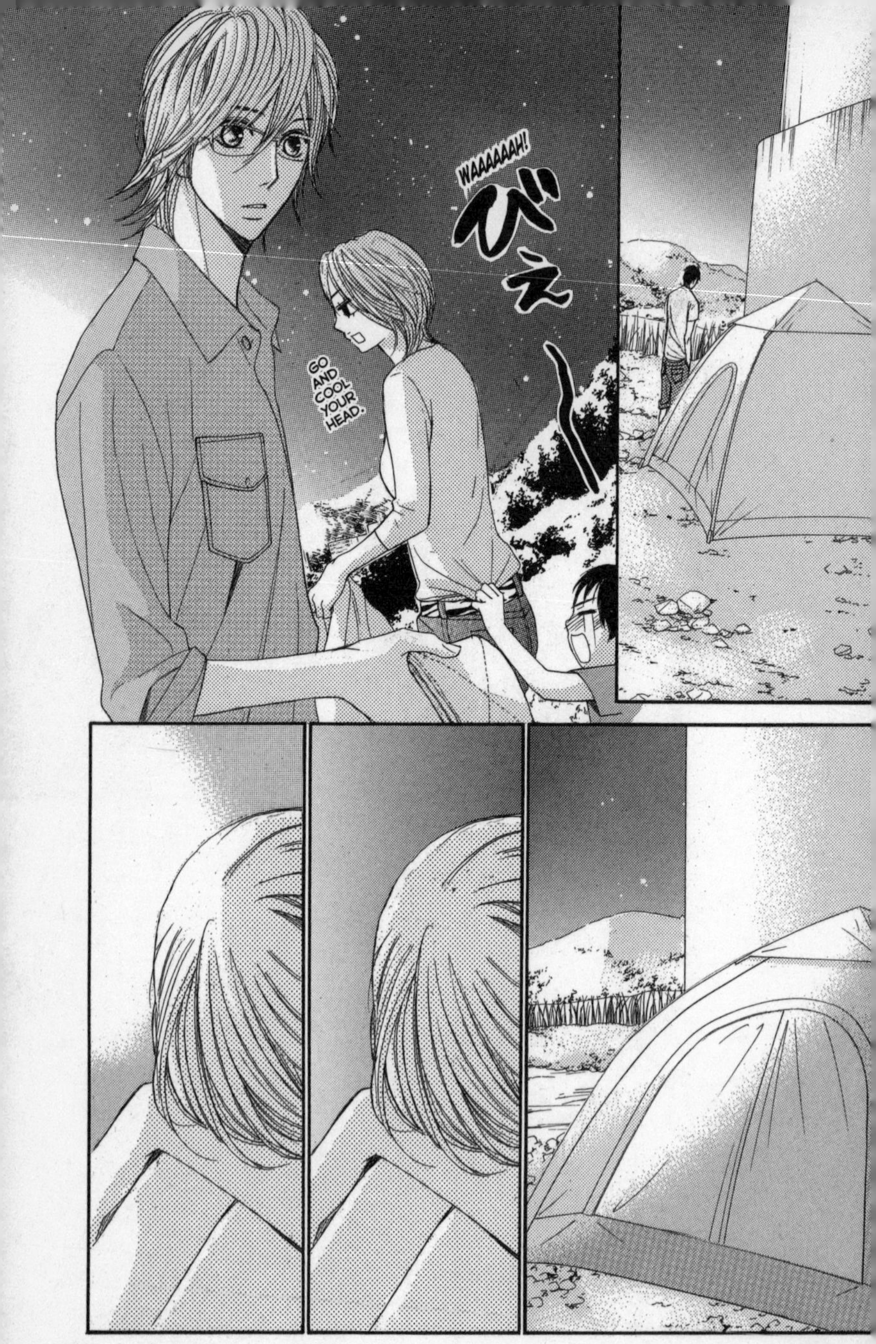
WAAAAAAH!
びえ
GO AND COOL YOUR HEAD.

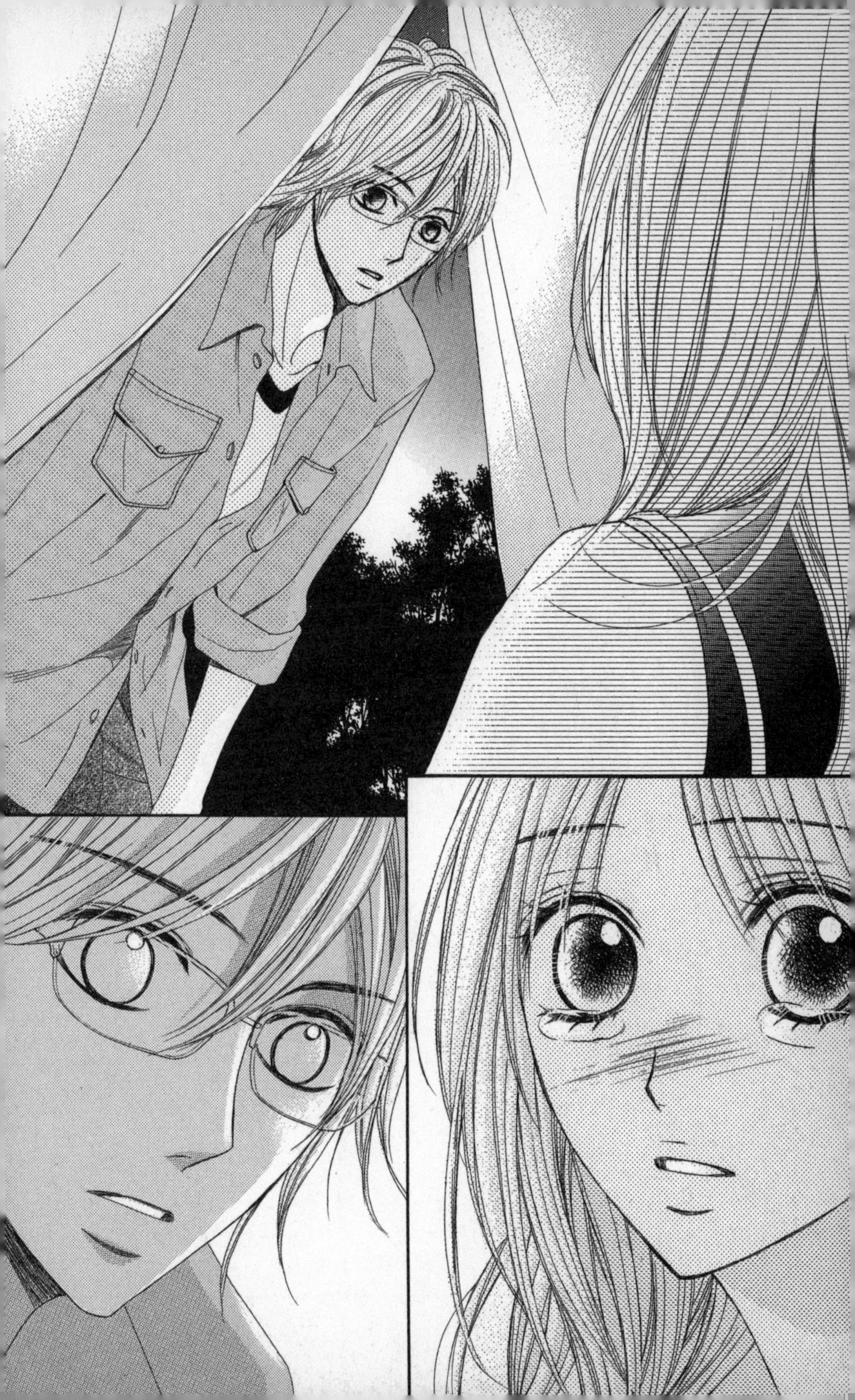

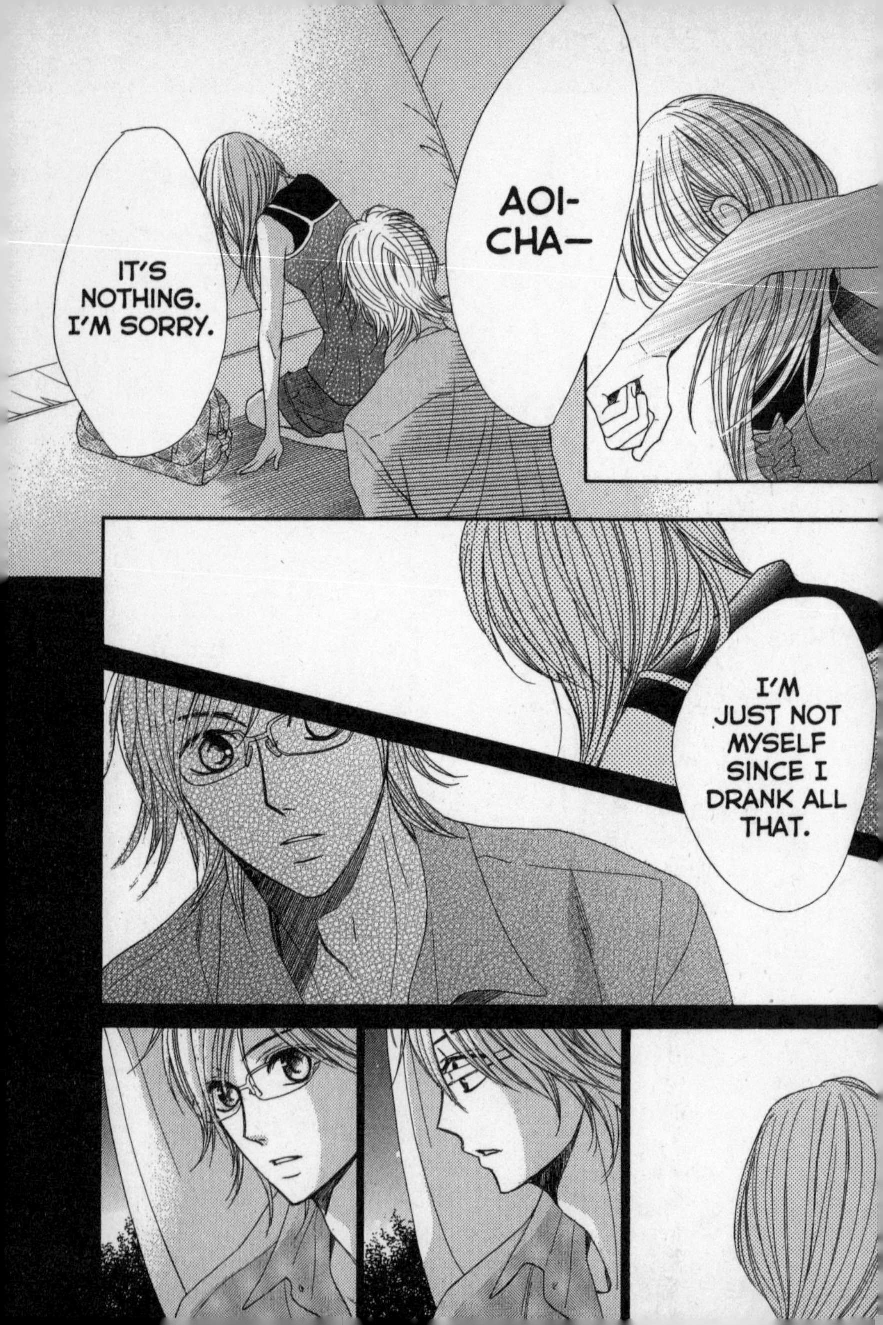
AOI-CHA—
IT'S NOTHING. I'M SORRY.
I'M JUST NOT MYSELF SINCE I DRANK ALL THAT.

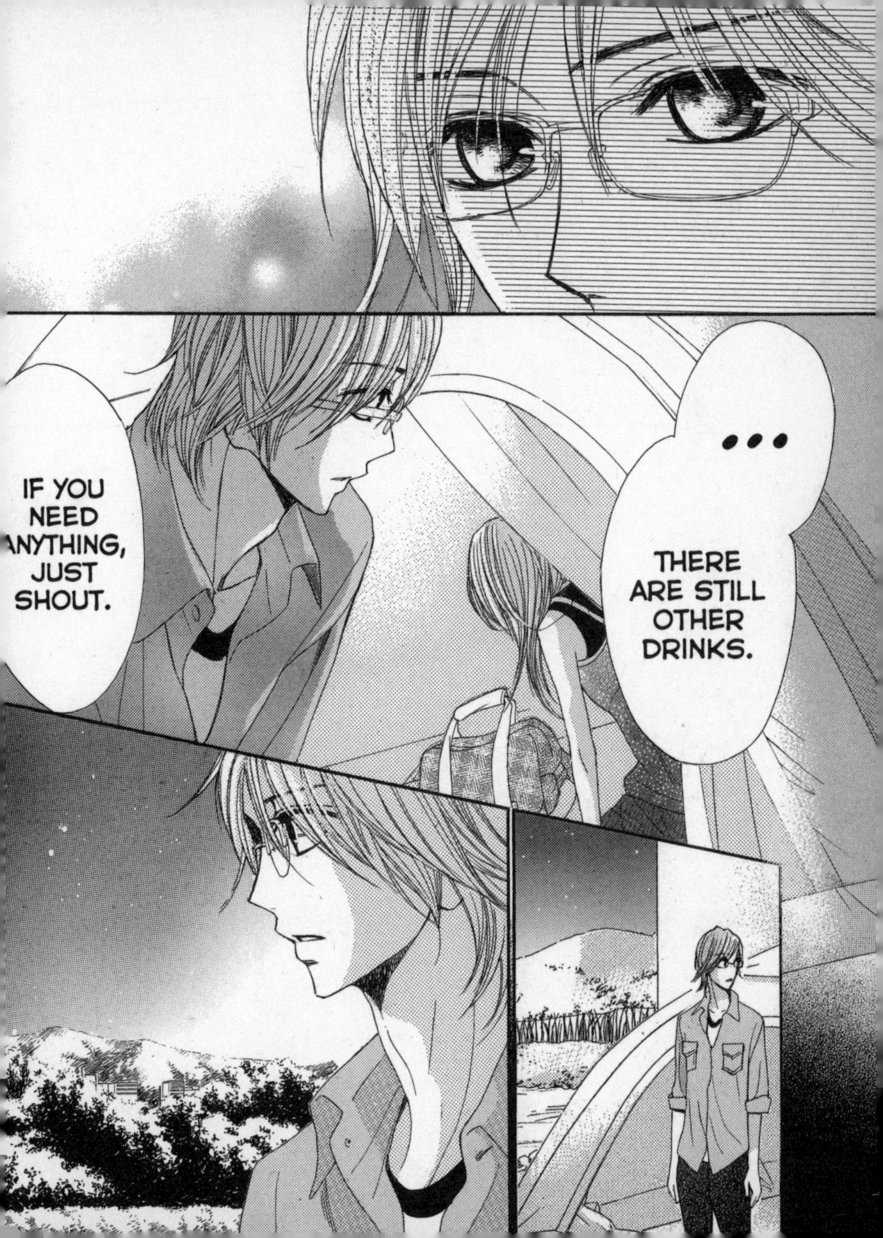
…
THERE ARE STILL OTHER DRINKS.
IF YOU NEED ANYTHING, JUST SHOUT.

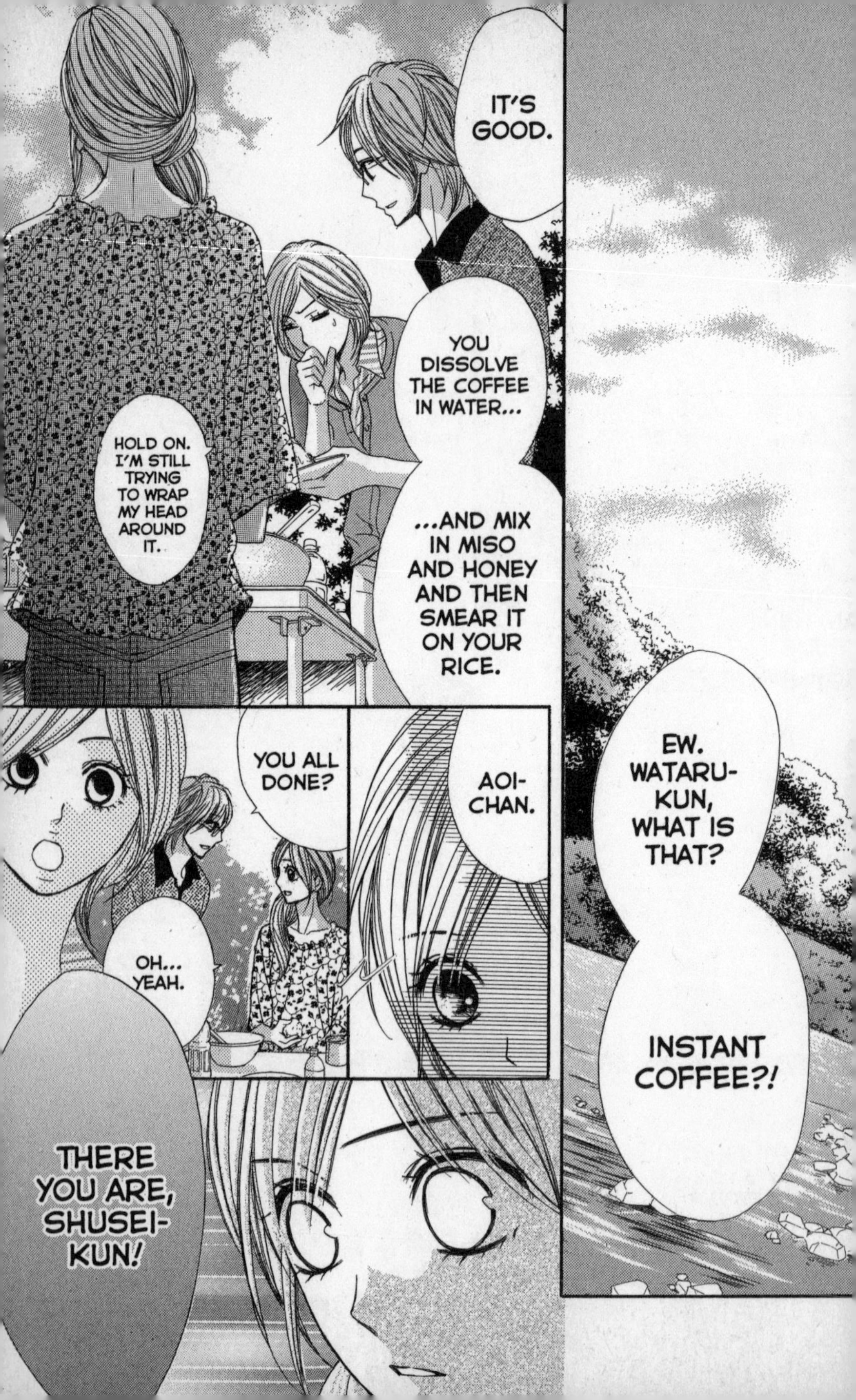
EW. WATARU-KUN, WHAT IS THAT?
INSTANT COFFEE?!
IT'S GOOD.
YOU DISSOLVE THE COFFEE IN WATER...
...AND MIX IN MISO AND HONEY AND THEN SMEAR IT ON YOUR RICE.
HOLD ON. I'M STILL TRYING TO WRAP MY HEAD AROUND IT.
AOI-CHAN.
YOU ALL DONE?
OH... YEAH.
THERE YOU ARE, SHUSEI-KUN!

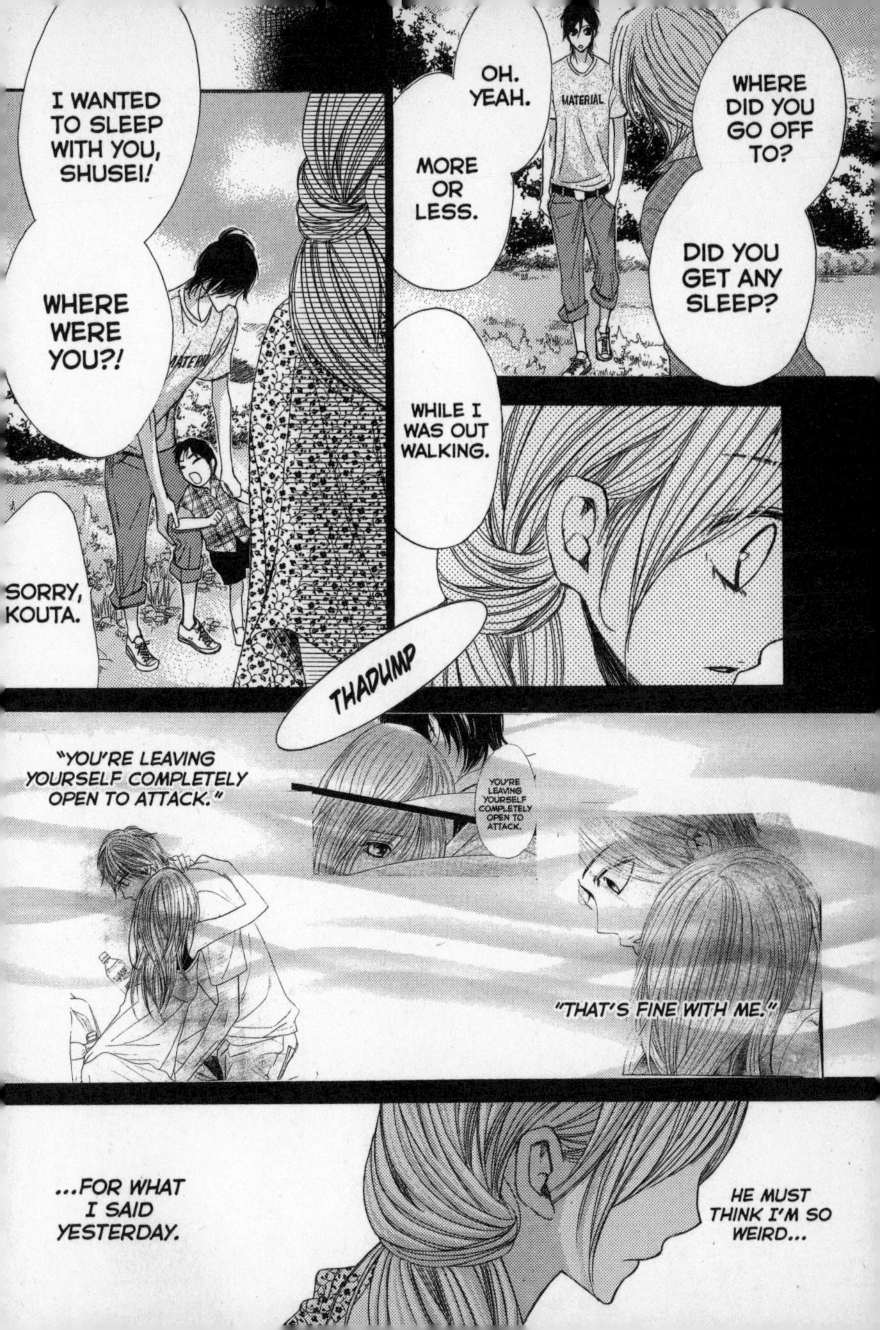
WHERE DID YOU GO OFF TO?
DID YOU GET ANY SLEEP?
OH. YEAH.
MORE OR LESS.
WHILE I WAS OUT WALKING.
THADUMP
I WANTED TO SLEEP WITH YOU, SHUSEI!
WHERE WERE YOU?!
SORRY, KOUTA.
"THAT'S FINE WITH ME."
YOU'RE LEAVING YOURSELF COMPLETELY OPEN TO ATTACK.
"YOU'RE LEAVING YOURSELF COMPLETELY OPEN TO ATTACK."
HE MUST THINK I'M SO WEIRD...
...FOR WHAT I SAID YESTERDAY.

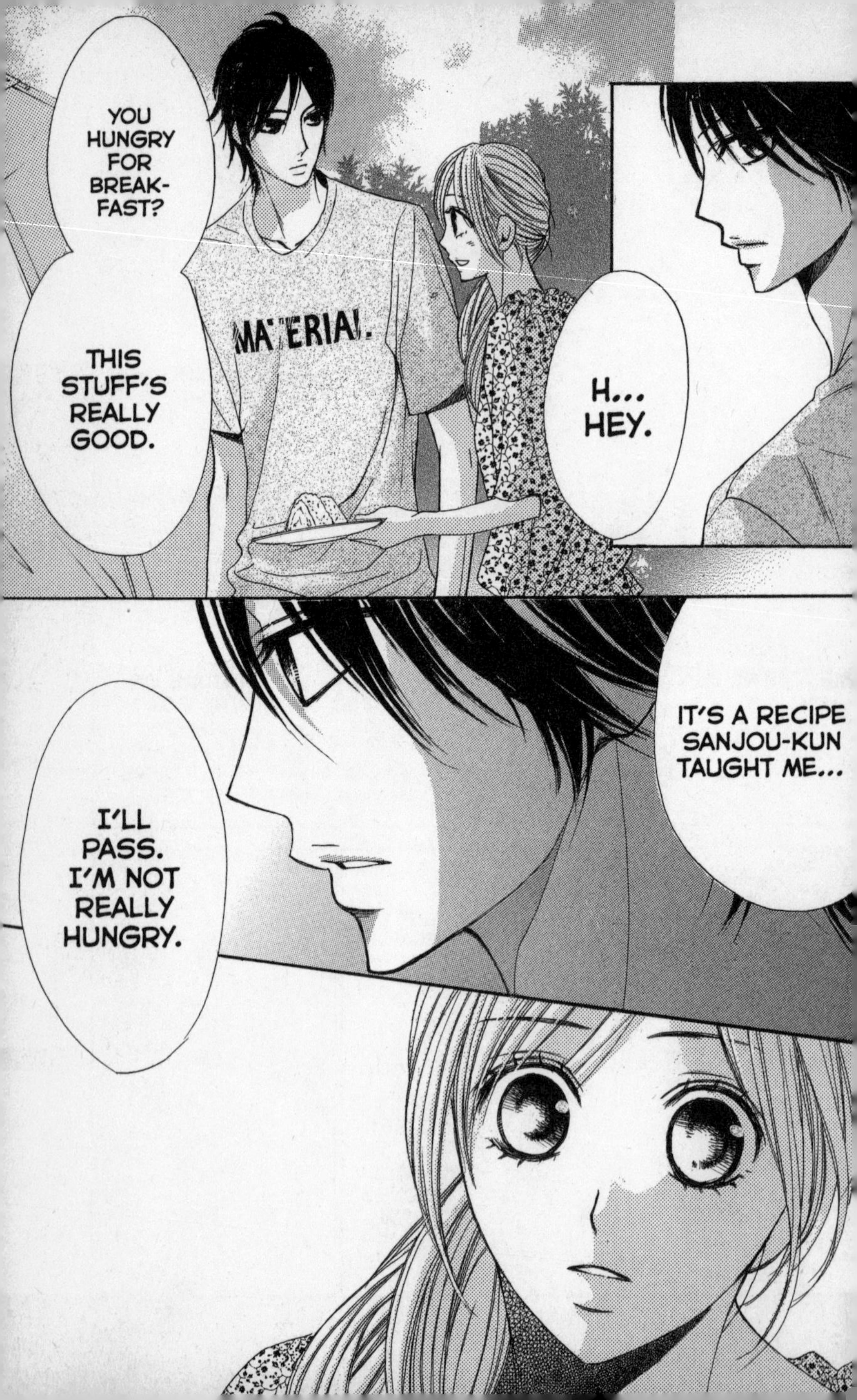
H... HEY.
YOU HUNGRY FOR BREAK-FAST?
THIS STUFF'S REALLY GOOD.
IT'S A RECIPE SANJOU-KUN TAUGHT ME...
I'LL PASS. I'M NOT REALLY HUNGRY.

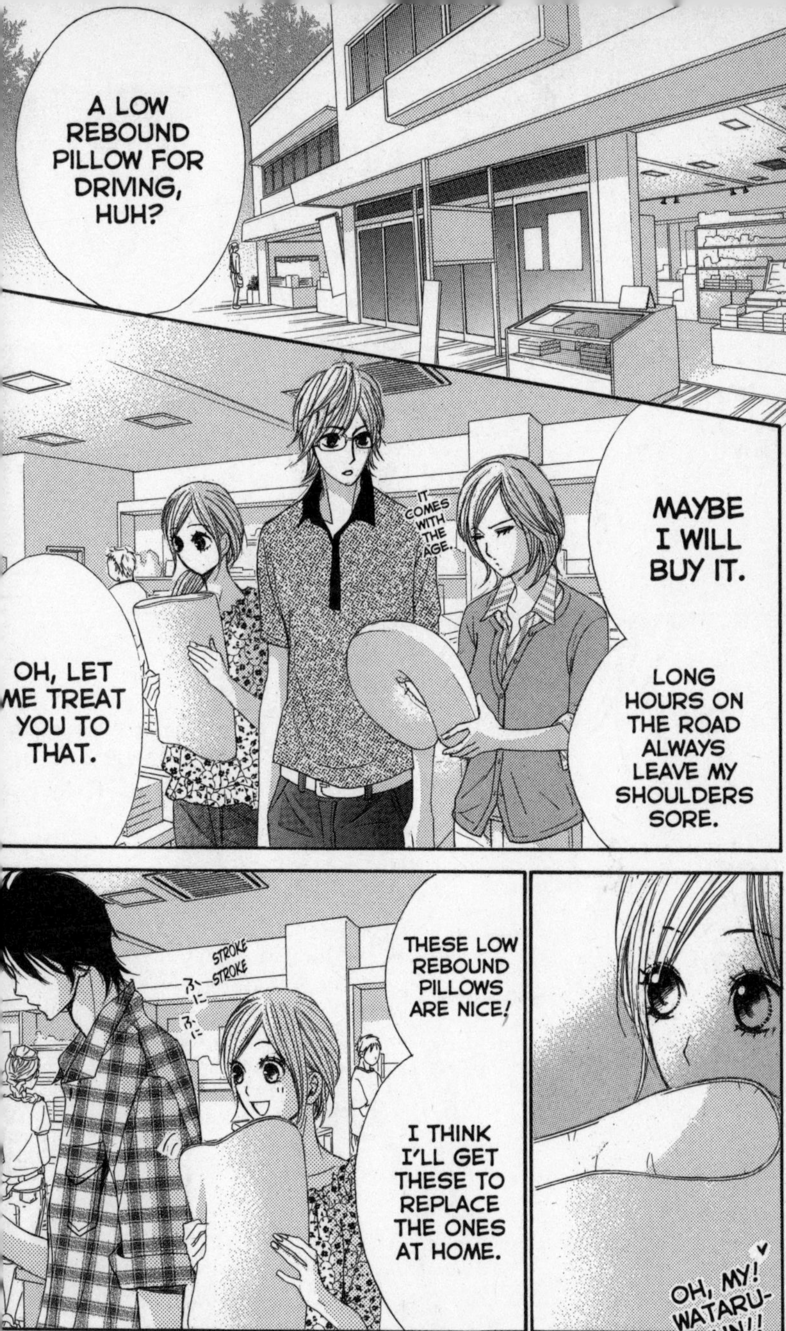
A LOW REBOUND PILLOW FOR DRIVING, HUH?
MAYBE I WILL BUY IT.
LONG HOURS ON THE ROAD ALWAYS LEAVE MY SHOULDERS SORE.
IT COMES WITH THE AGE.
OH, LET ME TREAT YOU TO THAT.
OH, MY! WATARU-KUN!!
THESE LOW REBOUND PILLOWS ARE NICE!
I THINK I'LL GET THESE TO REPLACE THE ONES AT HOME.
STROKE STROKE
ふにふに

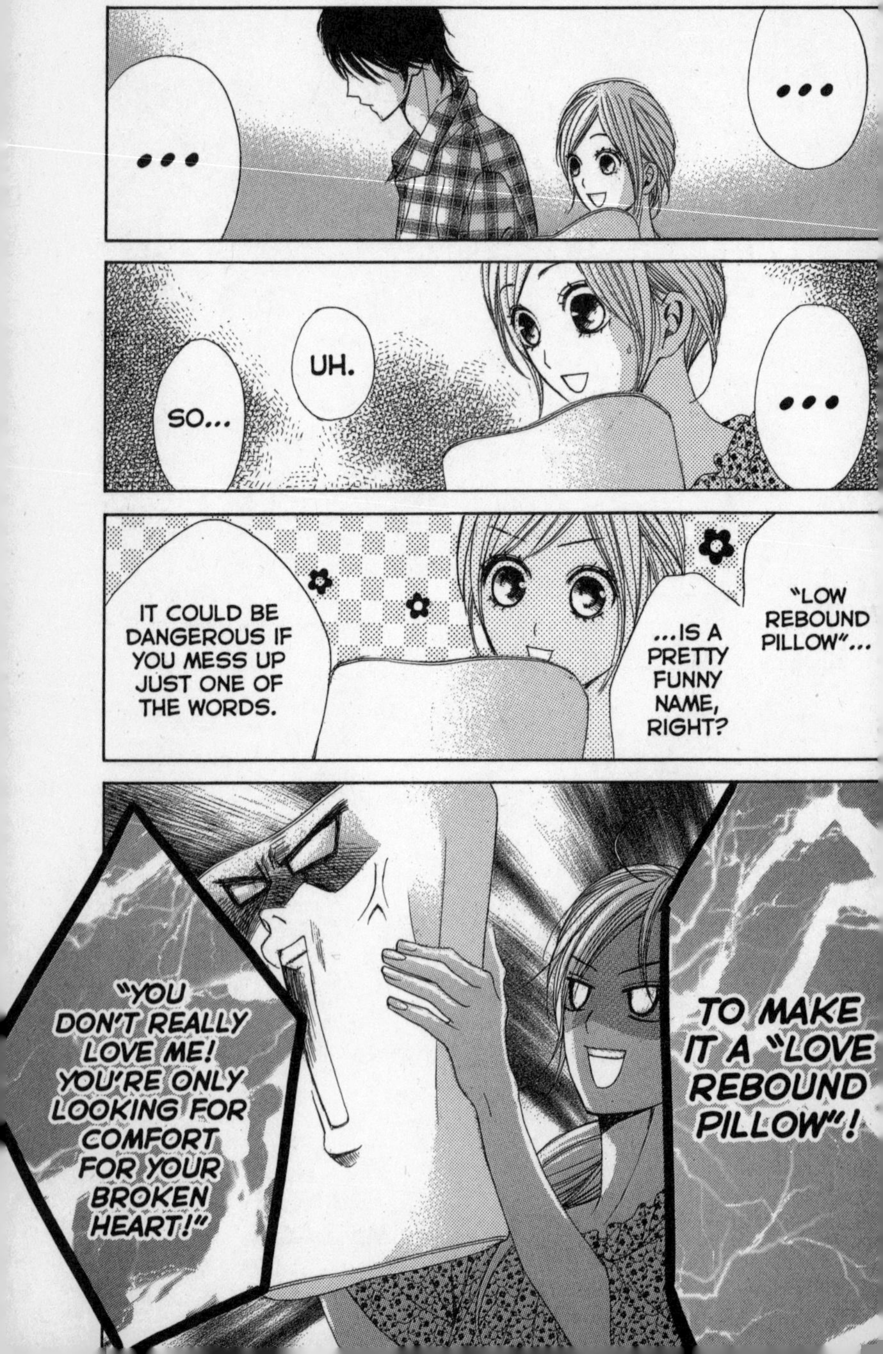
...
...
...
UH.
SO...
"LOW REBOUND PILLOW"...
...IS A PRETTY FUNNY NAME, RIGHT?
IT COULD BE DANGEROUS IF YOU MESS UP JUST ONE OF THE WORDS.
TO MAKE IT A "LOVE REBOUND PILLOW"!
"YOU DON'T REALLY LOVE ME! YOU'RE ONLY LOOKING FOR COMFORT FOR YOUR BROKEN HEART!"

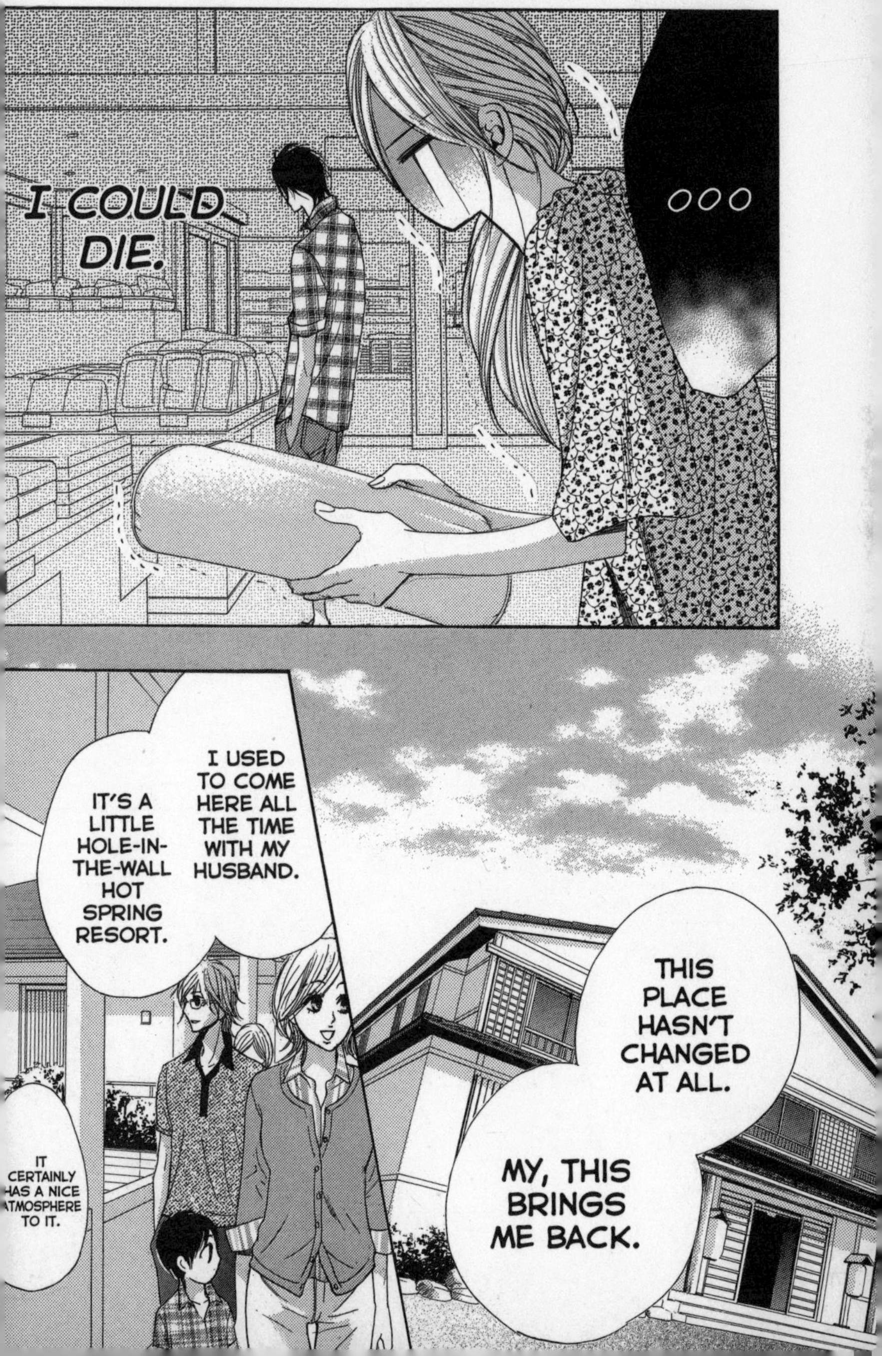
I COULD DIE.
THIS PLACE HASN'T CHANGED AT ALL.
MY, THIS BRINGS ME BACK.
I USED TO COME HERE ALL THE TIME WITH MY HUSBAND.
IT'S A LITTLE HOLE-IN-THE-WALL HOT SPRING RESORT.
IT CERTAINLY HAS A NICE ATMOSPHERE TO IT.

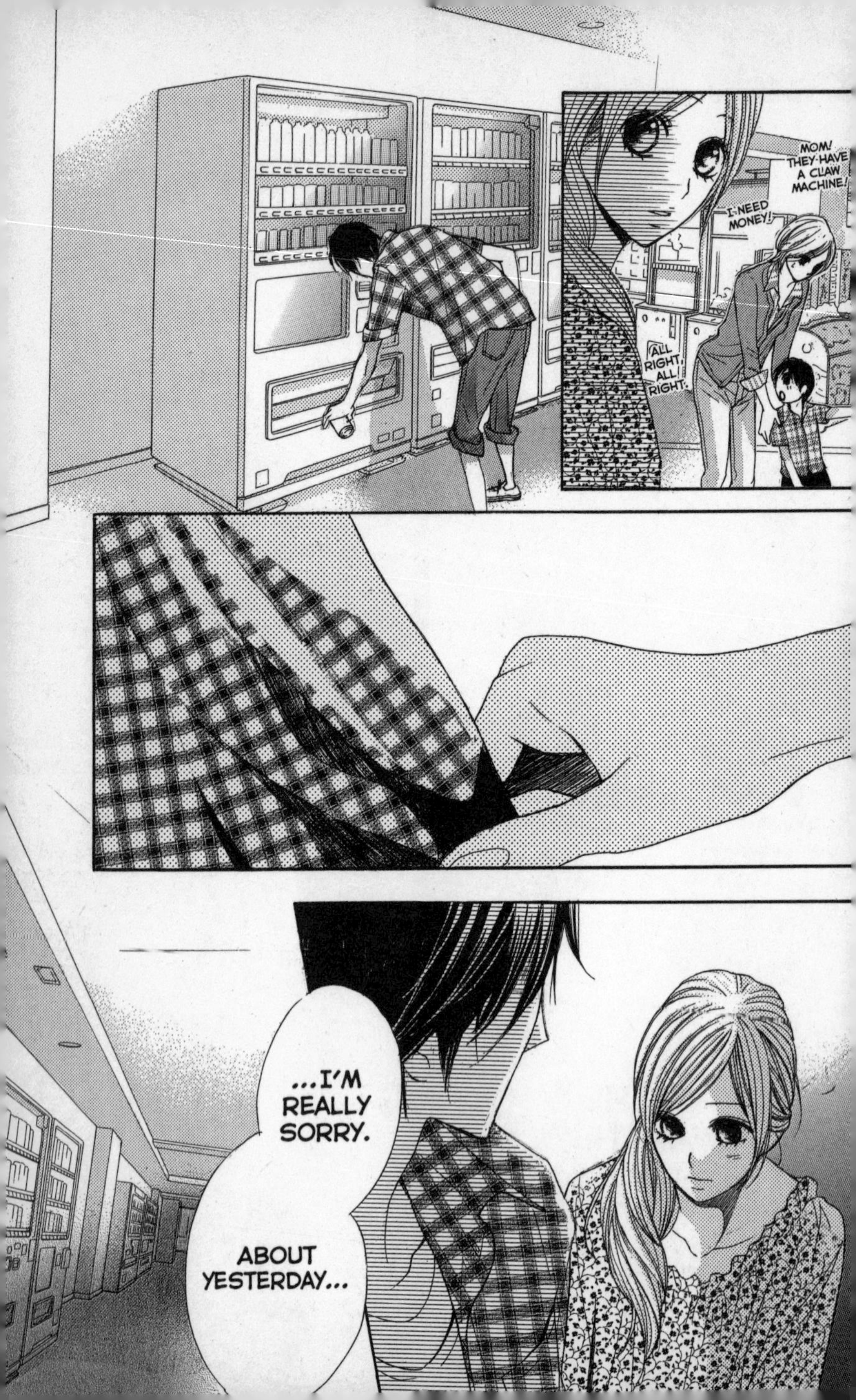
MOM! THEY HAVE A CLAW MACHINE!
I NEED MONEY!
ALL RIGHT, ALL RIGHT.
...I'M REALLY SORRY.
ABOUT YESTERDAY...

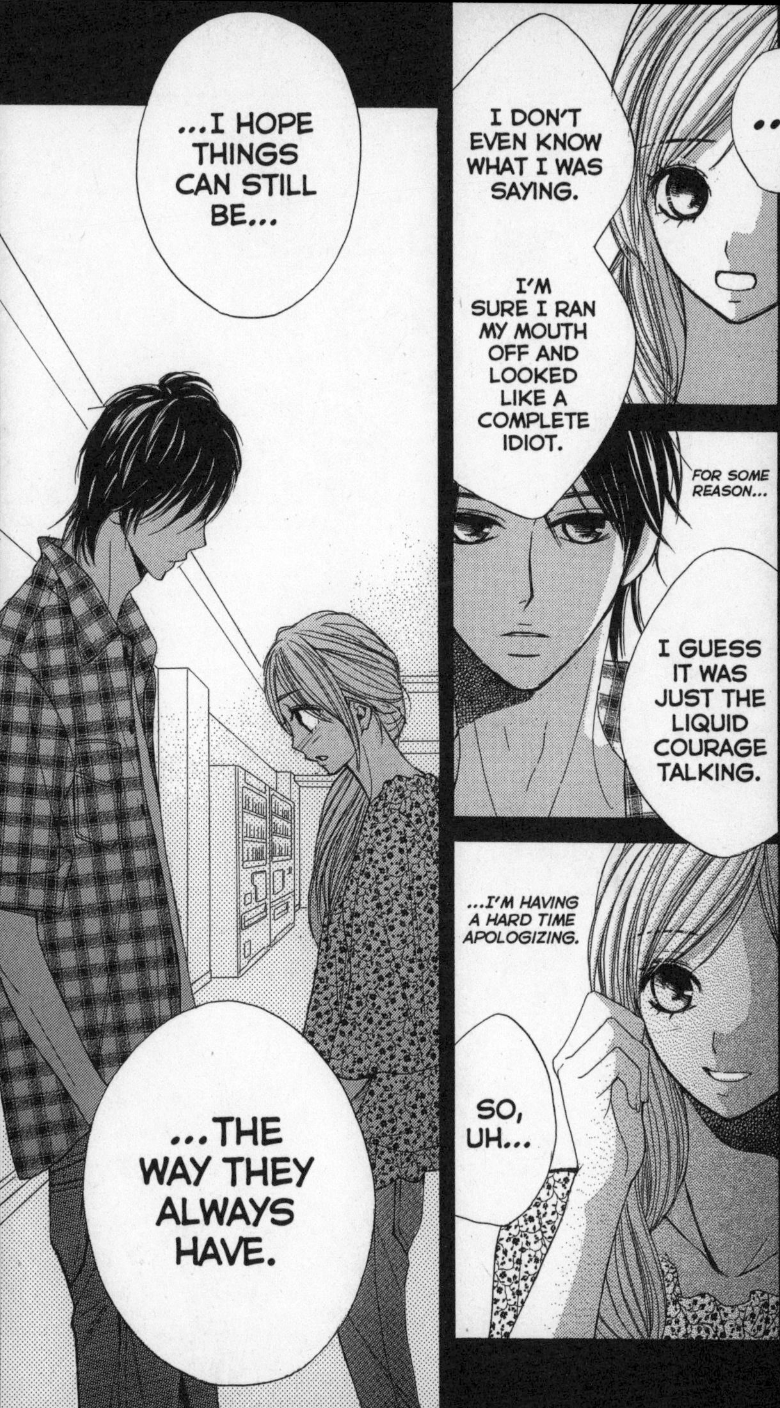
...
I DON'T EVEN KNOW WHAT I WAS SAYING.
I'M SURE I RAN MY MOUTH OFF AND LOOKED LIKE A COMPLETE IDIOT.
FOR SOME REASON...
I GUESS IT WAS JUST THE LIQUID COURAGE TALKING.
...I'M HAVING A HARD TIME APOLOGIZING.
SO, UH...
...I HOPE THINGS CAN STILL BE...
...THE WAY THEY ALWAYS HAVE.

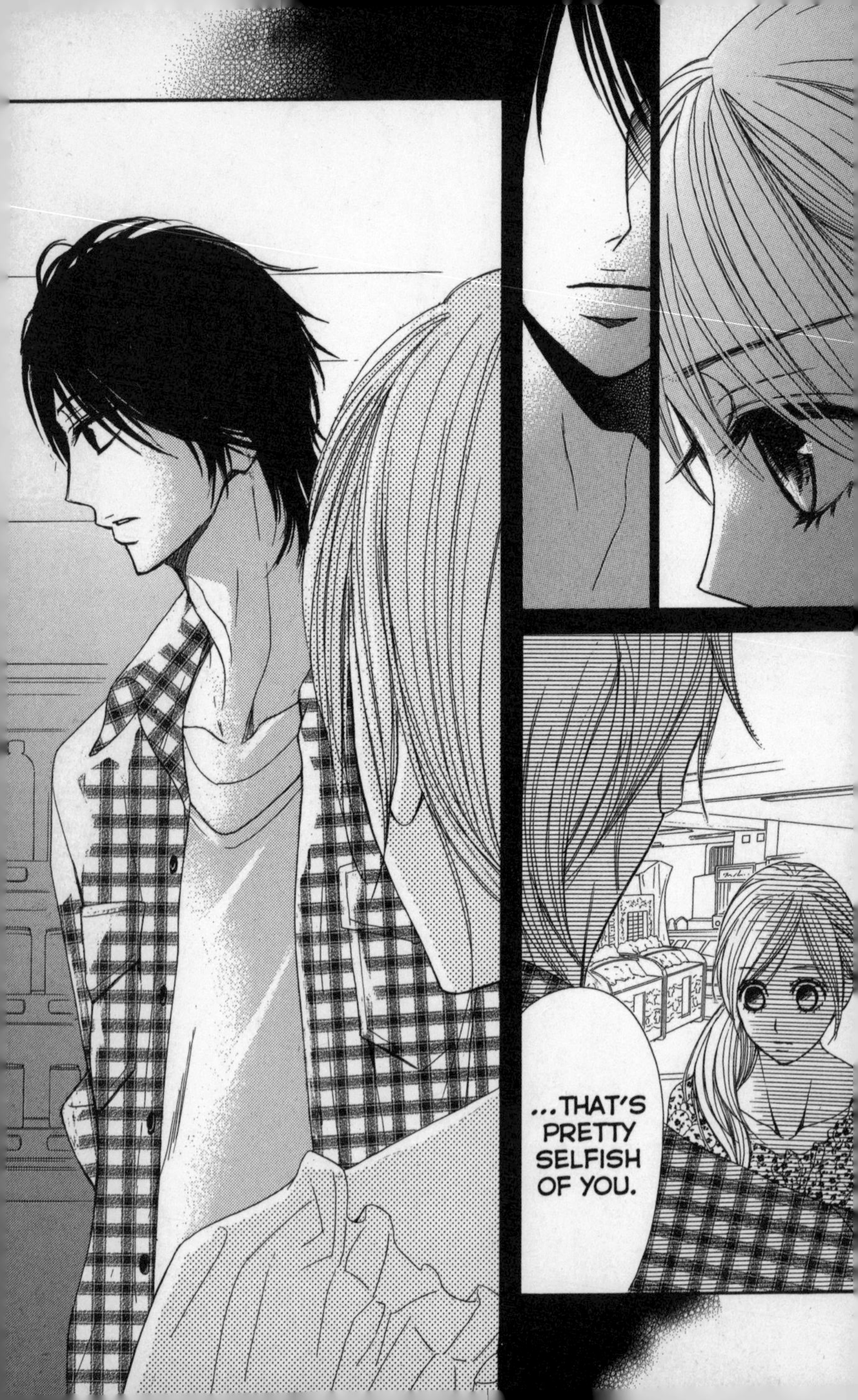
...THAT'S PRETTY SELFISH OF YOU.

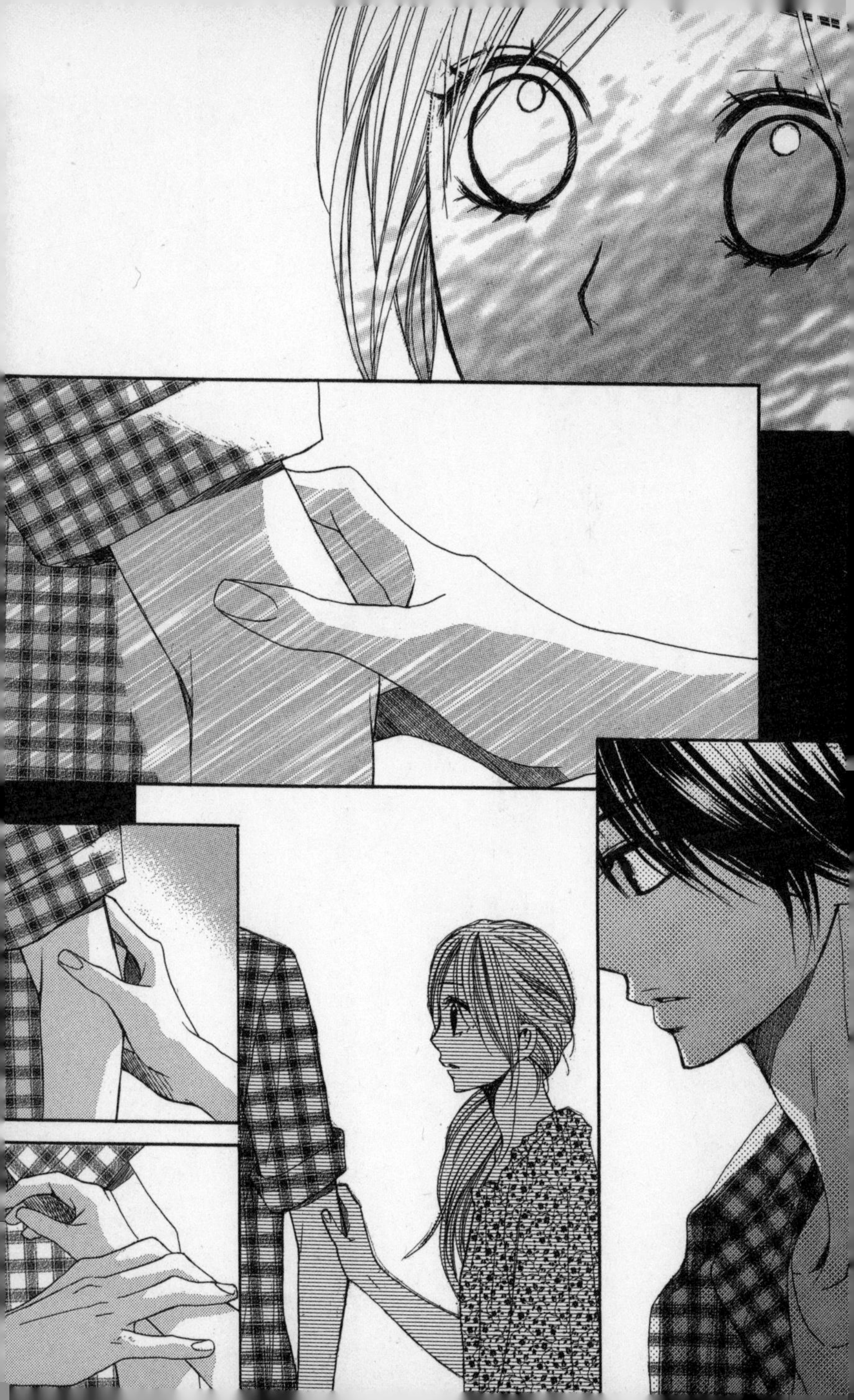

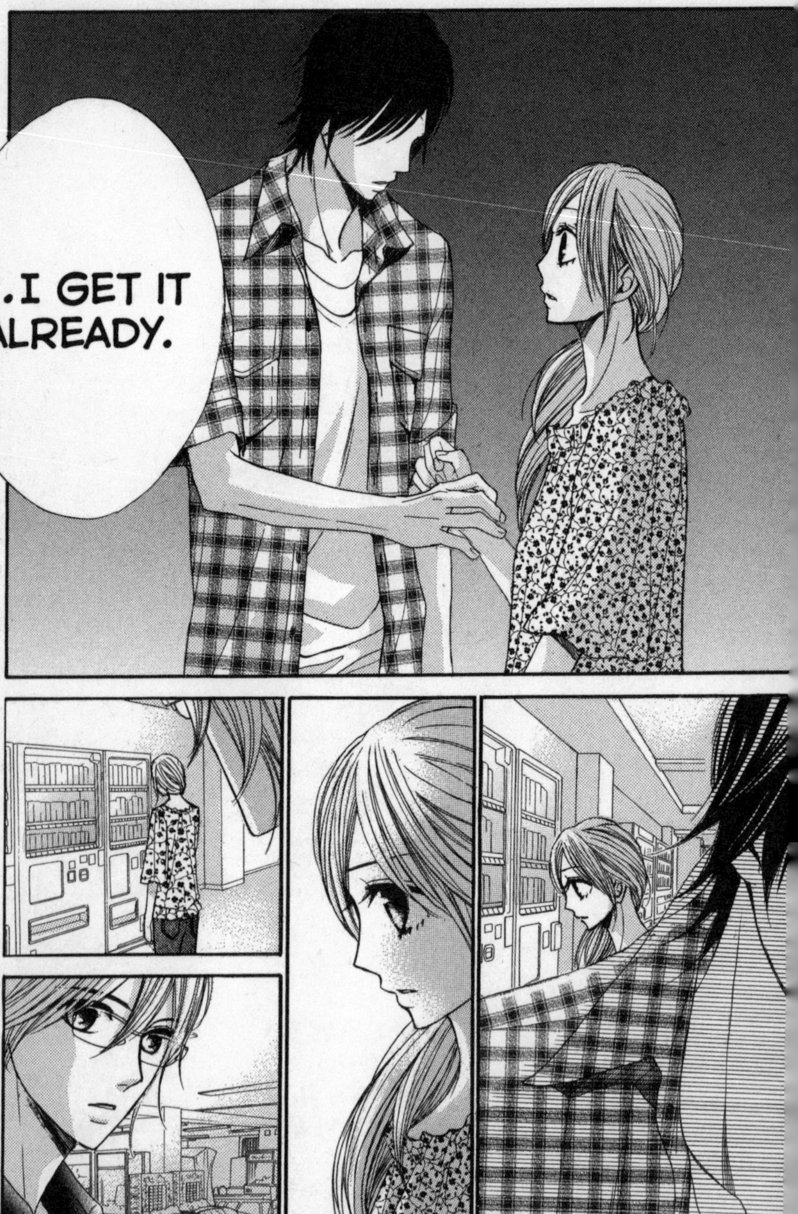
...I GET IT ALREADY.

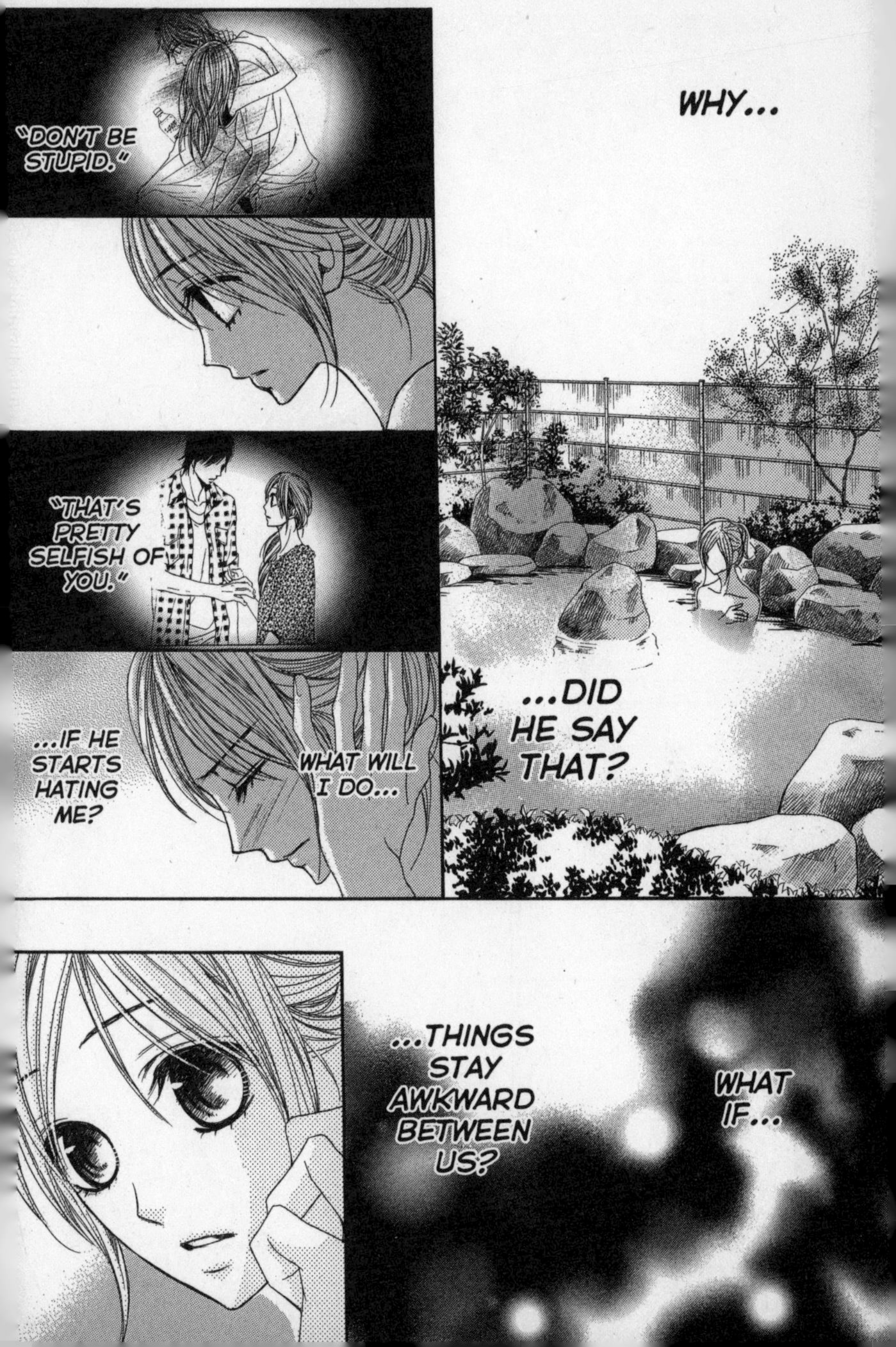
WHY...
...DID HE SAY THAT?
"DON'T BE STUPID."
"THAT'S PRETTY SELFISH OF YOU."
WHAT WILL I DO...
...IF HE STARTS HATING ME?
WHAT IF...
...THINGS STAY AWKWARD BETWEEN US?

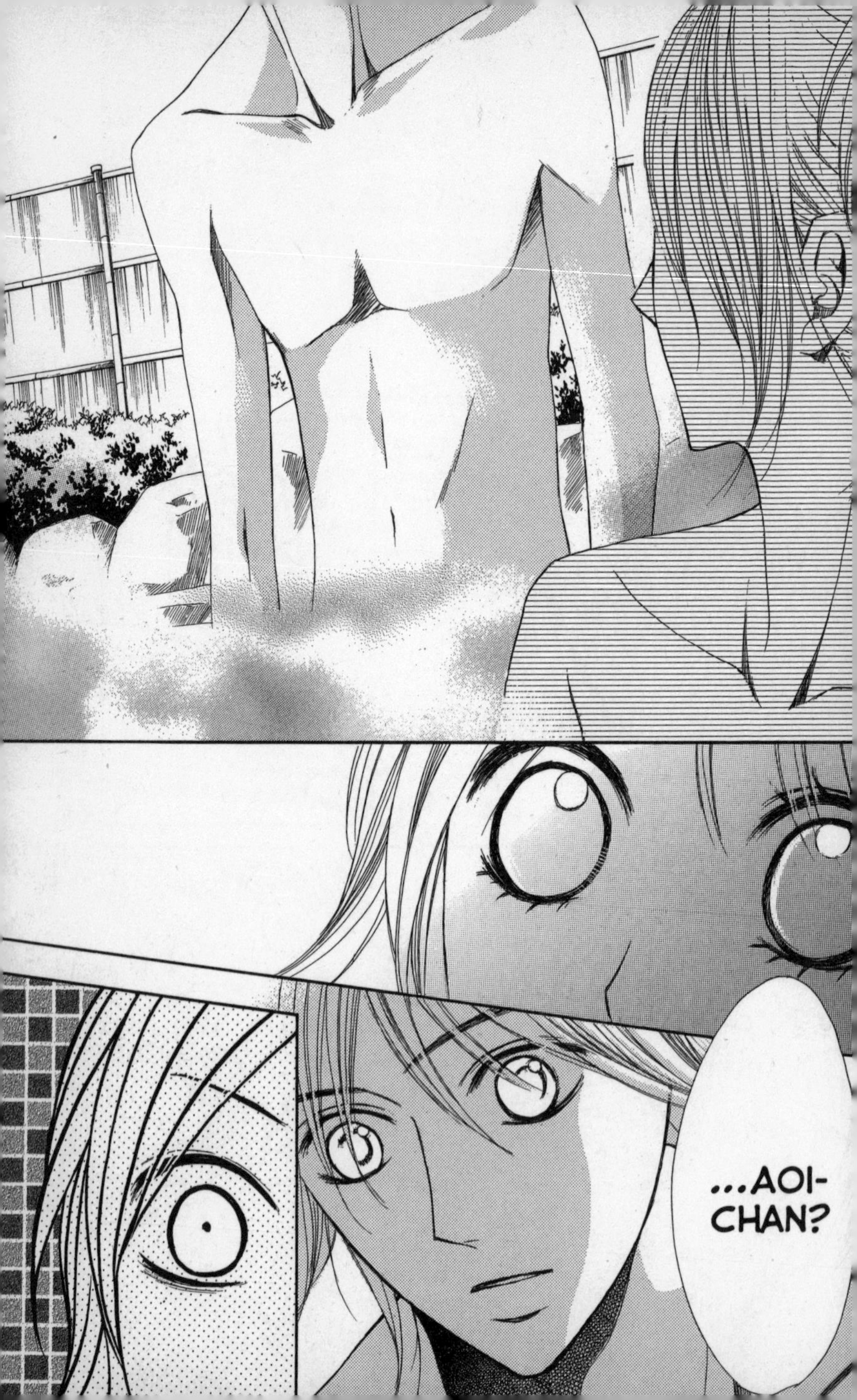
...AOI-
CHAN?

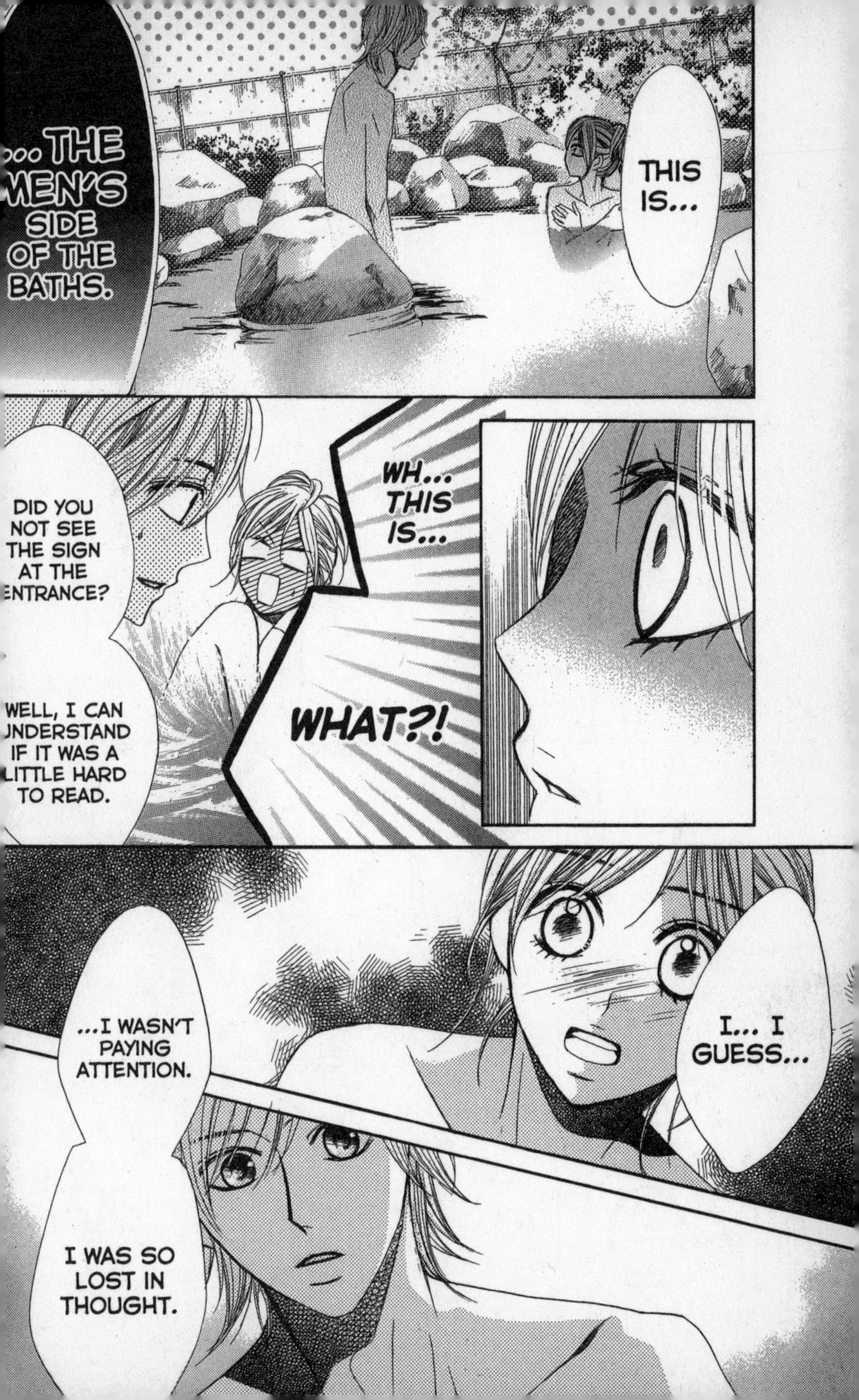
THIS IS...
...THE MEN'S SIDE OF THE BATHS.
WH... THIS IS...
WHAT?!
DID YOU NOT SEE THE SIGN AT THE ENTRANCE?
WELL, I CAN UNDERSTAND IF IT WAS A LITTLE HARD TO READ.
I... I GUESS...
...I WASN'T PAYING ATTENTION.
I WAS SO LOST IN THOUGHT.

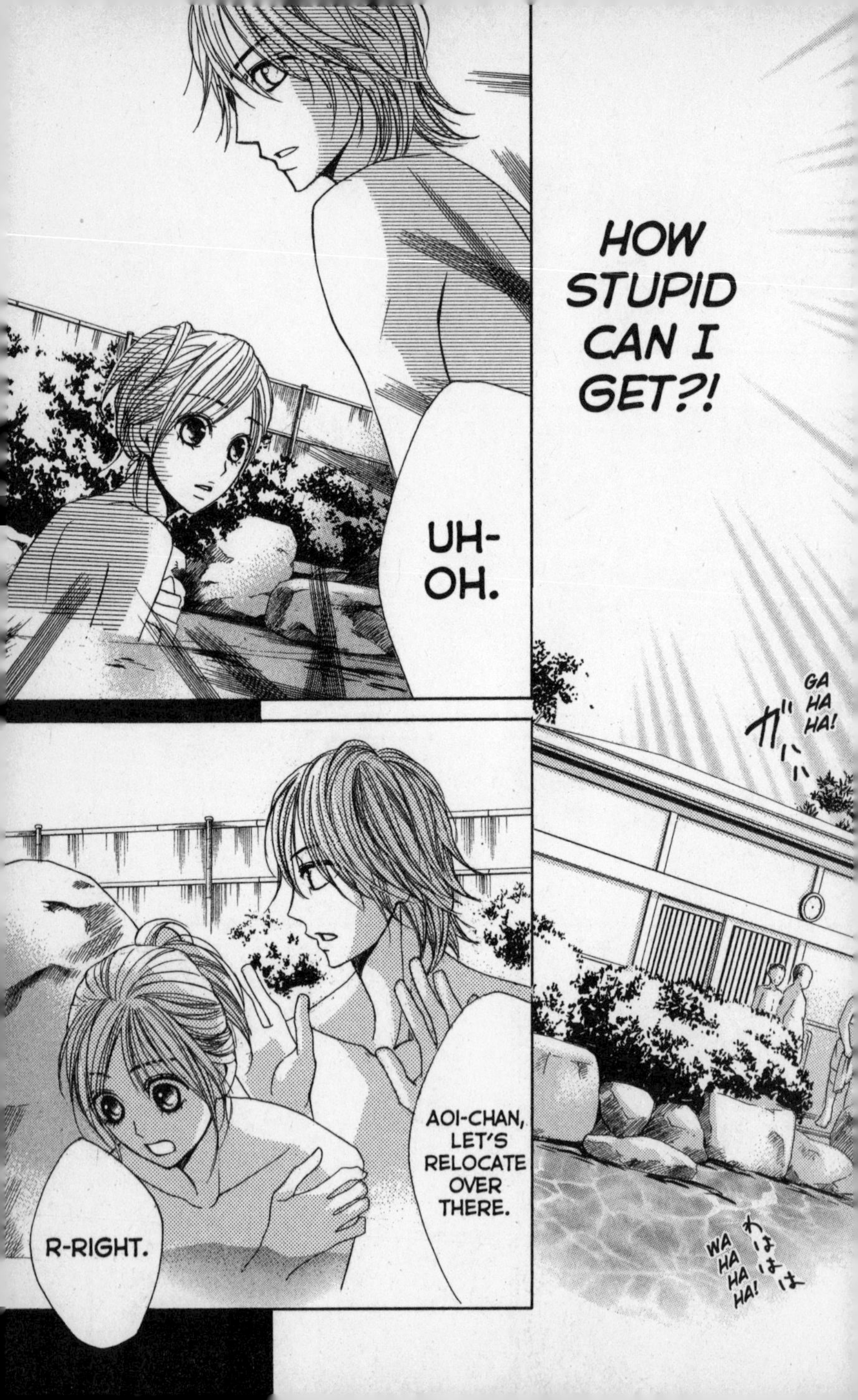
HOW STUPID CAN I GET?!
GA HA HA!
ガハハ
WA HA HA HA!
わははは
UH-OH.
AOI-CHAN, LET'S RELOCATE OVER THERE.
R-RIGHT.

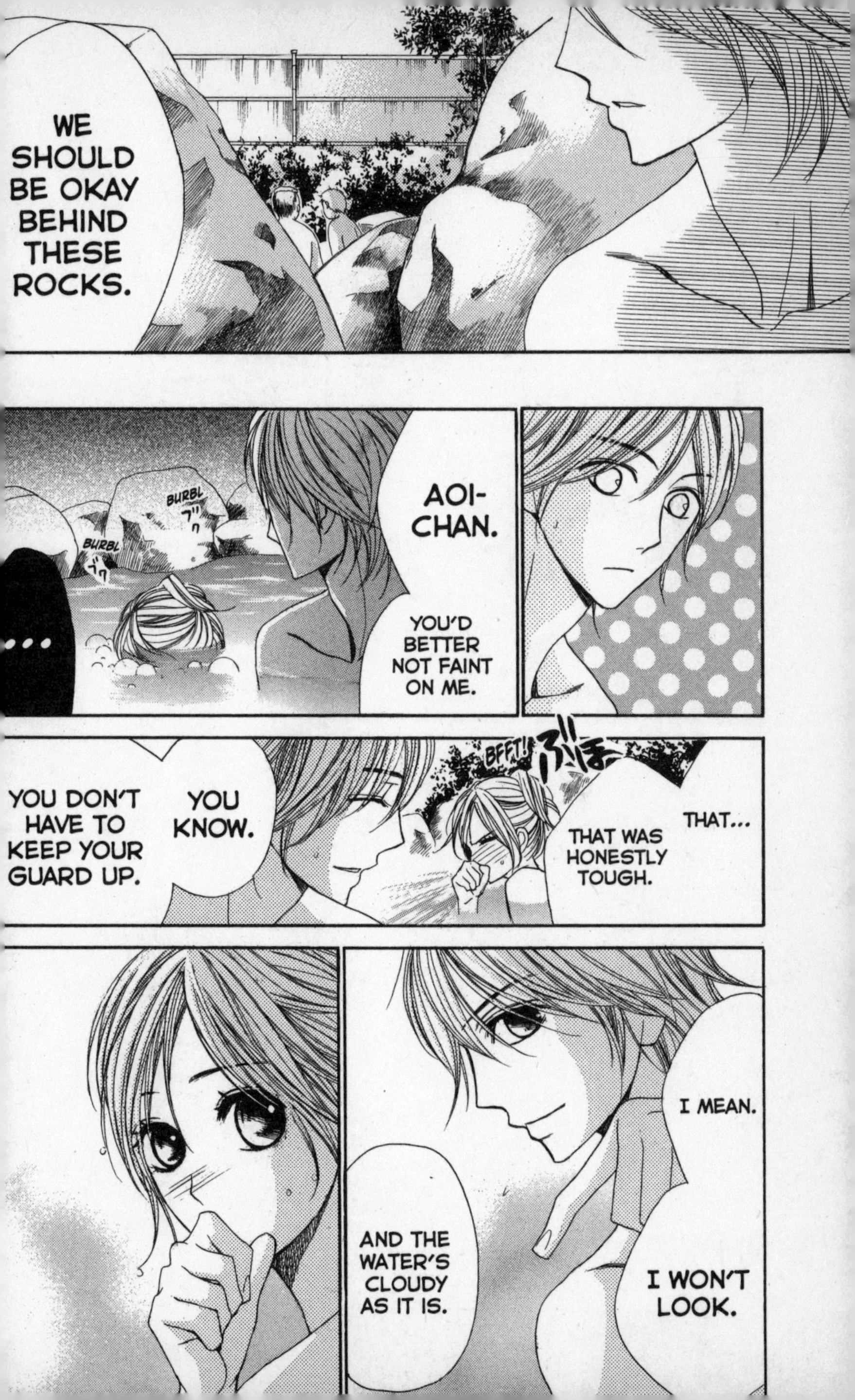
WE SHOULD BE OKAY BEHIND THESE ROCKS.
AOI-CHAN.
YOU'D BETTER NOT FAINT ON ME.
BURBL
BURBL
...
THAT...
THAT WAS HONESTLY TOUGH.
BFFT!
YOU KNOW.
YOU DON'T HAVE TO KEEP YOUR GUARD UP.
I MEAN.
I WON'T LOOK.
AND THE WATER'S CLOUDY AS IT IS.

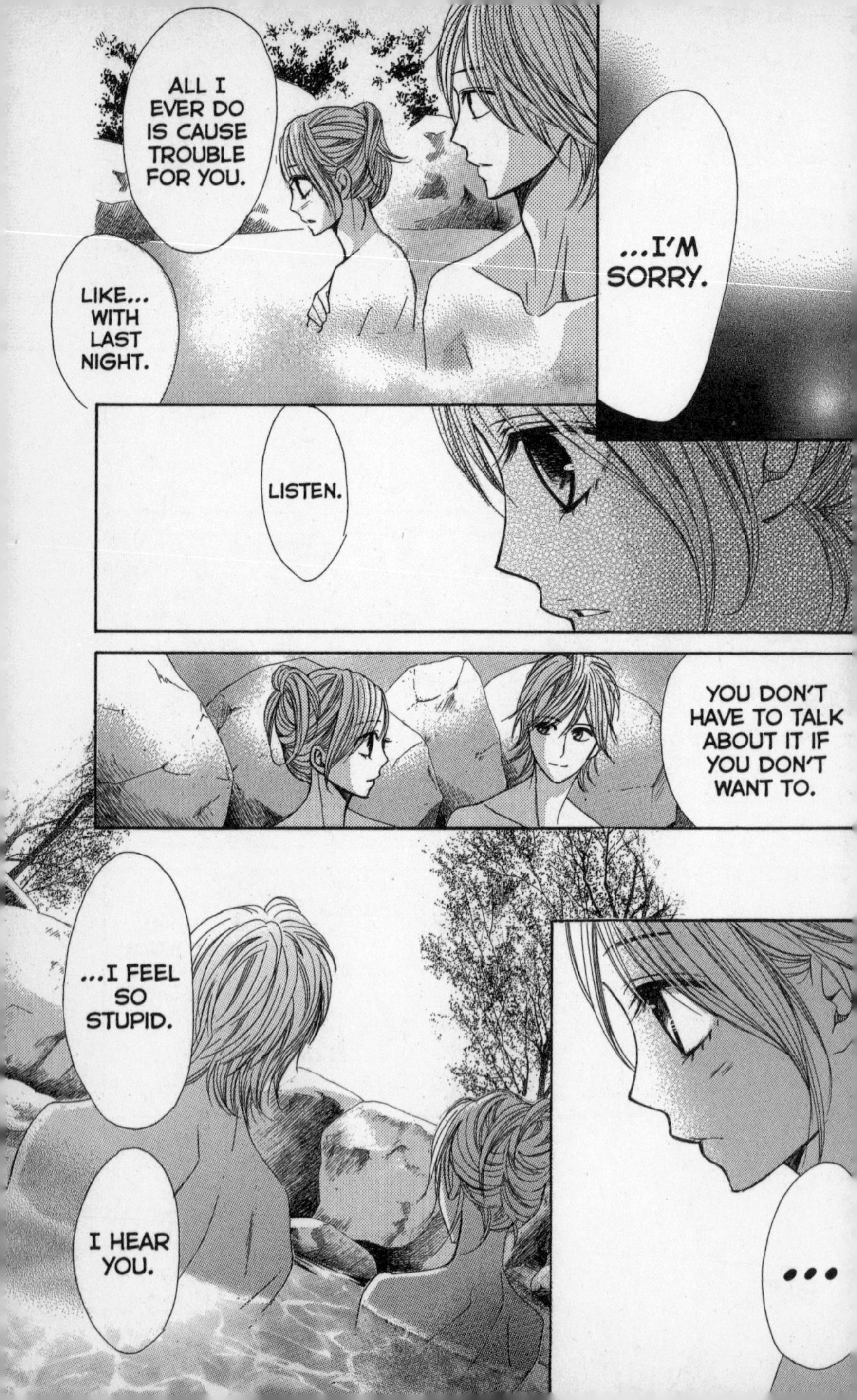
...I'M SORRY.
ALL I EVER DO IS CAUSE TROUBLE FOR YOU.
LIKE... WITH LAST NIGHT.
LISTEN.
YOU DON'T HAVE TO TALK ABOUT IT IF YOU DON'T WANT TO.
...
...I FEEL SO STUPID.
I HEAR YOU.

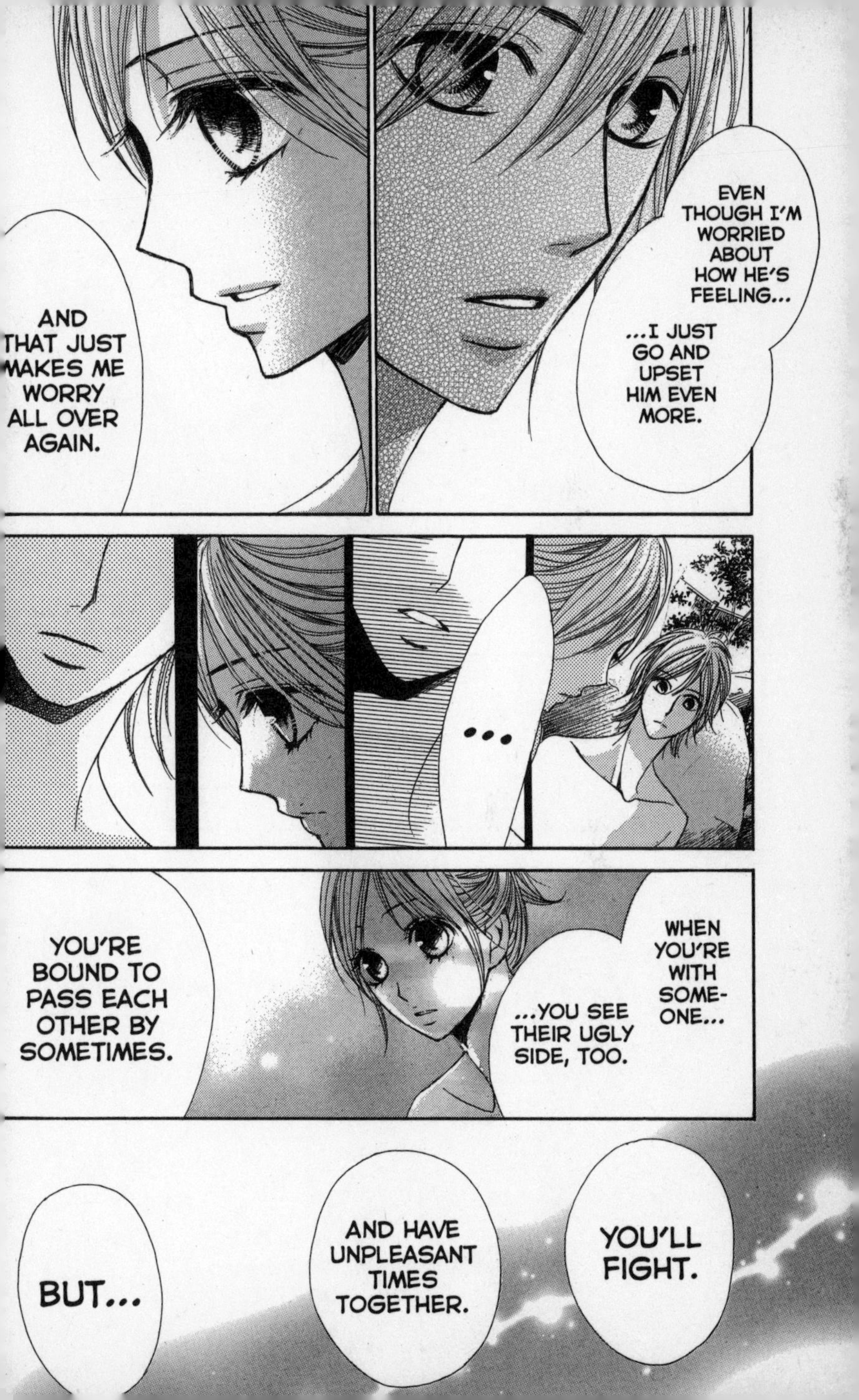
EVEN THOUGH I'M WORRIED ABOUT HOW HE'S FEELING...
...I JUST GO AND UPSET HIM EVEN MORE.
AND THAT JUST MAKES ME WORRY ALL OVER AGAIN.
...
WHEN YOU'RE WITH SOME-ONE...
...YOU SEE THEIR UGLY SIDE, TOO.
YOU'RE BOUND TO PASS EACH OTHER BY SOMETIMES.
YOU'LL FIGHT.
AND HAVE UNPLEASANT TIMES TOGETHER.
BUT...

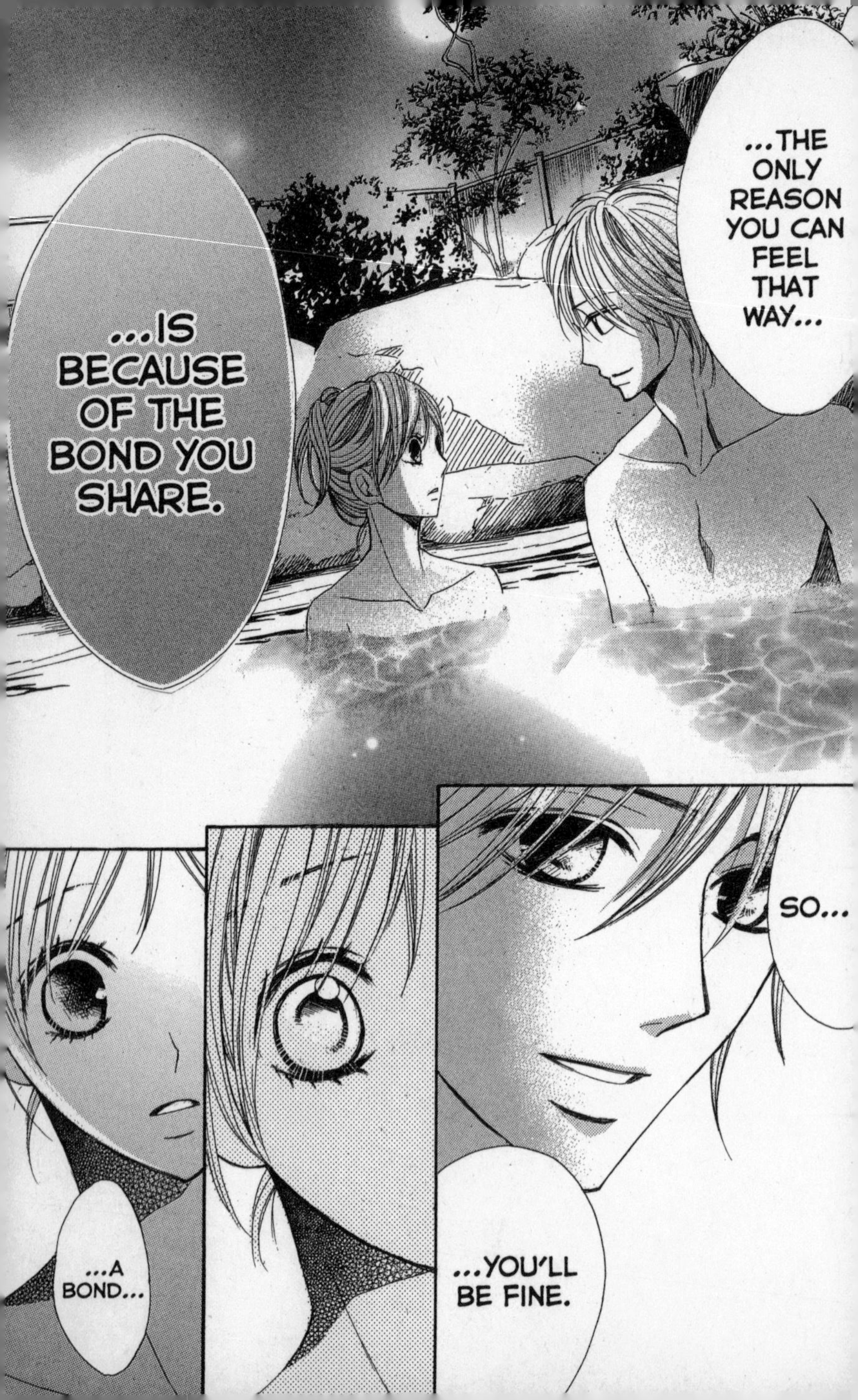
...THE ONLY REASON YOU CAN FEEL THAT WAY...
...IS BECAUSE OF THE BOND YOU SHARE.
SO...
...YOU'LL BE FINE.
...A BOND...

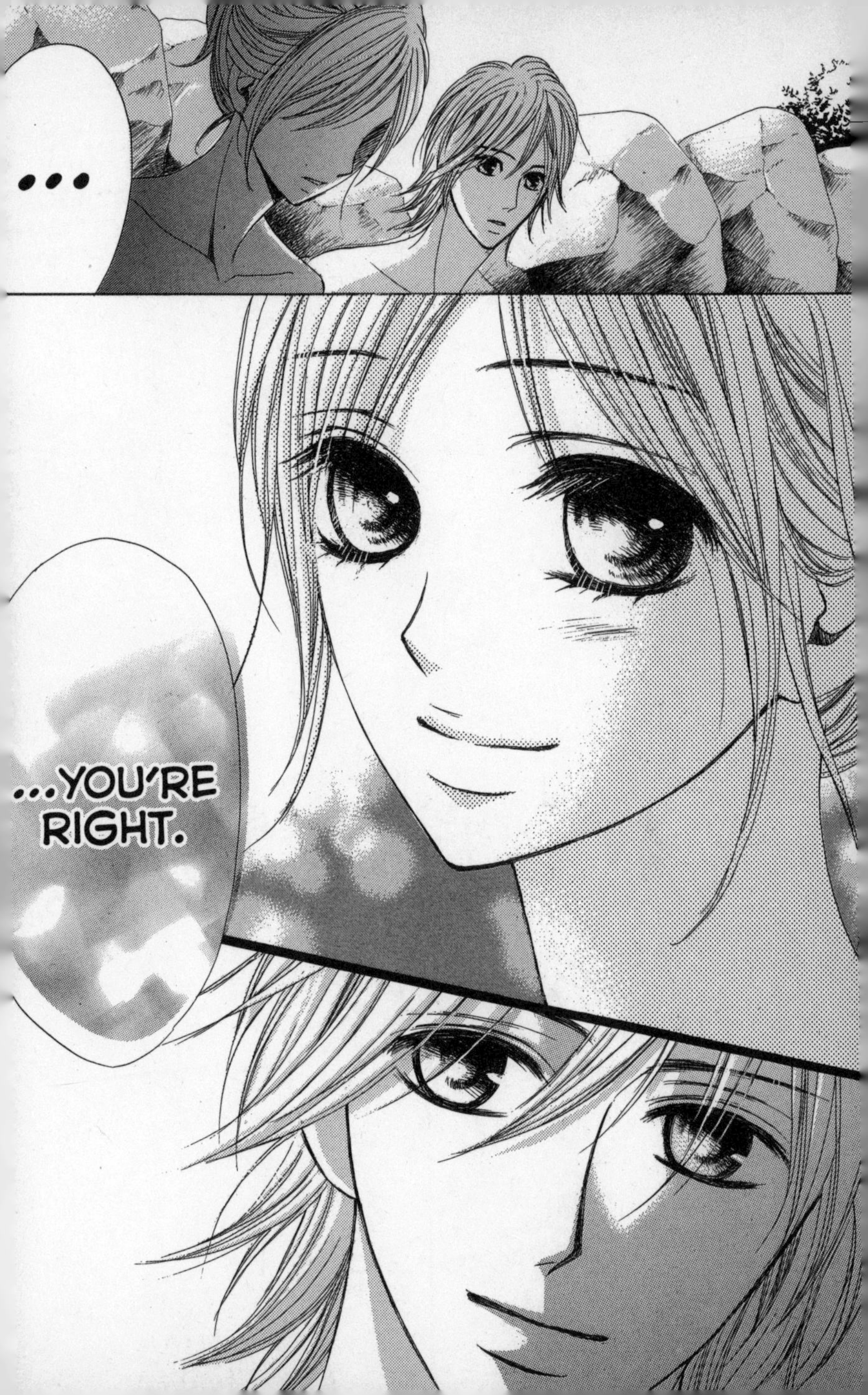
...
...YOU'RE RIGHT.

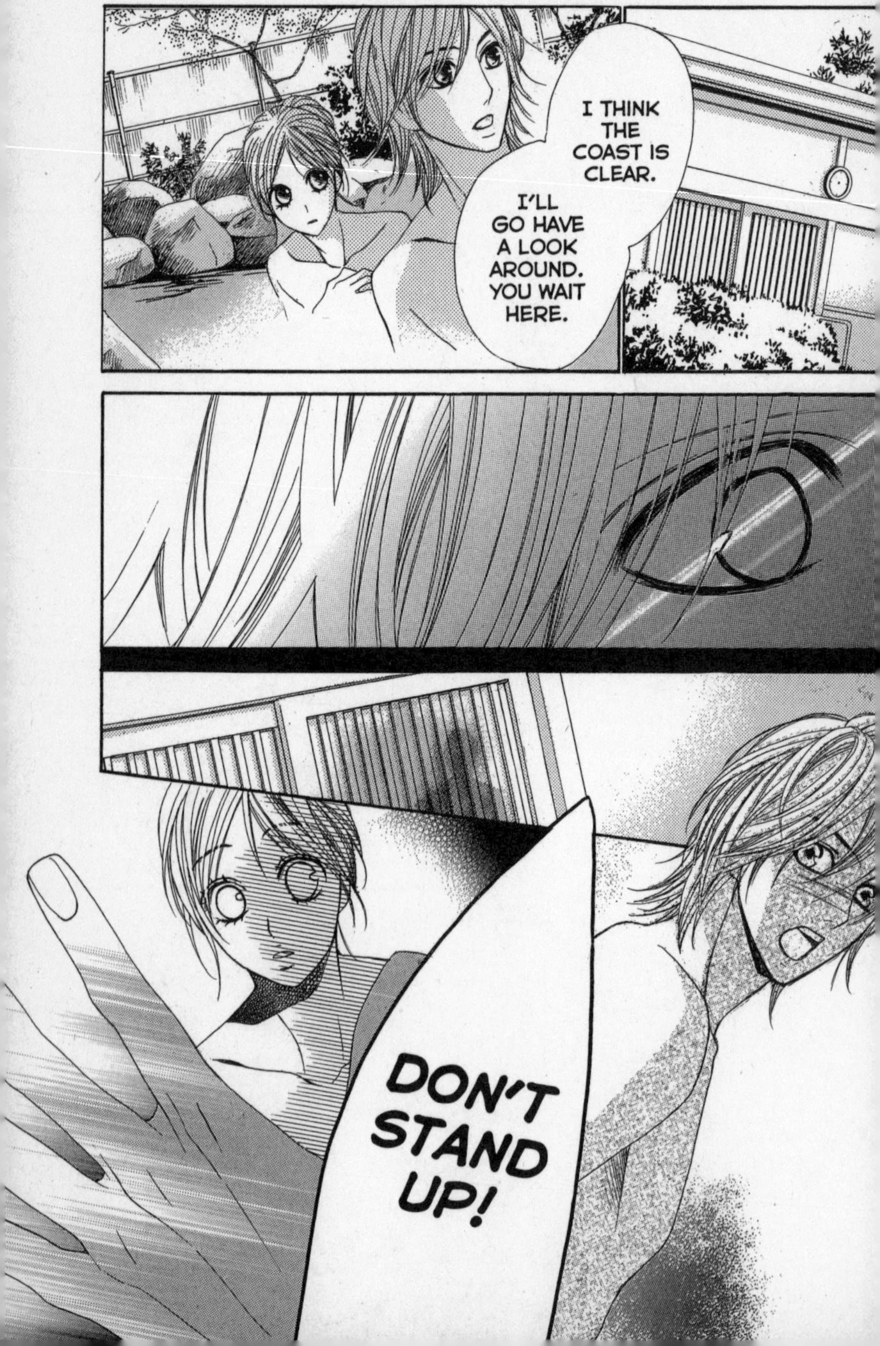
I THINK THE COAST IS CLEAR.
I'LL GO HAVE A LOOK AROUND. YOU WAIT HERE.
DON'T STAND UP!

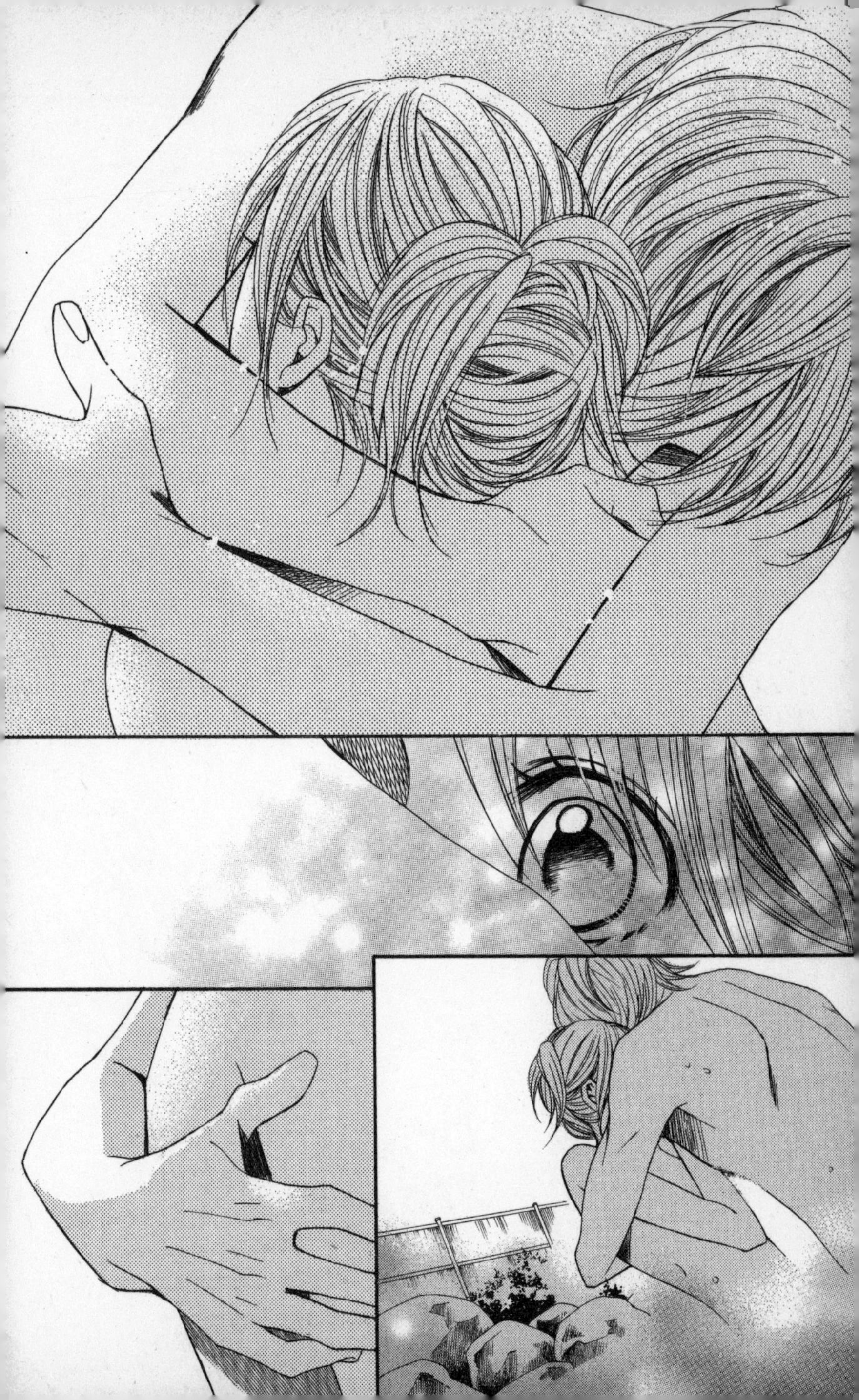

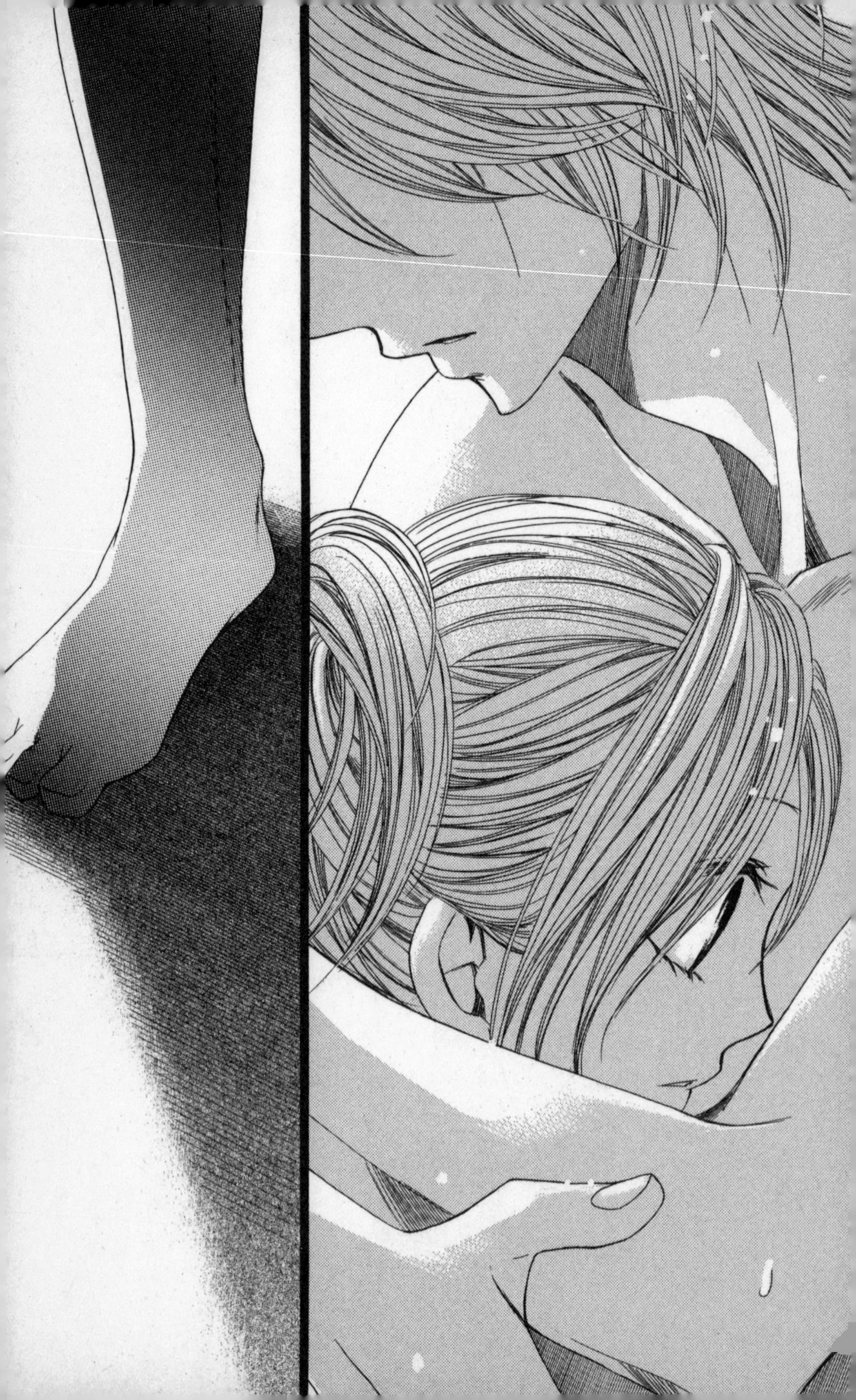

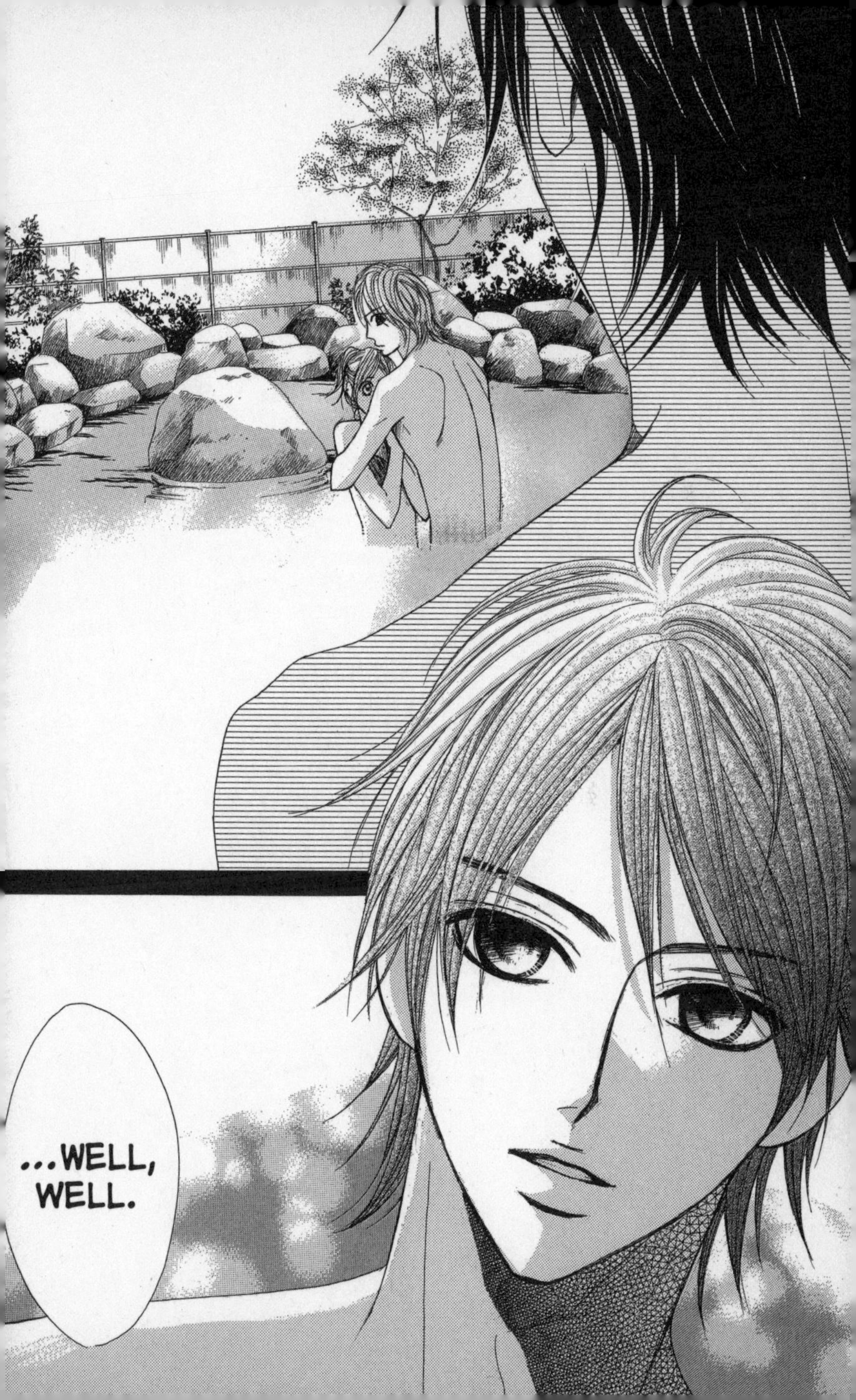
...WELL, WELL.

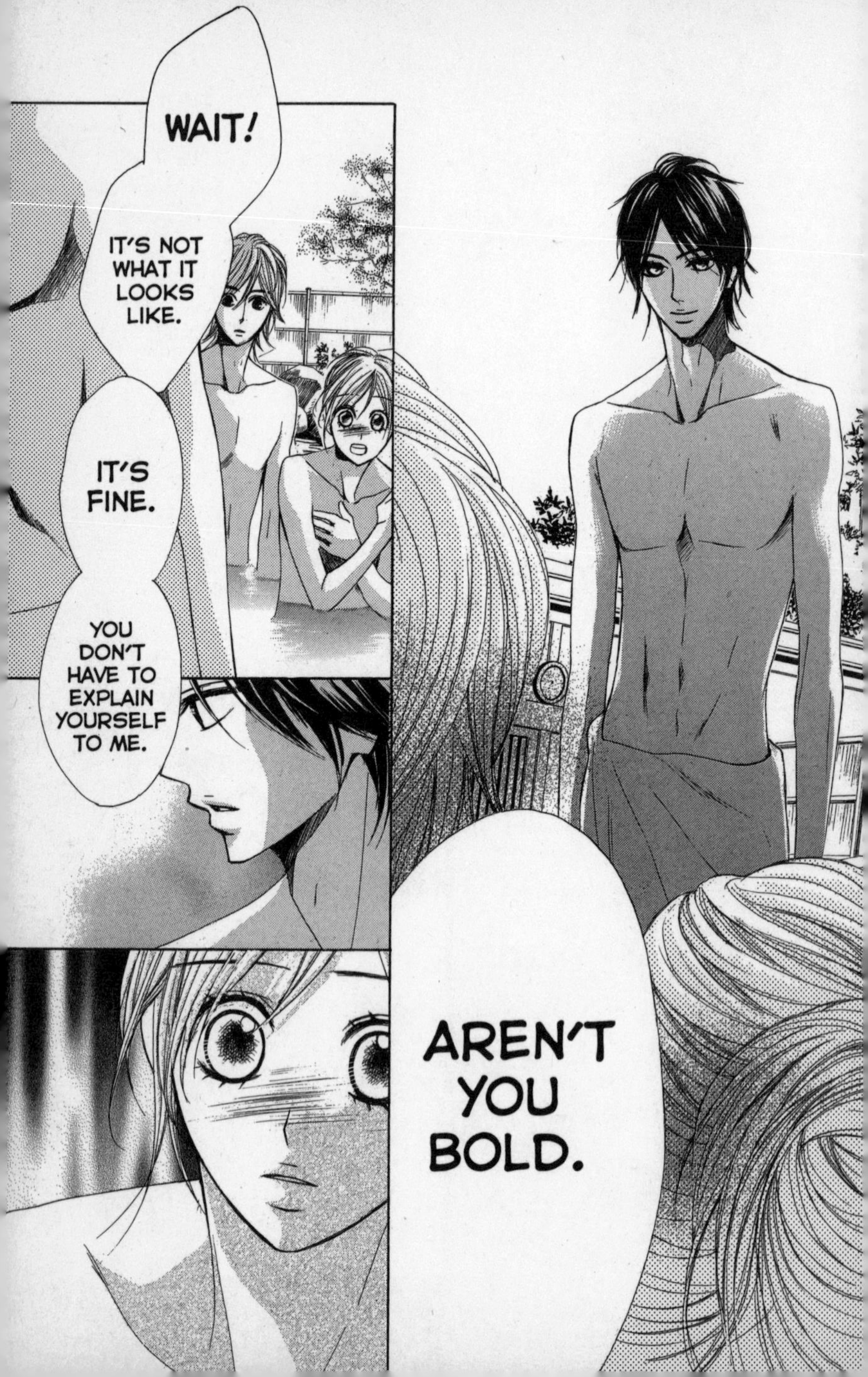
AREN'T YOU BOLD.
WAIT!
IT'S NOT WHAT IT LOOKS LIKE.
IT'S FINE.
YOU DON'T HAVE TO EXPLAIN YOURSELF TO ME.

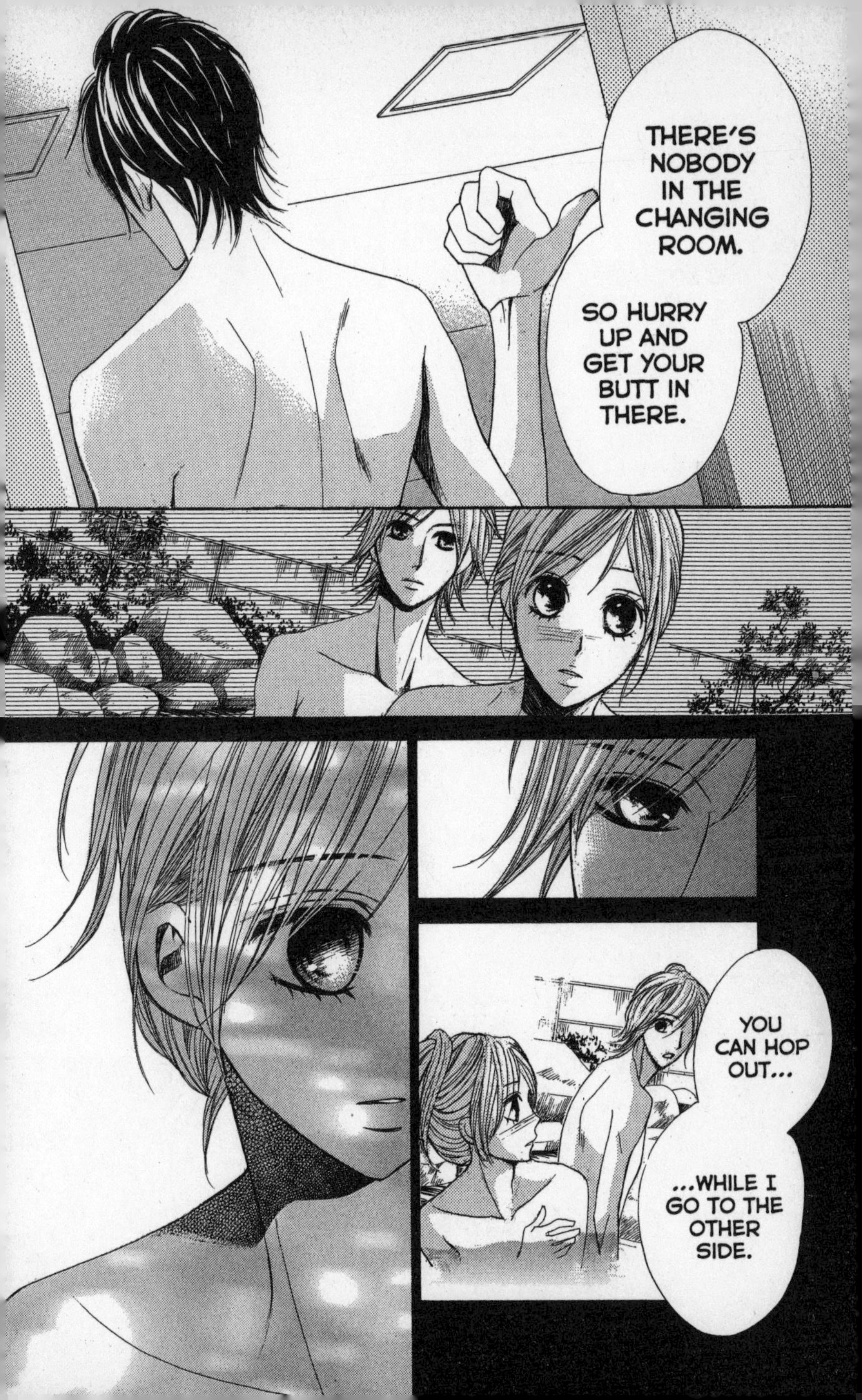
THERE'S NOBODY IN THE CHANGING ROOM.
SO HURRY UP AND GET YOUR BUTT IN THERE.
YOU CAN HOP OUT...
...WHILE I GO TO THE OTHER SIDE.

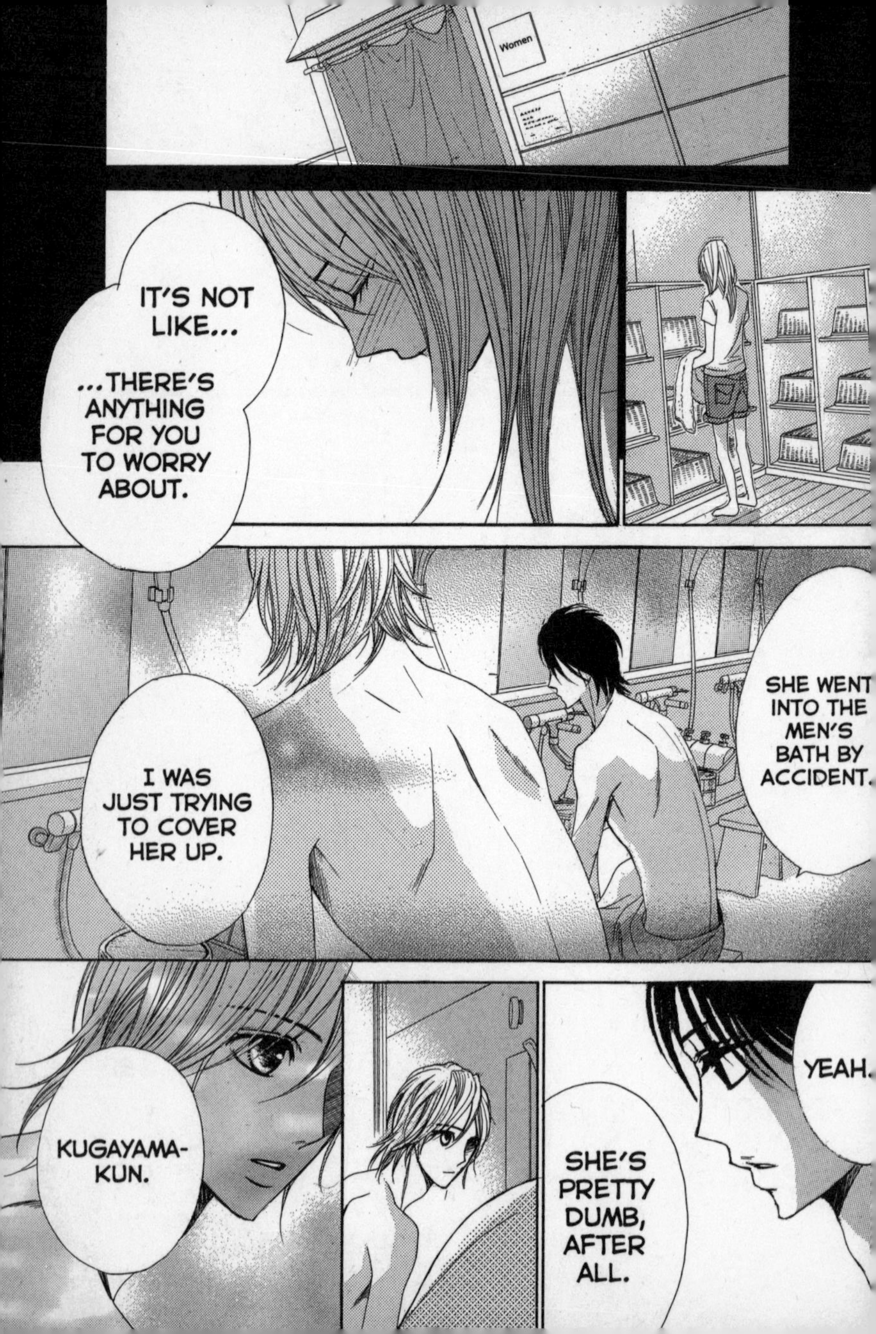
Women
IT'S NOT LIKE...
...THERE'S ANYTHING FOR YOU TO WORRY ABOUT.
SHE WENT INTO THE MEN'S BATH BY ACCIDENT.
I WAS JUST TRYING TO COVER HER UP.
YEAH.
SHE'S PRETTY DUMB, AFTER ALL.
KUGAYAMA-KUN.

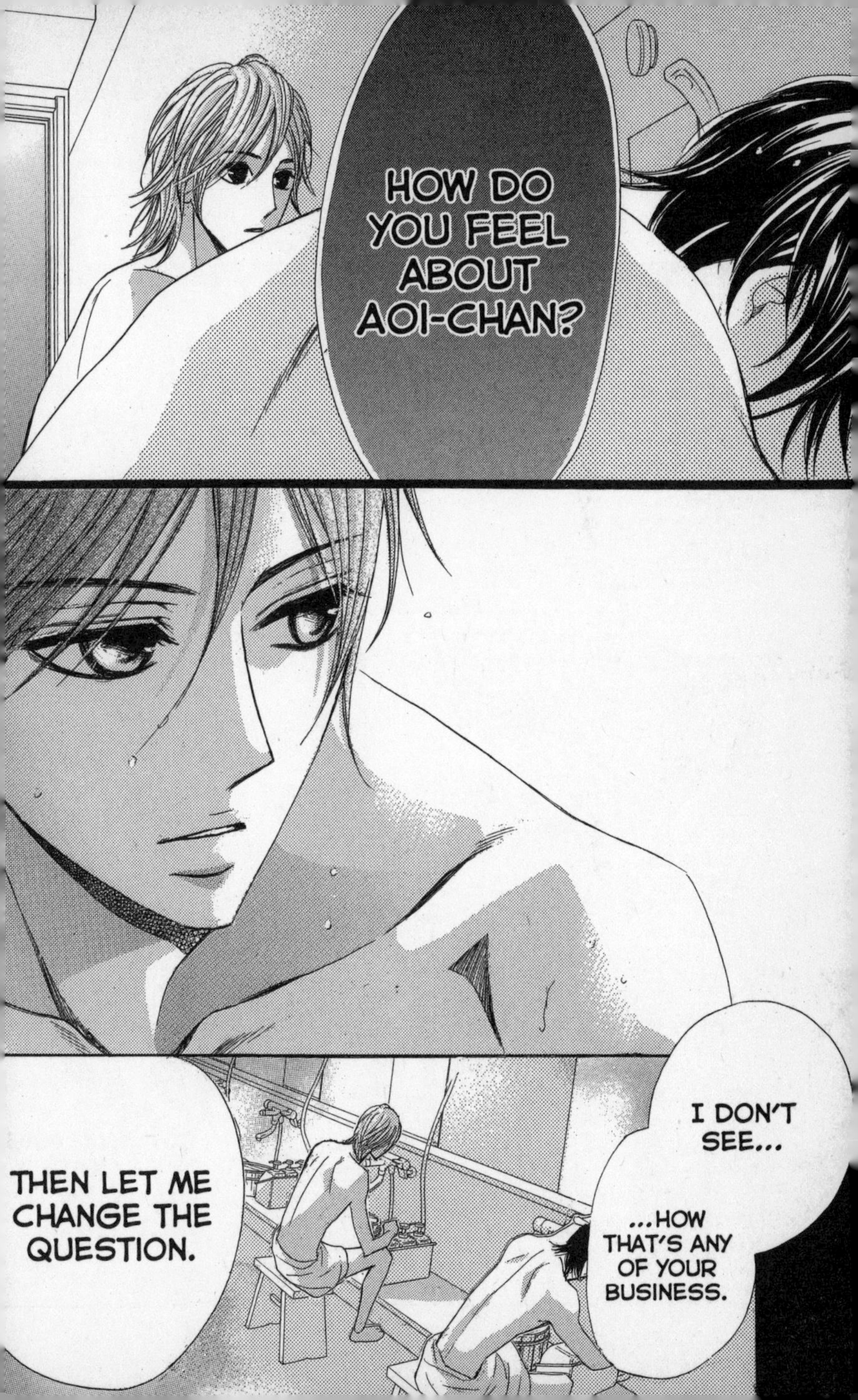
HOW DO YOU FEEL ABOUT AOI-CHAN?
I DON'T SEE...
...HOW THAT'S ANY OF YOUR BUSINESS.
THEN LET ME CHANGE THE QUESTION.

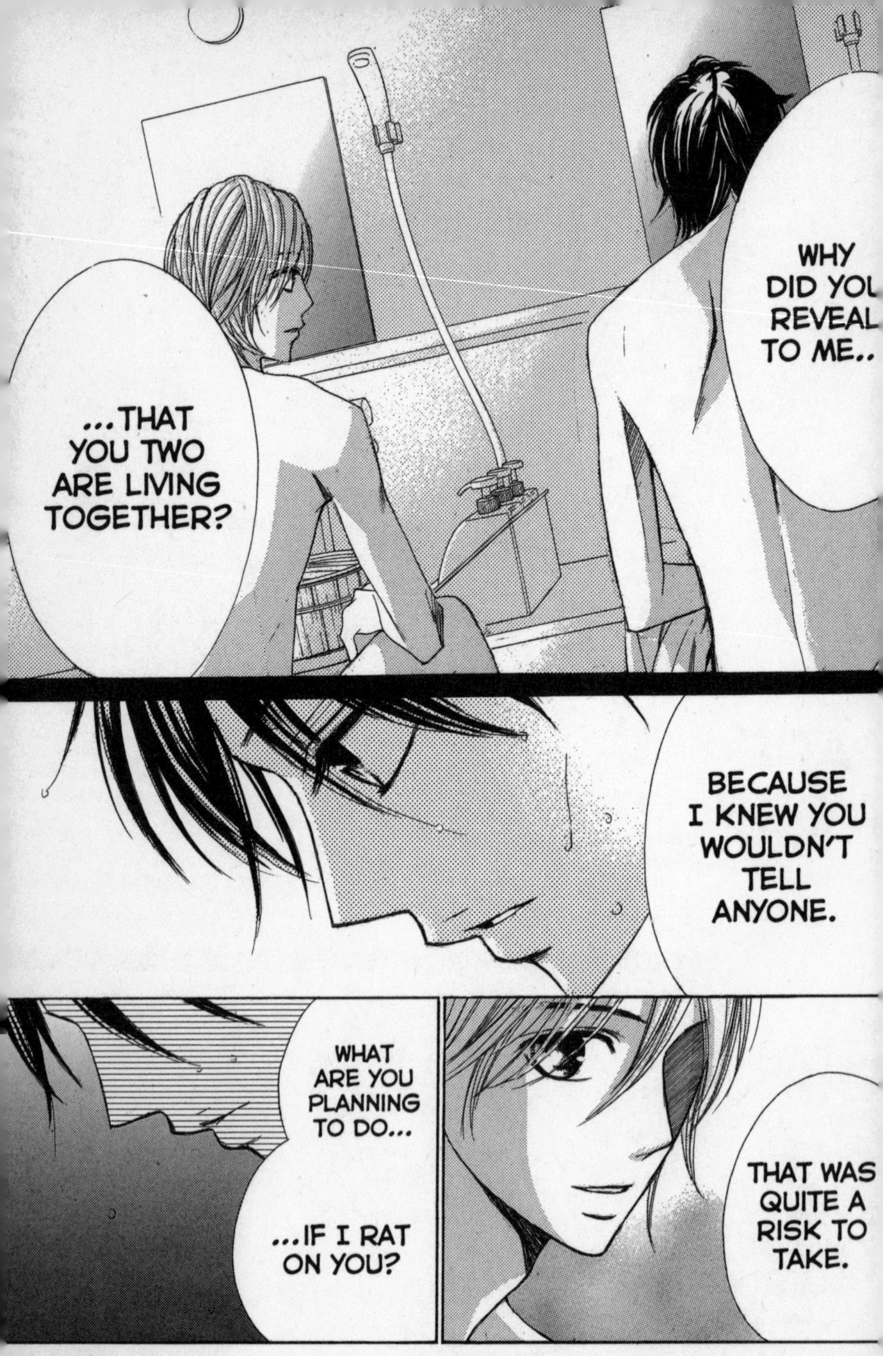
WHY DID YOU REVEAL TO ME..
...THAT YOU TWO ARE LIVING TOGETHER?
BECAUSE I KNEW YOU WOULDN'T TELL ANYONE.
THAT WAS QUITE A RISK TO TAKE.
WHAT ARE YOU PLANNING TO DO...
...IF I RAT ON YOU?

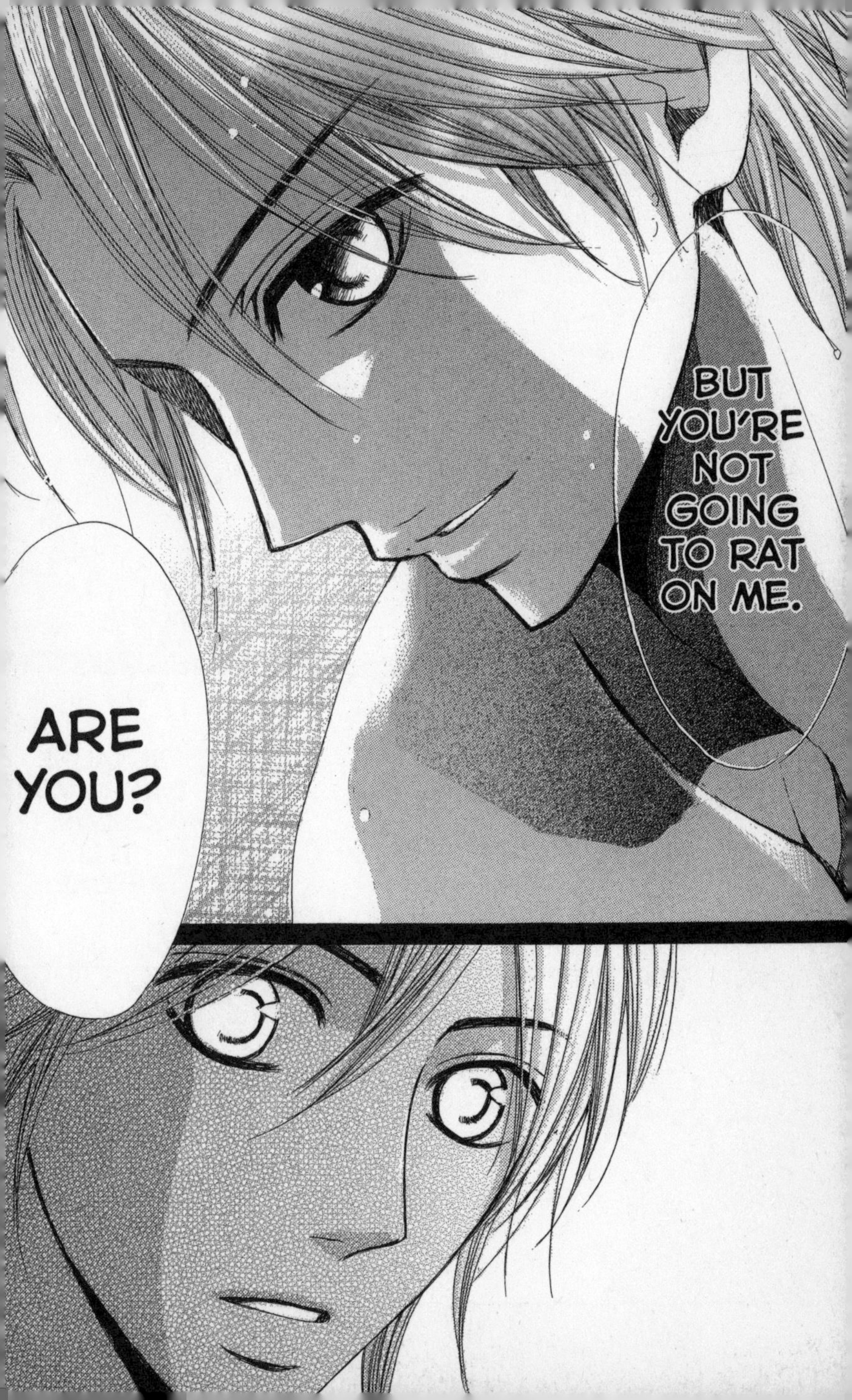
BUT YOU'RE NOT GOING TO RAT ON ME.
ARE YOU?

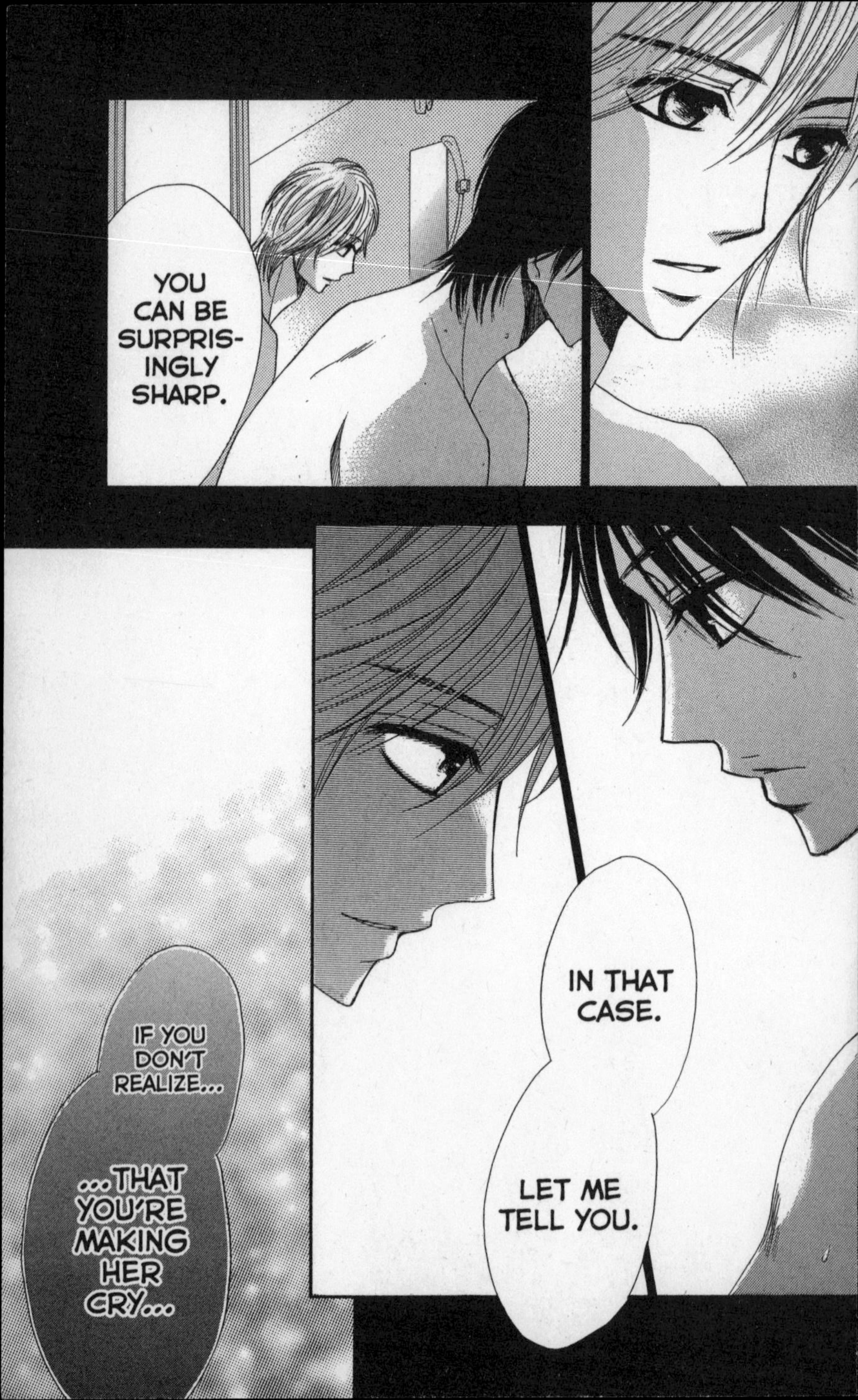
YOU CAN BE SURPRIS-INGLY SHARP.
IN THAT CASE.
LET ME TELL YOU.
IF YOU DON'T REALIZE...
...THAT YOU'RE MAKING HER CRY...

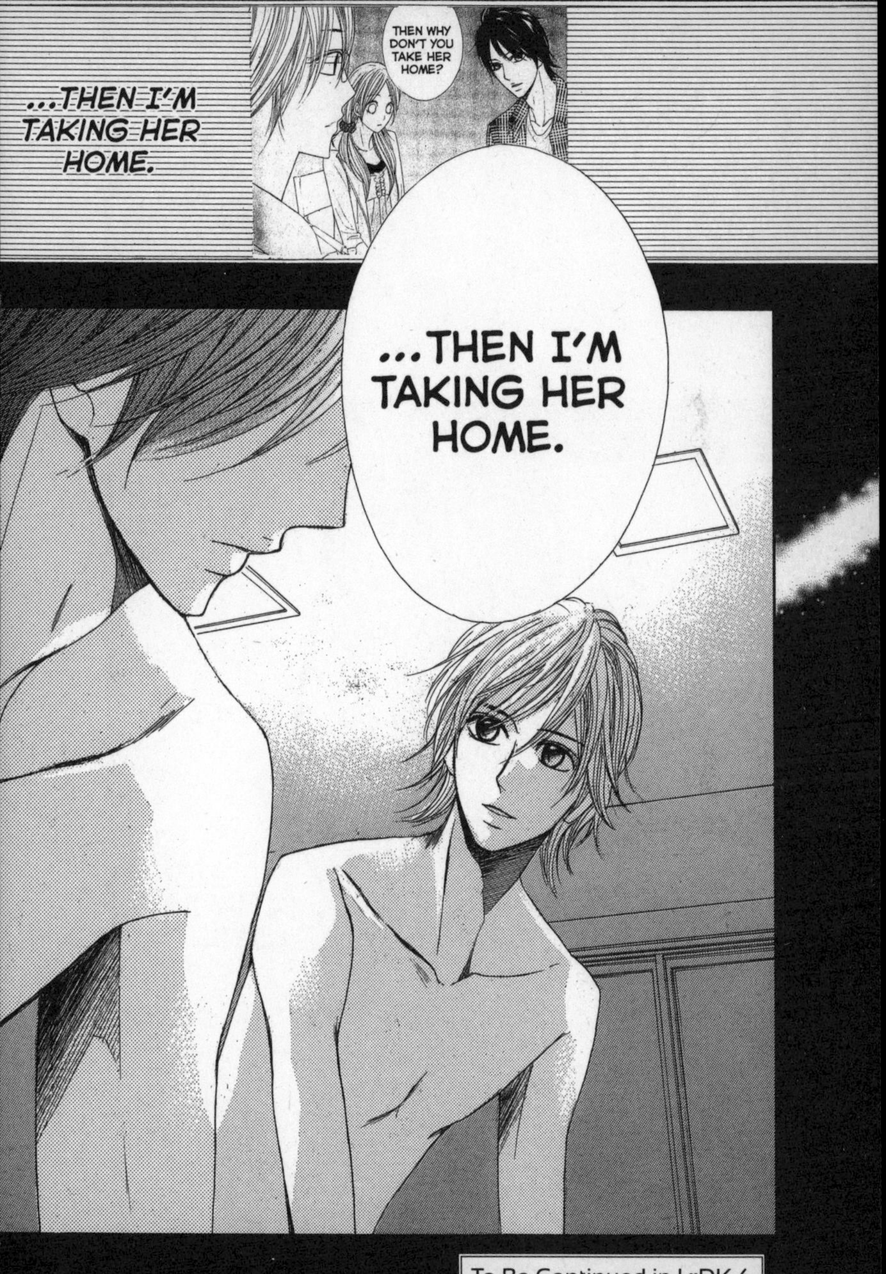
THEN WHY DON'T YOU TAKE HER HOME?
...THEN I'M TAKING HER HOME.
...THEN I'M TAKING HER HOME.

To Be Continued in L♥DK 6

L♥DK

GREETINGS

Hello, everyone. This is Ayu Watanabe. Sorry for not being able to do a Greetings column at the end of the last volume. Thank you very much for picking up Volume 5 of *LDK*!! Everyone's encouraging words are far more potent to me than any energy drink! I really appreciate you all!! Let's see. Going back to my diet that I mentioned in Volume 3, let's see how my weight change is going. Looking at it now...**I've gotten heavier.**
Nothing's easy in life, is it? Ha ha ha. When I get tired while doing my storyboards, I just reach for something sugary. Yep. That's my excuse. But I'm not giving up. I'm going to take to heart what they say about the state of your heart affecting the state of your body and will report back here again on the progress of my diet.
By the way, when the comic is set to go on sale, I have to do a lot of work revising the storyboards, and in my case this work is so grueling that it makes me wish I could just disappear. Starting with my mangaka friends, just about everyone says that "going over old storyboards is always difficult and humiliating." And I have to agree. I'm plenty humiliated by them myself. This is what it always looks like↓

DEEP BREATHS →
PHOOO. HAAAHH.
I'M SUPPOSED TO LOOK AT MY DRAWINGS FROM FOUR OR FIVE MONTHS AGO...
...WITHOUT PUKING?
EEEEK! STUPID! I'M SO STUPID!! I'VE GOT NO TALENT!
ROLL
ROLL ROLL
WAAAAH! THIS IS SO HUMILIATING!! I'M SO STUPID!!
GREAT AGONY
POINT
DOUBTING MY SKILL
MAKING WEIRD NOISES

I wonder why that is... It's not like I've improved that much (LOL) and yet no matter how much time passes, I can't get used to it! At the same time, I can look at the oldest storyboards and feel warmly toward them. It's odd. I must steel my heart and apply myself to the daily grind. And with that, I look forward to seeing you again in the next volume.

special thanks

K.Hamano
N.Imai
S.Sato

my family
my friends

M.Morita
A.Ichikawa
A.Yamamoto

AND YOU

Ayu Watanabe
Dec.2010

**Everyday Essentials, Item 5
Handheld Vac**

This thing gets a lot of action when things like eraser bits find themselves around my pillow. When I'm cleaning, my mind feels extra sharp. But I can't get rid of all the mess before sleepiness overtakes me...

BY TOMOKO HAYAKAWA

It's a beautiful, expansive mansion, and four handsome, fifteen-year-old friends are allowed to live in it for free! But there is one condition—within three years the young men must take the owner's niece and transform her into a proper lady befitting the palace in which they all live! How hard can it be?

Enter Sunako Nakahara, the horror-movie-loving, pock-faced, frizzy-haired, fashion-illiterate hermit who has a tendency to break into explosive nosebleeds whenever she sees anyone attractive. This project is going to take far more than our four heroes ever expected; it needs a miracle!

Ages: 16+

Special extras in each volume! Read them all!

VISIT WWW.KODANSHACOMICS.COM TO:
• View release date calendars for upcoming volumes
• Find out the latest about new Kodansha Comics series

Say I Love You.

KC KODANSHA COMICS

Mei Tachibana has no friends — and says she doesn't need them!

But everything changes when she accidentally roundhouse kicks the most popular boy in school! However, Yamato Kurosawa isn't angry in the slightest— in fact, he thinks his ordinary life could use an unusual girl like Mei. But winning Mei's trust will be a tough task. How long will she refuse to say, "I love you"?

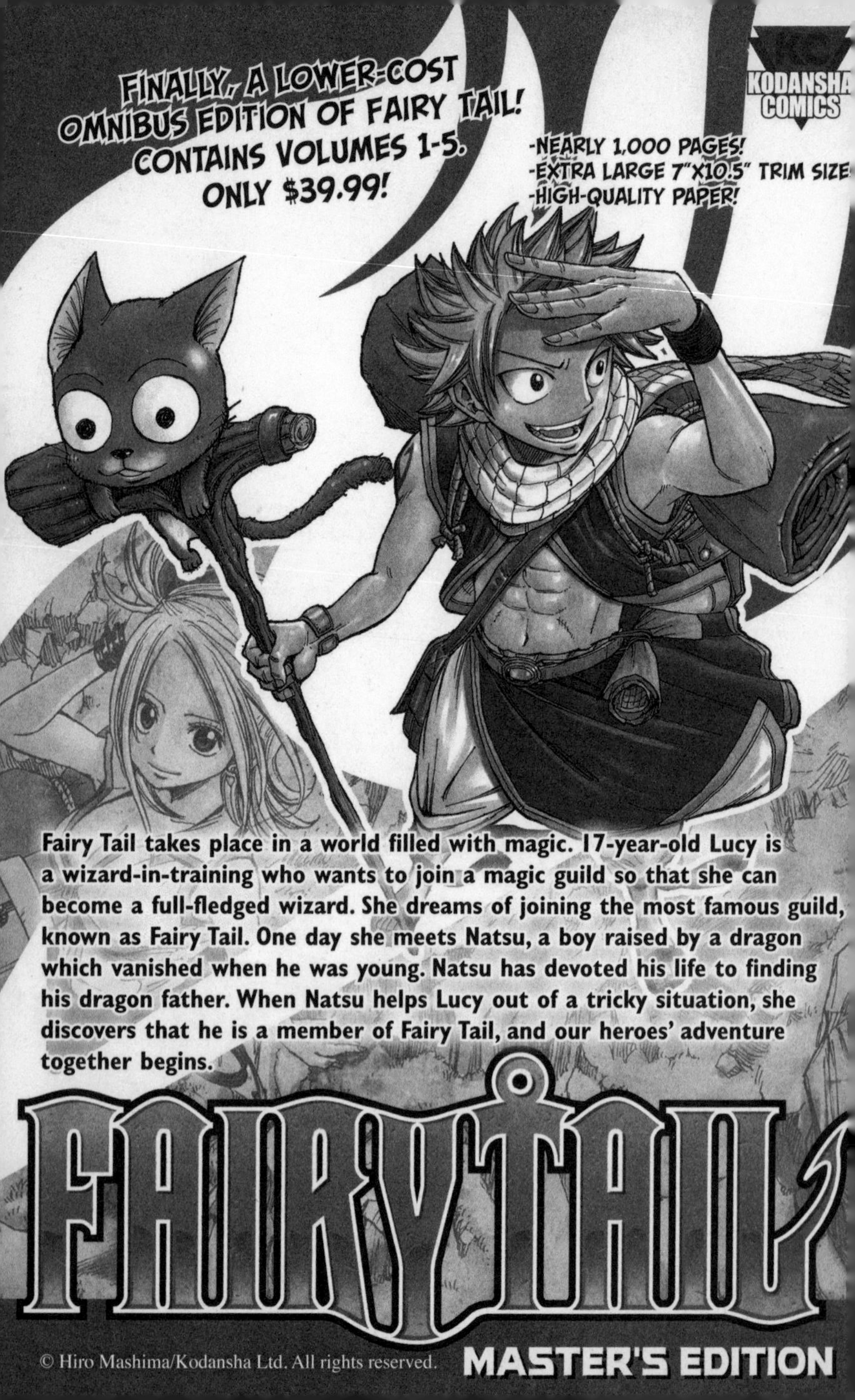
KODANSHA COMICS
FINALLY, A LOWER-COST OMNIBUS EDITION OF FAIRY TAIL! CONTAINS VOLUMES 1-5. ONLY $39.99!
-NEARLY 1,000 PAGES!
-EXTRA LARGE 7"X10.5" TRIM SIZE
-HIGH-QUALITY PAPER!
Fairy Tail takes place in a world filled with magic. 17-year-old Lucy is a wizard-in-training who wants to join a magic guild so that she can become a full-fledged wizard. She dreams of joining the most famous guild, known as Fairy Tail. One day she meets Natsu, a boy raised by a dragon which vanished when he was young. Natsu has devoted his life to finding his dragon father. When Natsu helps Lucy out of a tricky situation, she discovers that he is a member of Fairy Tail, and our heroes' adventure together begins.
FAIRY TAIL
MASTER'S EDITION

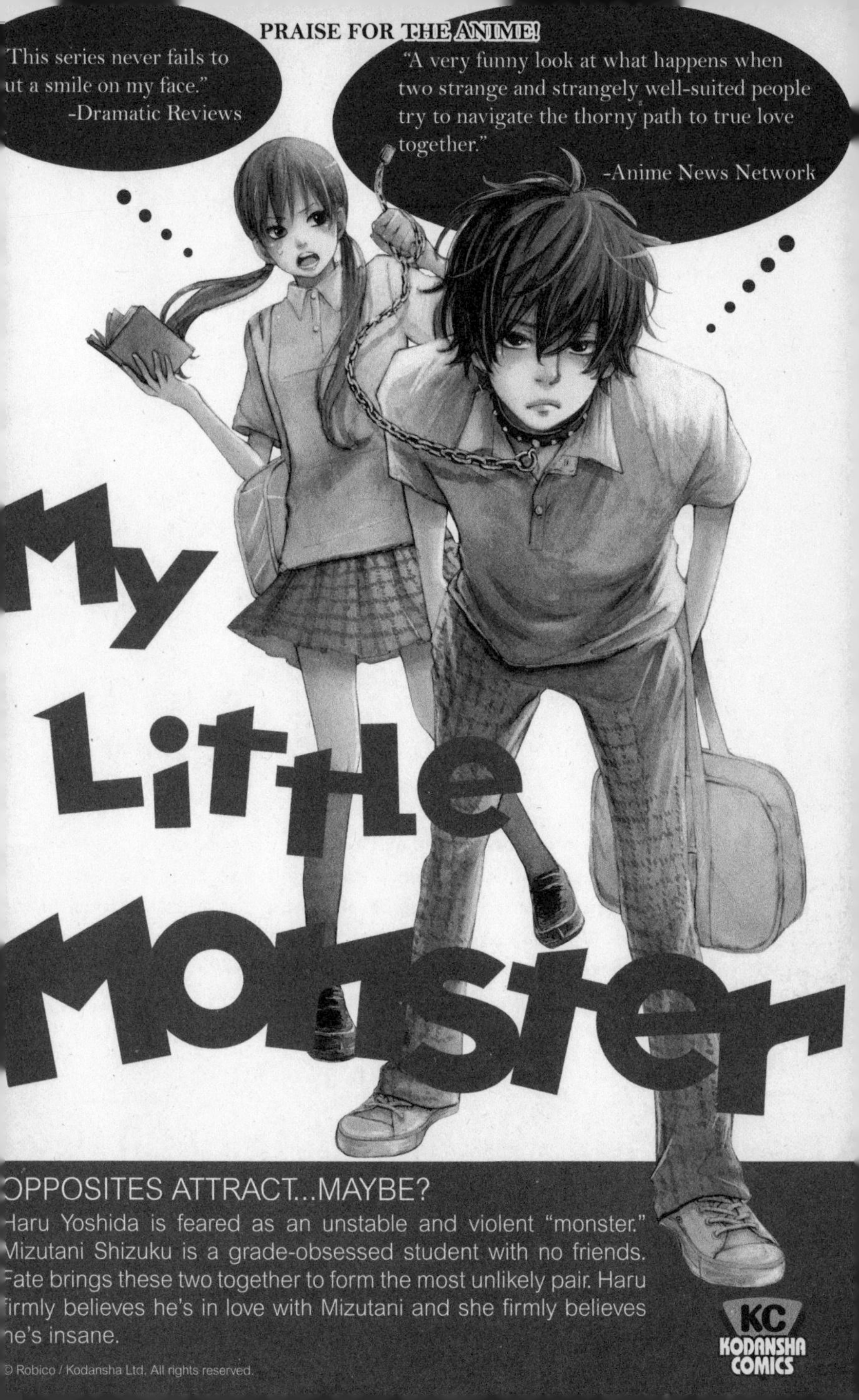
PRAISE FOR THE ANIME!
This series never fails to ut a smile on my face."
-Dramatic Reviews
"A very funny look at what happens when two strange and strangely well-suited people try to navigate the thorny path to true love together."
-Anime News Network
My Little Monster
OPPOSITES ATTRACT...MAYBE?
-laru Yoshida is feared as an unstable and violent "monster." Mizutani Shizuku is a grade-obsessed student with no friends. Fate brings these two together to form the most unlikely pair. Haru firmly believes he's in love with Mizutani and she firmly believes ne's insane.
© Robico / Kodansha Ltd. All rights reserved.
KC
KODANSHA COMICS

FAIRY TAIL
BLUE MISTRAL
Wendy's Very Own Fairy Tail!
The new adventures of everyone's favorite Sky Dragon Slayer, Wendy Marvell, and her faithful friend Carla!
KODANSHA COMICS
Available Now!
© Hiro Mashima/Rui Watanabe/Kodansha, Ltd. All rights reserved.

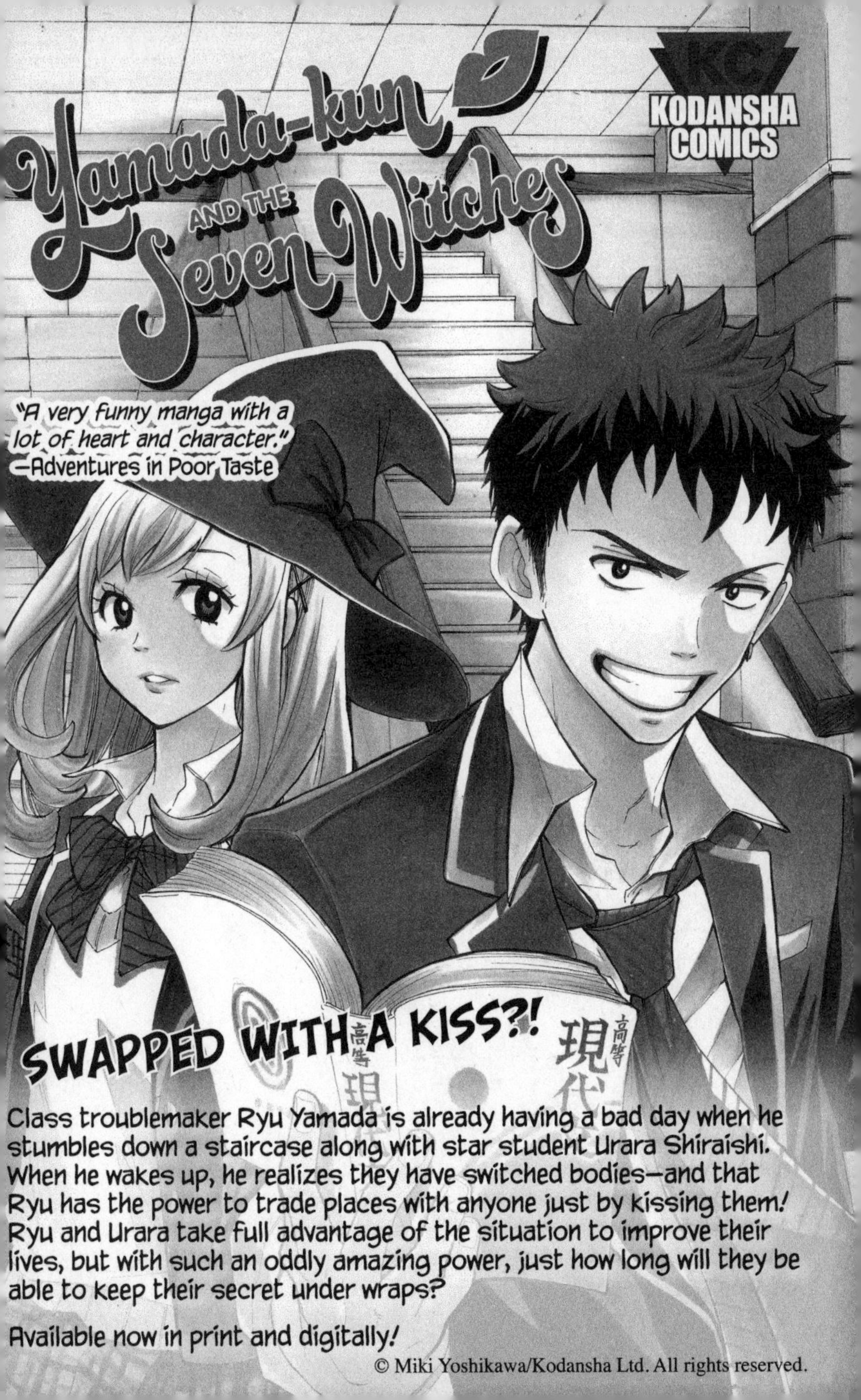
KODANSHA COMICS
Yamada-kun AND THE Seven Witches
"A very funny manga with a lot of heart and character."
—Adventures in Poor Taste
SWAPPED WITH A KISS?!
Class troublemaker Ryu Yamada is already having a bad day when he stumbles down a staircase along with star student Urara Shiraishi. When he wakes up, he realizes they have switched bodies—and that Ryu has the power to trade places with anyone just by kissing them! Ryu and Urara take full advantage of the situation to improve their lives, but with such an oddly amazing power, just how long will they be able to keep their secret under wraps?
Available now in print and digitally!
© Miki Yoshikawa/Kodansha Ltd. All rights reserved.

a Silent Voice

"The word heartwarming was made for manga like this."
–Manga Book-shelf

"A harsh and biting social commentary... delivers in its depth of character and emotional strength." -Comics Bulletin

"A very powerful story about being different and the consequences of childhood bullying... Read it."
–Anime News Network

Shoya is a bully. When Shoko, a girl who can't hear, enters his elementary school class, she becomes their favorite target, and Shoya and his friends goad each other into devising new tortures for her. But the children's cruelty goes too far. Shoko is forced to leave the school, and Shoya ends up shouldering all the blame. Six years later, the two meet again. Can Shoya make up for his past mistakes, or is it too late?

Available now in print and digitally!

NO.6

A PERFECT LIFE
IN A PERFECT CITY

r Shion, an elite student in the technologically sophisticated
ty No. 6, life is carefully choreographed. One fateful day, he
kes a misstep, sheltering a fugitive his age from a typhoon.
elping this boy throws Shion's life down a path to discovering
e appalling secrets behind the "perfection" of No. 6.

LDK volume 5 is a work of fiction. Names, characters, places, and incidents are the products of the author's imagination or are used fictitiously. Any resemblance to actual events, locales, or persons, living or dead, is entirely coincidental.

A Kodansha Comics Trade Paperback Original.

Published in the United States by Kodansha Comics, an imprint of Kodansha USA Publishing, LLC, New York.

Publication rights for this English edition arranged through Kodansha Ltd., Tokyo.

First published in Japan in 2010 by Kodansha Ltd., Tokyo, as *L♡DK*, volume 5.

ISBN 978-1-63236-158-5

Printed in the United States of America.

www.kodanshacomics.com

9 8 7 6 5 4 3 2 1

Translation: Christine Dashiell
Lettering: Sara Linsley
Editing: Lauren Scanlan
Kodansha Comics edition cover design: Phil Balsman

TOMARE!

止まれ

[STOP!]

You're going the wrong way!

Manga is a completely different type of reading experience.

To start at the *beginning,*
go to the *end!*

That's right! Authentic manga is read the traditional Japanese way—from right to left, exactly the *opposite* of how American books are read. It's easy to follow: Just go to the other end of the book and read each page—and each panel—from right side to left side, starting at the top right. Now you're experiencing manga as it was meant to be!